THE PUBLIC INTELLECTUAL AND THE CULTURE OF HOPE

The Public Intellectual and the Culture of Hope

EDITED BY
JOEL FAFLAK AND JASON HASLAM

UNIVERSITY OF TORONTO PRESS
Toronto Buffalo London

Toronto Buffalo London
www.utppublishing.com

ISBN 978-1-4426-4184-6

Library and Archives Canada Cataloguing in Publication

The public intellectual and the culture of hope / edited by Joel Faflak and Jason Haslam ; foreword by John Polanyi.

Includes bibliographical references and index.
ISBN 978-1-4426-4184-6 (bound)

1. Intellectuals – Social conditions. 2. Intellectual life. I. Haslam, Jason W., 1971– II. Faflak, Joel, 1959–

HM728.P82 2013 305.5′52 C2013-904063-3

This book has been published with the help of a grant from the Canadian Federation for the Humanities and Social Sciences, through the Awards to Scholarly Publications Program, using funds provided by the Social Sciences and Humanities Research Council of Canada.

University of Toronto Press acknowledges the financial assistance to its publishing program of the Canada Council for the Arts and the Ontario Arts Council.

University of Toronto Press acknowledges the financial support of the Government of Canada through the Canada Book Fund for its publishing activities.

Contents

Part Two: Public Performances

Part Three: Public Matters

Acknowledgments

We thank our contributors, whose engagement, enthusiasm, and commitment made this venture possible. Their writing for this volume, as well as their various intellectual energies as researchers, teachers, mentors, and interlocutors exemplify our best hope for the future vitality of public intellectualism. Each of us in turn owes a singular debt to John Charles Polanyi, whose dedication as academic and activist provided the inspiration for this volume, and we thank Dr Polanyi for his support of this project, as well as for his generous Foreword. We are grateful to the support of the University of Toronto Press, especially to Richard Ratzlaff for his unfailing commitment, advice, and assistance at every stage of this volume's development. We both thank the Social Sciences and Humanities Research Council of Canada for its generous support of our research. Finally, we thank our partners for their support intellectual and nonintellectual, public and private, and always hopeful.

Foreword

My life as a scientist (which continues) places me at several removes from this exceptional book. Nonetheless, the authors insist that I am implicated. They are, it is true, winners of an enduring Ontario prize for literature, with which I have a distant link. That is my good fortune since from this volume I learn, as will any reader, what it means to be professionally literate. It is an enviable condition of ebullience; enquiry; and, at times, eloquence. But that description does not do this book justice since, above all, it has a purpose.

The purpose is to be found in the title, which is, in fact, an essay. At the outset it addresses itself to "The Public Intellectual." This is a term unknown in my profession, but that is our loss. For what the term describes is a fundamental contract between society's creative class and its consumers. The contract extends back to the time, thirty thousand years ago, when cave painters were accorded time off from the hunt. It has endured because humanity demands food for the mind, as well as the body. The precise terms of the contract remain, however, a matter for negotiation.

The rest of this book's title makes a still more subtle point, since it conjoins the bargain between the intellectual and the public with the need for a "Culture of Hope."

What does that mean? We are provided with a clue in the opening phrase of the Introduction, which attributes to Aristotle the proposition that "Hope is a waking dream." This brings us to the heart of the problem faced by the Public Intellectual: who among the public will exchange a tangible good – a portion of bison – for a waking dream – a painting on the wall? Clearly it must be someone in whom the anticipatory joy that we term "hope," is strong.

But is that such an exceptional condition? The authors of this book think not, nor do I. Rather than being rare, hope is better described as a condition for life. It is evident in the infant who must engage in feats of discovery that would give pause to Isaac Newton. Similarly the adult committed to creative endeavour nourishes the hope that order can be made out of chaos, and, as a professional, makes a promise to deliver on that hope.

It is the purpose of the teacher (all the authors of this book are teachers) to foster hope and deliver on the promise of enlightenment. This too was the purpose of the Province in planting the seeds that led to this book. It did so liberally, since it did not ordain the outcome. In acting as it did, and as it resolutely continues to do, it has become a notable subscriber to the "Culture of Hope."

John Polanyi,
University of Toronto

THE PUBLIC INTELLECTUAL AND THE CULTURE OF HOPE

Introduction: Public Hopes

JOEL FAFLAK AND JASON HASLAM

Hope is a waking dream.

– Aristotle

Here's Hoping

One of the original inspirations for this volume, as the second clause of our title likely gives away, was the 2008 U.S. election, specifically the discourse of hope that surrounded Barack Obama's campaign. Famously captured and propagated by Shepard Fairey's poster of a stylized Obama with "HOPE" written underneath, this atmosphere of expectation for positive change was voiced by supporters as an inspiring moment in American and global politics, and derided by its opposition as an empty – and possibly even cynical – campaign slogan. Combined with this sense of "hope," though, and often supporting it, was a sense of a return to a positive vision of intellectualism. In this narrative, Obama, the Harvard-educated lawyer and published author, the man often seen with books, the "articulate" speaker and debater (with all of the racial overtones of that statement)[1], was set against George W. Bush, represented not as the Yale-educated businessman and former governor but as the stumbling and inarticulate "bubba," an image later so grandly embodied by Sarah Palin (as the uninformed beauty queen, with all the gendered implications of that image). A clear cultural line between the intellectual and the "people's man" was, it seemed to us, once again being paraded in its stark primary colours, in this case only added to by the racial dynamics of the election. But, through the discourse of "hope," intellectualism was being tied to the people – that is, to the public – in an enthusiastic way, and this was heralded by many as a positive sign of a new United States to come.[2] Nonetheless, in the depths of the so-called Great Recession – with its joblessness, hollowed-out urban centres, and war on several fronts – the suspicion that "hope and change" was *just* a campaign slogan has been gaining steam. Perhaps the "culture of hope" in our title was to become a dated and ironic clause, pointing to the ways in which intellectual efforts to bring about change in the public sphere can be sold back to the public in the empty, ideological forms of culture, or, at best, emptied of material possibility by the pragmatics of political and economic reality (the latter a common reactionary response to the "ivory tower" of intellectualism).

While the 2008 U.S. election brought this binary vision into focus as we began this volume, the 2010 Canadian election, as we were reading contributions, repeated the formula. The representation of Michael Ignatieff, like Stéphane Dion before him, focussed on his background as an academic and intellectual. More significantly, for both Ignatieff and Obama, this formula was tied to the representation of them as having "foreign," rather than "national" interest at heart. In Obama's case this figure was clearly based on a racist logic while, in Ignatieff's, it was tied to a general appeal to Canadian anti-Americanism. But, in both, there was the implication that the (liberal) intellectual had "global" rather than "local" interests that were, in some way, directed contra the nation. From the image of a possible national salvation through the uniting of the political and the intellectual, with which we started thinking about the volume, we arrived, while composing the volume, at the representation of the intellectual as foreign agent, as Manchurian Candidate. In other words, in relation to the public, the intellectual was always the exotic and threatening other, posing as "one of us" (where that pronoun, so seemingly inclusive, is very much exclusive). The hierarchized binaries continue to propagate from there, and the feeling of hope falters in the face of debt crises, joblessness, and cultural malaise.

But a strange thing happened on the way to the press. Another singular moment (one is even tempted to call it a "singularity") occurred: the Arab Spring. If both Canadian and U.S. politics, under a certain interpretation, point to a hope-less and at best a-intellectual state, then the Arab Spring could be held up as their mirror image. A series of revolutions, resistances, demonstrations, and regime changes instigated by resistance to the oppression dealt out under (often Western-supported) regimes on the Arab peninsula and Northern Africa, the Arab Spring can easily be seen as an exercise through which the public both intellectually and physically asserted its right to be what Jürgen Habermas has called "the carrier of public opinion" (2). While many of these revolutions are still violently ongoing at the time of this writing, still "the public" and "hope" seem more than empty phrases bracketed by "scare quotes": they are material facts for which people are willing to die. And the members of these rebellions are using (rather than just being used by) the tools that the marketplace made available, employing a combination of "old" and "new" media technologies in part to publicize their movements, to make heard their thoughts – the expression of their intellects that was denied by their former oppressors.[3] In these events, a public is presented that is always intellectual, if by that one means capable of rational thought – and of rational sentiment and emotive thought – as evidenced by the voicing, the publicizing of thoughts of hope and change even when the expression of those thoughts can lead to death.

Hope, however, as the saying goes, is fleeting. As we awaited readers' reports on the book, the Arab Spring turned to winter, as many began to feel that the military regime maintained too much control in Egypt, and Western televisions were inundated with shaky cell-phone video of slaughters in Syria. But, hope also springs eternal, as Alexander Pope would remind us, and the Occupy movements, starting at Wall Street in New York, hoped to thaw the grip of twenty-first-century robber barons on democratic political structures, while later still students took to the streets in Quebec to fight for the right to accessible education. But that hope falters in the face of its opposition, while tents are cleared and the Quebec government imposes laws against demonstrations, as another spring opens around – or closes upon – us.

Even the strongest hope seems faint, then, and we are left wondering if the promise of hope is itself a feint. As you read this introduction, necessarily in our future, some of the items above will be dated: some will be remembered for a long time to come, others will fade more quickly, even as our readings of them may later seem naive or overly cynical, overwrought or underdeveloped. Such is the risk of topicality. But we present this discussion of what to us are recent events in order to make a larger thematic point about hope as a cultural and political category. These recent – and other, more historical – events present cycles of hope and despair, change and retrenchment, which constitute political or other social moments and processes. All statements of political and even personal hope are necessarily immediately dated, because hope is very much the result of the material conditions of one's specific historical moment. But, it is also the means by which one projects the endlessly conditional but always immanent future.

Hope, in other words, is a prime mechanism through which the immaterial becomes the material, to borrow the parlance of contributor R. Darren Gobert. Of course, in this regard, hope, being a species of desire, finds its demonic reflection in repression and violence, serving to render other, more sinister kinds of "forward thinking" material. But hope, unlike the exercise of repressive power and unlike the stultifying effects of utopia, revels in its very conditionality. Whereas traditional definitions of hope would see it only as a forward-looking entity, we argue that hope is hope because, while it keeps one foot in the immaterial future, it gains its strength from the foot pushing off of its rootedness in our moment. Hope recognizes itself as the first step, always unfinished but therefore always moving. Hope is thus the Janus face of culture itself, looking forward and backward at the same time, rendering any conditional thoughts on the present into "datedness" the minute they are formed.

How, then, to make sense of the relationship between the public, the intellectual (both the person and the condition), and hope, when all of these terms apply to the radically different situations described above, and when the final term is so very slippery? For, while not negating the profound significance of Obama's election, we are not suggesting, as some would, that the "hope" of the Obama campaign and the "hope" of the Arab Spring are equivalent, because of the simple fact that the material expression of such a sentiment by a people who are violently repressed will never be the moral equivalent of a campaign slogan in the Global North, however sincere and authentic it may have at first been[4] (though one could point to Obama's election as a singular moment in a civil rights history that experienced – and still experiences – its own violent state repression). Regardless, slogans and images were necessary to all of these moments, and hope and change were their expressions.

From a critical perspective, of course, what fascinates is the troubled nature of all of these terms. Not only do "public" and "intellectual" join together into what many of the present essays see as the complex and often contradictory figure of the public intellectual, but the very terms "public" and "intellectual," not to mention "hope" and "culture," each have their own lengthy history of critical study, debate, and definition. In what follows, we want not only to explore aspects of the specific history of the "public intellectual" as it relates to this volume, but also to gesture towards the ways in which all four terms, taken together, constitute both the field that this volume takes as its subject and the methodologies used to study it. To this extent, and despite its primary position in our title, the "public intellectual" per se is not our ultimate concern (though we discuss the history of the term below), so much as the role of public intellectualism in the development and dissemination of culture. In short, we wish to discuss the way in which culture, and specifically the study of it, is the simultaneously material and ephemeral figure through which an always already intellectual public generates – even if under erasure – the simultaneously ephemeral and necessarily material figure of hope.

Finding Hope

Closer to home, a more immediate inspiration for this volume was to celebrate research by winners of the John Charles Polanyi Prize, established in 1987 by the Government of Ontario to honour Polanyi's 1986 Nobel Prize in Chemistry for his groundbreaking work on the physics of chemical reactions. All of the over one hundred Prize winners, drawn from the five Nobel areas of Chemistry, Economics, Literature, Medicine, and Physics, owe a profound debt not only to Polanyi's brilliant scholarly achievement but also to his keen social conscience.[5] At least in part a festschrift for Dr Polanyi, this volume takes its cue from his commitment to both research and social action as they epitomize the scholar as citizen. We thus asked contributors to reflect upon the challenging and often-vexed work of intellectualism within the public sphere. Earlier scholarly work usually begins by destabilizing the category "public intellectual,"[6] often by questioning its presupposed isolation of an academic "ivory tower" separate from the "real world" of non-academic life. Less often does this work ask the question raised by recent political and cultural developments: when did the "public" become *not* intellectual? The founding documents of the American and French republics, or of later liberation and suffrage movements, reflect the Enlightenment principle that *all* individuals are rational beings engaged in producing and maintaining a functioning public life. To separate the "public" from the "intellectual" thus raises several questions: Is there a distinction between rationality and intellectualism? Is one the more perfect form of the other? Does one's position within the hierarchies and nodes of a stratified public sphere determine one's response to those questions?

To answer these questions we proceeded by two assertions: the intellectual *is* part of the public and the public *is* intellectual, both in its structural formation as a sphere of (inter)action and in its constituent, individual parts. If the public sphere is an intrinsic part of intellectual life, culture becomes the space that connects the two. Accordingly, we approached Literature winners of the Polanyi Prize, whose research constitutes a diversity of methodological and critical approaches to the study of culture and whose academic home is Arts and Humanities, a field that seems more than ever pressured, arguably more than most others, to explain and justify to "the outside world" the kinds of intellectual activity it undertakes. This is not necessarily to mount an *apologia* for the Arts and Humanities. Many within and outside the academy are happy to challenge the university's entrenched critical, institutional, and professional positions at a time when increased specialization often isolates the university from social or political relevance. In a country whose academic institutions exist nearly exclusively by public funding (albeit decreasingly), this isolation offers no quarry for the public intellectual, who exists outside of the specialist or professional boundaries that define academic teaching or research. The debate over scholarly vs. public intellectualism is by no means new, as we shall see in the next section, but the current pressures of unprecedented technological, economic, cultural, and environmental change gives the debate a particular urgency. And certainly, one aspect of recognizing the always already intellectual nature of the public is also to recognize the necessity, and the desirability and fruitfulness, of making clear to the world at large these labours' value as it has always existed (be it through such initiatives as Western University's "Public Humanities@Western," McMaster University's "Public Intellectuals Project," or the simple act of engaging in academic work in the open, so to speak, in public lectures at libraries or science fiction conventions, conversations on social media, or on buses and street corners. . .). This is not a matter of reviving a notion of (a potentially elitist) public intellectualism, but of mobilizing the resources and spirit of public intellectualism within a public already intellectual, a relationship that has always sustained the academy's scholarly labours.

This volume, by people who have won provincial awards, then, aims to avoid provincialism. The following chapters ask what influence intellectual life has (ever) exerted in the public sphere. They avoid engaging in partisan, polarizing, and ultimately self-defeating debates about the greater relevance of some fields over others, but rather speak from the Arts and Humanities as a case study for addressing a larger set of issues about the role of the public intellectual in reflecting, analysing, and reimagining social and cultural identity at a time when hope is perhaps our world's most urgent concern. One of our key assumptions is that one of a country's greatest natural resource is its intellectual energy: the ability of scholars to anticipate and conjecture about the future, to seek out new areas for thought and new ways of thinking without always knowing where these paths might lead. Polanyi's work and career exemplify how pure research produces valuable social capital, but must also risk this profit in order to pursue unexpected or unthought discoveries that innovate new modes of knowledge. As citizens of the world, scholars are public intellectuals answerable to society in the present. However, their effectiveness also depends upon the freedom to detach from the present in order to challenge conventional wisdom within a broader history that looks at once backward and forward. The public intellectual also has the responsibility to reflect society otherwise; to predict rather than dictate its outcomes; to remain astute and alert, not prescriptive. Thus we draw upon researchers from the Arts and Humanities as fields driven by critical and cultural speculation and thus by a passionate commitment to express and envision the world differently.

The chapters in this volume explore how cultural materials – from foundational Enlightenment writings to the populist media spectacles of the twenty-first century – frame intellectual debates within the clear and ever-present gaze of the public writ large. For instance, while it is impossible to summarize their importance to subsequent scholarship (including the editors' own work), the Frankfurt School – and (perhaps more so) the critics who followed them – treated "popular culture" in terms of a public sphere largely emptied of agency.[7] Against this trend, this volume demonstrates how all forms of culture constitute not just the media but also the intellectual messages of a society. If we do not posit an inherent split between the public and its intellectuals, neither do we merely praise individuals who seem to bridge this nonexistent gap (though certainly they will be one area of interest). Instead, this volume examines how the public sphere is constitutively intellectual at every level, a kind of fractal pattern of reflexive thought that is both mirrored in and constituted by culture itself. Following Jacques Rancière, the volume will analyse the formal complexity of culture without adopting the notion of a separate, nonpolitical cultural sphere. In this argument, "culture" becomes at once the source, end point, and evolving matrix for the hope generated by an intellectual public life.

Because our contributors meditate in diverse ways on the role of culture in the interplay of our title's other three terms, we have organized chapters both thematically and historically in order to suggest both synchronic and diachronic dialogues on culture. In hopes of mobilizing what Len M. Findlay calls "daring to know," with its necessary suspicion of academic intellectualizing (we will return to Findlay below), we have positioned chapters to speak both with and against each other and the arguments taken up in this introduction. The themes of our three sections can be read as a rough chronology of the development of the modern public, its relationship to the intellectual, and their promotion or refusal of hope in the space of culture. But we also organized the sections to debate, resist, and rupture any straightforward chronology or critical expectations about the definition and role of the public intellectual. It is our hope that this equally nonsynchronic approach will illuminate how past cultures can shed light on present and future issues, as well as how current debates can reframe our approaches to older subjects. To this end, each section includes one chapter at a temporal remove from the others, and the thematic concerns of each section overlap, in order to allow for a reader-generated "map" of the book. The opening three chapters in our first section, "Public Readings," thus explore how texts circulate and educate in the public sphere by focussing on the emergence of the modern intellectual and public in the Romantic period, while a fourth chapter reads this evolution forward to address the role of storytelling in the formation of the public and private histories of the Partition of India in 1947. Turning back to the seventeenth century and then reeling ahead to twentieth- and twenty-first centuries, the four chapters in our second section turn from public "readings" to "Public Performances" of culture in musical, dramatic, and cinematic acts that at once model and refract public concern and debate. Our final section, "Public Matters," returns to the figure of the public intellectual by turning to contemporary politics and by focussing on the relationship between intellectual acts and the material world. When we speak as intellectuals to our material surroundings in order to answer a market demand for relevance, do we then turn away from the immaterial thoughts and pleasures of culture as a separate sphere? Our final four contributors offer productively divergent answers to this question.

Looking Back

The concept of the public work and influence of the intellectual, as widely deployed as it is, is not easily defined, and goes back a long way in cultural history. We could start with Socrates. Among other of his legacies is Socrates's famous profession of his own ignorance as his only philosophical certainty, the basis of the "Socratic method," the dialectical strategy of which was insistently to test and eventually undermine the presumptions and assumptions of his students' knowledge – what today, after Marx and Engels's dialectical materialism, itself a revision of Hegel's dialectic, we might think of as a process of demystifying all ideological positions. Hegel's method ultimately privileges the *Aufhebung* or "overcoming" of the negative moment of Socrates's thought in order to isolate what remained productive within an idea, and so marks the most profoundly idealist mode of intellectual activity. In both Socrates and Hegel, nonetheless, we can see intellectual activity as a certain *refinement* of thought. Yet locating this work in the public sphere was rather problematic. In his own time (the early nineteenth century) and country (Germany), Hegel enjoyed immense popularity as philosopher and lecturer for much of his career – this despite the monumentally abstract nature of his thought and writing. Socrates was equally prominent within Athenian society. But such prominence also made him a target. In the *Apology*, Plato's account of Socrates's trial speech, the younger philosopher refers to his mentor as a "gadfly" who dissents from state authority. Bucking the status quo, and remaining unrepentant to the end, Socrates was found guilty and punished to death by drinking hemlock.

Socrates had been charged with "corrupting the young, and [...] not believing in the gods in whom the city believes, but in other *daimonia* that are novel" (24b), but the less "official" offence came before this when the Delphic Oracle announced there was no individual smarter than Socrates. Insisting upon his lack of wisdom made him the paragon of intellectual and academic humility. It also, paradoxically, threatened those less aware of their own ignorance, a shortcoming of insight always anticipated by Socrates's ignorance. No one likes to be told he's stupid, but the sting was especially irksome coming from a man who, at least ostensibly, professed to be stupider than anyone else. Socrates's point was more subtle and noble, of course, but it smacked of being rather patronizing, and so set the stage for public intellectualism as double-edged sword: on one hand, the ideal of or standard against which a state might measure its cultural and political achievement; on the other hand, both gadfly *and* threat to state legitimacy for reminding the state that the knowledge buttressing its authority always rested on debatable grounds.

Which is what makes rather bogus the official charges against Socrates, the tenor of which resonate to our present day. By holding positions contrary to the status quo, or by questioning the very position *of* the status quo (Edward Said has been one of our most famous contemporary players of this role), Socrates was said to hold "daemonic" beliefs. In classical thought a "daemon" hovered indeterminately, arbitrarily, and thus suspiciously between the mortal and divine realms – a figure of dubious, misleading, and thus threatening moral quality. Ironically, of course, such an accusatory word, as Socrates's own philosophical method suggests, points to the abstract or groundless nature of all "official" beliefs taken as absolute truth. Such truth can only be signified by the Good, by which moral compass all human endeavour might be directed and thus reminded of its fallibility. It was this ideal, however, that the state perverted in its second charge against Socrates: corrupting the minds of its youth. Not so carefully veiling the crime of pedophilia lurking within the already debatable practice of pederasty in ancient Greek culture, the charge protects adolescence as a precious but malleable alloy. The young are susceptible to bad outside influence but also receptive to a kind of Althusserian interpellation, a reaction formation incited by the state's moral outrage (think of the aftermaths of the unsettling representation of adolescent – or earlier – sexuality in the public art of Robert Mapplethorpe). The charge thus implicitly fetishizes (male) youth as an impressionable stage between the absolute ignorance of earliest innocence and the maturity of later experience. This (gendered) sense of intellectual *cum* moral progression is endemic to classical ethical, aesthetic, and political thought (think of Plato's or Aristotle's anxieties about the potentially de-rationalizing and emasculating effects of metaphor) and becomes a potent way for culture to mark its civil and civilizing aspirations. But such imperatives also infantilize and thus discipline citizens as a mass body at once capable and in need of education. "To educe," of course, means to evolve or develop a latent or potential capacity, but stems from the Latin *educere*, which means "to lead" and thus, by implication, "to form" and "to conform," and by negative implication, "to lead away or astray."

Despite two thousand years between ancient Athens and late capitalism, whose notions of democracy are rather different, we might call

Socrates one of the first victims of free speech, a martyrdom that marks the dangerous ideals of intellectuals who speak on behalf of society. As our earlier nod to Habermas indicates, however, modern notions of the "public" can be traced specifically to the eighteenth century and to an explosion of populations, political allegiances, and print cultures that radically altered the formation of social bodies and their modes of disseminating knowledge. This phase of cultural development, influenced by the legacies of early modern global exploration, Renaissance humanism, and a later Enlightenment scientific empiricism, fuelled debates in moral philosophy and political economy about the essentially progressive and benign character of civil society. It also reflects a profound desire to manage a rapidly expanding public sphere. Samuel Johnson, author of the first comprehensive English dictionary, typifies this managerial response. Recapitulating an ancient fear of fiction's ability to persuade its audience with counterfeit versions of "the truth," Johnson's essay "On Fiction" warns against the rise of the novel as speaking more directly (i.e., more realistically and in more quotidian fashion) to its readers (against the supposedly more elevated, abstract, and thus elitist values expressed by poetry). Given that this audience subtended an increasingly literate working class informed by an expanding print culture (pamphlets, newspapers, magazines, as opposed to the "official" authority of books), its supposed susceptibility to political and moral suasion meant that it might be persuaded otherwise against the entrenched values of a ruling elite. Indeed, Johnson invokes the same ancient Greek anxiety about a malleable youth reader and thus about a potentially infantilized, infantalizing – but also infantalizable – readership.

It is no coincidence, then, that Katherine R. Larson's chapter for this volume traces the (gendered) role of the public intellectual to early modern culture, the development of which extends to Romantic culture, the focus of chapters by James Robert Allard, Angela Esterhammer, and Julia M. Wright. At this historical point the intellectual gets redeployed not only as either spokesperson or gadfly of state knowledge, values, and authority, but also as *arbiter* of public opinion. With accelerating literacy rates and exploding media for the dissemination of knowledge, the intellectual as rarefied scholar or philosopher gets pressured to speak for an expansive, diverse, and thus unwieldy array of single and collective identities, political, cultural, economic, and otherwise. Or rather, the intellectual begins to emerge *as* this presence, and intellectualism as a certain mode of cultural and civilizing refinement. The intellectual must adopt some sort of response to her everyday public, often to help this public make greater sense of the increasingly complex matrix from which it emerges and develops, but usually to take some kind of stand either for or against the status quo. The sociopolitical intentions of such efforts were never transparent. As Larson's chapter demonstrates, Margaret Cavendish deployed the figures and rhetoric of music and musicality to speak in the cultivated and cultivating (and thus often implicitly feminizing) voice of a somewhat latter-day female courtier loyal to the ruling class. But in her desire to "transgress" and thus overthrow "reformist" social trends, she both knew and didn't know to know her place.

Such an extra-verbal influence persists in Esterhammer's examination of the performative figures and strategies deployed by British periodical culture. Esterhammer focusses on a crucial, yet overlooked historical moment in the intellectual transformation of the public sphere. The 1820s are wedged between a post-Revolutionary culture that produced Napoleon's troubled global dreams and a Second British Empire whose intellectual life – and military might – help to discipline global cultural life well into the twentieth century. The rise of periodicals during this time, like our own intermedial culture, triangulates technological, cultural, and political change to produce a social vision at once progressively cosmopolitan and increasingly reactionary. For Wright, the public intellectual's terrain is equally vexed for Samuel Taylor Coleridge, who was an English sympathizer with the French Jacobin cause, but whose later career turns towards censoring and thus correcting such "adolescent" or gothic impulses in order to parent more mature English cultural values. Wright makes explicit what are in Larson's chapter the implicit spectres of colonialism and imperialism haunting the intellectual's response to increasingly non-Western ideas and influences, which response promulgates what Edward Said calls the orientalising representation and assessment of the East as "other" to Western identity. A similar training of the social will takes place in Allard's exploration of the emergence of the modern doctor as an arbiter of his field's professional authority as well as of its progressive desire to heal what ails the bodies and body politic of civil society.

Coleridge is key to this evolution, for in later sociopolitical writings such as *Aids to Reflection* (1825) and *On the Constitution of the Church and the State* (1826), he argues for an informed intelligentsia as secular clerisy. Eliding Blumenbach's idea of the epigenesis of life and Schelling's idea of a world spirit, Coleridge sees philosophy as a kind of national theology expressing the state's *Bildungstrieb*, its "formative urge, impulse, or force" (*Constitution* 48n). He calls this the "nisus formativus of the body politic, the shaping and informing spirit, which educing, i.e. eliciting, the latent man in all the natives of the soil, trains them up to citizens of the country, free subjects of the realm" (48). Reading Marx back to Coleridge, we can say that Coleridge's political thought expresses the purest form of ideology – ideology without being ideological. Like "nation" and "progress," Church and State are psychological concepts that citizens learn to internalize, as if unconsciously, in order to preserve a society's "permanent" cultural knowledge (*Biographia* 185). Disseminated through a broader "national education" (*Constitution* 48), such ideas "powerfully influence a man's thoughts and actions, without his being distinctly conscious of the same, much more without his being competent to express it in definite words," which is why "it is the privilege of the few to possess an idea: of the generality of men, it might be more truly affirmed, that they are possessed by it" (12–13). Thus, the task of expressing a nation's vital interests falls to a "National CLERISY" who oversee the nation's "continuing and progressive civilization" and who "remain at the fountain heads of the humanities, in cultivating and enlarging the knowledge already possessed" (42, 46, 43). Keeping the national trust as a type of revealed religion, the Cleric is a hierophant who speaks for culture's civilizing potential as well as for the status quo of its acculturating imperatives, the effects of which became so influential on such Victorian public intellectuals as Thomas Carlyle and Matthew Arnold. Yet this public intellectual speaks *above* or *beyond* as well as *to* or *of* the public sphere, as in Arnold's notion of the necessarily disinterested critic.

Two different models emerge later in the nineteenth century, each of which pays a certain price for public involvement. One is the ironic result of Arnold's disinterestedness: Oscar Wilde's notion of the critic as artist detached from the affairs of the everyday, a retreat that eventually betrayed Wilde's other, punishable entries into public life. The other is what is often cited as the first instance of modern public intellectualism. In 1894 Alfred Dreyfus, a French military captain of Alsatian Jewish descent, was convicted of treason and sentenced to life imprisonment. In *J'accuse*, an open letter to the French president published in the Paris newspaper *L'Aurore* in 1898, writer Émile Zola focussed public outrage over accusations that the military court had framed Dreyfus, resulting in his subsequent retrial and exoneration in 1907. Expressing the force of public opinion against official state knowledge, Zola's text evokes intellectual activity as a vanguard or avant-garde force. Zola's role in the Dreyfus Affair also galvanized the role of the writer as a public intellectual who directly influences and foments political action, an agitation that Wilde sought through less direct, but by no less inflammatory means.

Such transgressions both within and against the public sphere also take place within the context of the emergence of the modern university (at first in nineteenth-century Germany, and later elsewhere) as the result of a desire to organize and professionalize the accumulation and dissemination of knowledge among disciplines. One result of this specialization has been to polarize public and academic intellectual pursuits. As Russell Jacoby argues in *The Last Intellectuals* (1987), "As professional life thrives, public culture grows poorer and older" (8). Jacoby privileges the public intellectual life that flourished in American from roughly the 1930s to 1960s, associated with bohemian communities in Greenwich Village or San Francisco, and fuelled by intense pre- and post-WWII economic, political, and cultural debate. A similar case might be made for the prominence of the public intellectual in Britain in the first half of the twentieth century. In both examples public intellectualism expresses profound social value by shoring up the universality of human thought against tumultuous historical change. We might, like Neil McLaughlin, resist Jacoby's nostalgia for this golden age, and remember that the work of the intellectual necessarily reflects as much as moulds its own time. "Being a public intellectual is not an occupation" (McLaughlin 115), for she can function in diverse settings, from government, to business, to the arts. "Being a public intellectual is not a profession," moreover, for "the intellectual is not subject to a licensing procedure, educated by formal credentials, or represented by a professional association." The authors and coeditors of the present volume might take exception to McLaughlin's second definition. But such a response itself indicates how academics (which includes everyone in this volume) are increasingly anxious about their relation (or lack thereof) to the "outside world," especially because our positions come at the expense of state largesse.

The extent to which academics can or should expect this largesse, and what price intellectualism might pay for inevitable change, is the focus of this volume's chapter by Patrick Deane, head of one of Canada's research universities. A number of perspectives matter here, but one is the thought that the current academic "crisis" – we might qualify this term by saying that the very nature of academic debate is what fuels this crisis and is thus somehow the academy's constitutive possibility – is part of a broader evolution in the productive development of a culture's intellectual life. In taking up the role of the global public intellectual, McLaughlin notes three forces of current transformation: technological, political, and educational-institutional (119). Daniel Coleman similarly reminds us that the simple act of reading, by scholars in their libraries or children on their beds reading *Harry Potter* novels, constitutes public intellectual activity of the most powerful sort. But Coleman's further point is that reading, not unlike Socrates's dialectical method, always opens us to cultural texts and spaces that we have, within a certain exclusionary Western tradition, at once explored, colonized, and written over, but which can be learned from anew – in this case the vexed yet rich history of indigenous Canadian cultures.

Eventually McLauglin puts in simplest terms the ongoing dilemma of public intellectualism: navigating the "tension between specialization and general knowledge" (131). Unlike field specialists, the public intellectual is charged with galvanizing public sentiment and refracting it back to society. He must be *erudite,* so as to critique and challenge received views, and thus address the risks of oversimplifying the sociopolitical complexities of an increasingly global culture. But she must also be *transparent,* so as to make sure that a diverse public not trained in specialist vocabularies still gets the point. For Imre Szeman, David Suzuki exemplifies the social activism that public intellectualism, at its best, can mobilize to bridge between "lay person" and "expert." Yet Suzuki's activism, deploying media and technology to foment public reaction to such crucial global problems as environmental decline, risks being compromised by the same ideological assumptions it seeks to debunk (Al Gore is similarly caught between the Scylla of a public armed with scientific fact and the Charybdis of one rendered complacent by the comforts of late capitalism).

R. Darren Gobert argues persuasively against this compromise. Taking up Esterhammer's concern with the power of public performance and Deane's with attacks against the supposed elitism or irrelevance of intellectual life, Gobert explores how the "immaterial" space of theatre "matters," a term that recalls Judith Butler's complex usage. Gobert considers how the play of ideas, the otherwise "frivolous" and "inconsequential" domain of intellectuals stuck in their own minds, can effect shifts in material circumstance (arguably more so) as much as the "useful" empiricism of scientific fact that drives debates and policy about higher education and cultural institutions. Certainly Aristotle knew of this "immaterial" force when he articulated how tragedy effects a powerful communal transformation of negative into productive affect, which catharsis Antonin Artaud and Berthold Brecht read to different, but no less potent political and cultural effect, in the twentieth century. Like Coleman's account of the simple act of reading, the simple act of seeing and feeling, Gobert reminds us, remains at some level a human endeavour of the most profound intellectual and material consequence.

It is to this more public or popular, and thus supposedly inconsequential, form of cultural expression that three further chapters in this volume address themselves. Both Joel Faflak and Andrea Most turn to a pivotal moment in the cultural history of the previous century – the rise of what Simcha Jacobovici calls "Hollywoodism"[8] in 1920s and '30s American cinema – to address how mainstream Hollywood film, otherwise thought to be hegemonic, innocuous, or stupefying, in fact critically negotiates a fraught and by no means monolithic ideological and political terrain. As one form of public intellectualism, popular film is taken to account in Jason Haslam's analysis of a return to what Jacobovici might call the primal scene of popular culture, the Holocaust, in Quentin Tarantino's controversial *Inglourious Basterds* (2007). Tarantino, like Suzuki, emerges at the triangulation between Antonio Gramsci's organic intellectual, who foments political action as an integral part of his social sphere; Said's amateur intellectual, who transgresses the bounds of official or institutional intellectual practice; and the intellectual as celebrity, who wields cultural autonomy and authority but risks compromise by the same technological and ideological demands she seeks to overturn.

Looking Forward

Nandi Bhatia takes on literary representations of a different trauma in twentieth-century history – the 1947 partition of India and Pakistan – by returning us to the targets of a vexed intellectual campaign to police the moral boundaries of Western cultural life. Children become witnesses to and purveyors of this life's all-too-human capacity for traumatizing itself and others (think of the cult of the child that defines Michael Jackson's persona), precisely at a moment of fragile and vulnerable national infancy haunted by its genealogy, compelled to parent its future, and thus able to snuff out as much as nurture its own hopeful visions. It is eventually to this capacity for culture to function as a mode of (hopeful) intellectual expression and critique that this volume turns its attention. The stakes of this public intellectualism are high, for hope risks being misled *by* its own hope for a future that has not or might not ever come. As Sara Ahmed argues, there is an "intimacy" and constitutively necessary relationship "between hope and anxiety" (183). For if "[h]ope is a feeling that is present (a pleasure in the mind) but is directed toward an object that is not yet present," then "[i]n having hope we *become* anxious, because hope involves wanting something that might or might not happen. Hope is about desiring the 'might,' which is only 'might' if it keeps open the possibility of the 'might not'" (183). As Erin Wunker writes, hope is both "necessary and slightly delusional" (13). Put another way, hope resides precisely with the spectres of its own (im)possibility, for the "failure of transcendence constitutes the necessity of a political struggle" (Ahmed 187). The place of hope in the work of culture, as expressed by the public intellectual, comes precisely with reminding society – the public, whether inside or outside the academy – that hope cannot be sentimentalized or simplified as a derivatively utopian concept. Nor can it be the object of an incessant derision or ironization – a fine line that Jon Stewart or Stephen Colbert walk each time they take on an increasingly complacently polarized audience in the forum of political satire performing as entertainment.

At this point we can turn to one of the starting points of the reexamination of culture as popular myth in the late structuralism of Roland Barthes. Each in their own way, and when placed together, the terms "public," "intellectual," "culture," and "hope" take on a mythological element. In his analyses of objects, events, and texts, ranging from Einstein's brain, to wrestling matches, to the cover of *Paris Match* and beyond, Barthes argues for a vision of culture as a series of interrelated myths, all largely empty of meaning on their own, but which shape and form the public's vision of itself, all the while bypassing the critical function of the intellect. "Myth," Barthes writes, "*is depoliticized speech.*" He continues: "One must naturally understand *political* in its deeper meaning, as describing the whole of human relations in their world, social structure" (143; emphasis in original). For Barthes, myth takes the specificity of political situations (say, for example, the Western support of repressive regimes in the Arab peninsula) and "makes them innocent, it gives them a natural and eternal justification, it gives them a clarity which is not that of an explanation but that of a statement of fact" (143). The myth of the "Western values" of freedom and democracy is presented as a fact that necessarily denies the material actions of the West on behalf of nondemocratic, violently repressive governments.

In this guise, then, our three terms – public, hope, intellectual – could be read as myth when it comes not only to the specificities of the Obama campaign, but to the formation of Western global hegemony: offering the promise of *change* and delivering the reality of the *same*.

In actual revolutionary spaces, however, hope and change through the active exercise of one's intellect become tangible, real things. "If myth is depoliticized speech," Barthes writes, then "that which *remains* political" can never be considered myth (145): "This is why revolutionary language proper cannot be mythical. Revolution [. . .] *makes* the world; and its language, all of it, is functionally absorbed in this making" (146; emphasis in original). So, our dilemma seems solved. Obama's hope and change = myth; the hope and change of the Arab Spring = material revolution. While the comparison is unjust and uninformed, the signing of the Magna Carta (1215), after all, while a singular moment, should not be considered the same kind of push for the recognition of rights as the Peasants' Revolt (1381). We say this comparison is unjust because the moment of an African American being elected as president of the United States *is* undeniably a hopeful moment, and the similarity in rhetoric – *in the cultural representations* – offered of and by these disparate moments haunts. And it haunts not just our linguistic registers, but material reality as well. After all, Obama's presidency gave him the ability to address the Arab world in his speech in Cairo in a way that inspired many, and the Arab Spring led to changes in U.S. policy as directly as their actions led to change at home. In part because of the deeply held myth of freedom, and the political ramifications thereof in the face of revolution, the West as a whole, Canada included, could not continue to support Mubarak's regime, for instance (even as the West, perhaps, exploited the same to move quickly into Libya, and ignored the same while looking at numerous other states). But the distinction between myth and revolutionary language begins to fade, and it does so in large part because of the global and immediate nature of information exchange at the present moment. Perhaps, here, there is a hope that literally materializes itself out of thin air.

But cynicism haunts us as well, as it haunts all academic endeavours that, however vaguely, remain constrained by the scepticism of the scientific method that we can trace at some level all the way back to Socrates. And, if we are to follow Barthes, we must "become estranged if [we] want[ ] to liberate the myth," and so be "condemned to live in a theoretical sociality" wherein our "connection with the world is of the order of sarcasm" (157): as academics – institutionalized intellectuals – we must, in other words, like Stan Marsh in the tenth-season finale of *South Park,* diagnose ourselves as having "the condition known as 'being a cynical asshole'" ("You're Getting Old"). Hope for social change here, problematically, becomes a function of academic and political cynicism. In this sense, perhaps what the state was really giving Socrates was the chance for a graceful, if dramatic, exit.

And so to test the hypothesis of hope, we turn again to definition. It is difficult, in many ways, even to consider defining the terms "public," "intellectual," "culture," and "hope" separately, for the minute one talks about, for example, the public, one finds oneself invoking the notion of culture, which then, in turn, requires a definition that either relies on or denies the notion of an intellectual quality to that culture. As Michael Warner has recently stated, "Behind the common sense of our everyday life among publics is an astonishingly complex history. The idea of a public is a *cultural form,* a kind of practical fiction" (8; our emphasis). Publics, cultures, our other terms, and their social effects are inextricably tangled. Take, for example, the incorporation of the study of popular culture into academic institutions. While this move has, since 1963 at least, become more and more (dare we say) popular, debates still occur as to whether this field is a progressive one, aiming to knock down boundaries between the (intellectual) academy and the public (figured often as "the masses"), or if it is simply an academic bowing to capitalist market pressures in what is represented as an ever-increasing demand to put "bums in seats," as the common academic parlance would have it.

But even at the level of historical definition, the terms become intertwined in this way. To start again with the "public" to indicate this entanglement, the passage from Warner's study, above, continues by noting that "There are ambiguities, even contradictions in the idea" of a public, and "[a]s it is extended to new contexts and new media, new politics and new rhetorics, its meaning can be seen to change" (8). In his foundational study of the history of the Western public, Habermas takes a similar position, stating that the terminology surrounding the concept of the "public," as it is used today, is

> most commonly associated with [. . .] expressions like "public opinion," an "outraged" or "informed public," "publicity," "publish," and "publicize." The subject of this publicity is the public as carrier of public opinion; its function as a critical judge is precisely what makes the public character of proceedings – in court, for instance – meaningful. In the realm of the mass

> media, of course, publicity has changed its meaning. Originally a function of public opinion, it has become an attribute of whatever attracts public opinion. (2)

But how to distinguish between "mass media" of the connected world and "common[ ] associat[ion]"? To move to one of the other points on the polygon of critical inquiry, if Jean Baudrillard is right about the public sphere being "constituted" as an endless mediation of signifiers through other signifiers, then does the public become an endless reflection of what is said about it by and in "the media," rather than a dialogic body that reflects on the reality in which it finds itself? Is the function of a "critical judge," of Barthes's "mythologist," simply transformed into *South Park*'s "cynical asshole," rendered meaningless – in a pay-for-vote phone call to *American Idol,* for instance? If Coleridge's Cleric or Arnold's critic smack of elitism, neither is there much hope for a democratic citizenry in the image of such a populist intellectual: Philip K. Dick made a living off of presenting just such a world in his futurist dystopias.

Our concern, then, is with the role of these expressions – ultimately with the role, that is, of our last term: culture. We note that this is a volume composed of essays by "humanists": certainly not necessarily all humanists in the theoretical sense, but scholars who inhabit the space of the humanities in the academy, the space of the study of the ephemera known as cultural products. If there is a place for the "public intellectual," and for the intellectual hopes of the public, then it is one that is at least mediated through culture: while differing as to its role, both Arnold and Frederic Jameson would agree to at least that. Where they would differ, of course, is on the question of hope. Can hope be captured in culture? Is culture Pandora's box, in other words, granting expression to all the evils of the world, while clinging to hope as its final true possession? The question comes down to one that roughly frames our volume: is culture to be viewed through an Enlightenment-refracted Romantic lens – does culture reflect, as in M. H. Abrams's mirror, the hope of a nation, while lighting the way, through its lamp, for a hopeful enlightenment to come (be it spiritual and/or intellectual)? Or is culture instead the glittering disco ball of the late-capitalist, postmodern, and carceral age – does it endlessly reflect the structure of an economically stratified society, turning back onto the public not an enlightened lamp, but Althusser's policeman's flashlight, hailing us to our pre-given spot in the ideological matrix of a divided world? Or can it be both and neither at the same time? The green light on Daisy's dock can close out this series of allusive and illusive definitions of culture: shining forth both the verdant hope and the lifeless glare of Gatsby's world, the green light perhaps highlights the tenuous division between the fractured mirror and the enlightened lamp.

To bridge this divide, building on Abrams's metaphor while borrowing from Rodolphe Gasché, we'd like to position culture instead as the tain of the mirror, the dull, unreflective, impermeable surface that is nonetheless necessary to create reflection and (perhaps only the illusion of) depth. The public, the intellectual, and hope are all reflections of and on a material world that is only brought into existence by its cultural tain, through which its reflections are made possible (a state which also makes attacks on culture – such as cuts to public funding for archives, to choose a recent example – into attacks on the public itself, something Orwell showed all too well). In this we return – as so many so often do – to Wilde. Perhaps the critic is the artist, as the public is the intellectual, but both are functions of their medium, which is culture "itself," something that is ultimately not regulated by any one discourse, but not free of them either. More to the point, as Vivian states in "The Decay of Lying," "to pass from the art of the time to the time itself is the great mistake that all historians commit" (1091). We read this to say that it is a mistake to think that either culture or history are so easily understood that one can fully contain either in any set of discourses, and surely the figure of the public/intellectual is that of the person who points to the failings of dominant discourses in her attempt to contain or circumscribe specific regimes of signification. And, as does Wilde's Algernon, we define culture here widely: to limit the study of culture to a select group of canonical works, figures, or tropes is a hopeless endeavour since "more than half of modern culture depends on what one shouldn't read" (*Importance* 360). Our hopes lie in the culture that has escaped Pandora's box.

We position these hopes in the plural because it is only too easy to slip into universalizing language due to the mythological elements of the terms we are dealing with. In a recent piece arguing for the necessity of the development of "Indigenous humanities," Len M. Findlay has pointed precisely to this problem:

> The Canadian humanities' deep complicity with colonialism has now morphed more emphatically into a complicity with, or subjection to, the imperatives of 21st-century capitalism. The situation is far from hopeless.

> But the audacity of hope associated with Obama must be critically connected to its veracity, as expressed in Kant's use of the Horatian tag, *sapere aude,* dare to know. And daring to know means daring to know the limitations of your white enlightenment universals, the provinciality of your Eurocentrism, and the implications of your ignorance of Indigenous languages and knowledge systems.

Daring to know and daring to hope become the necessary tain for each other, and they are tied to a deep suspicion of received intellectual wisdom and its material baggage.

The "public," "intellectual," and perhaps especially "hope," may well be myth: empty vessels that only signify within particular social and cultural matrices (be it Kant's Enlightenment, the United States in 2008, Canada in 2010, the Arab peninsula in 2011, or the classroom of tomorrow). More importantly, though, they are all necessarily imbricated with each other: despite claims to the isolation of the intellectual, the denial of the possibility of an intellectually engaged public, or the assertion that hope is only and always a utopian fiction used to mollify the masses, each of the public, the intellectual, and their various hopes are necessary for the others' reflection of/on society. Culture isn't a simple mimetic reflection of any of them, so much as it is the medium that enables our reflections, the alchemical agent that can make the public and the intellectual, hope and criticism, into mutable forms of each other. Perhaps these reflections, based on a cultural tain that is tied to but never at one with the material world, can intellectually bend, alter, or twist that world towards or away from its various publics' various hopes.

NOTES

1 Joe Biden, Obama's future vice president, was quoted in 2007 as having said of Obama that "you got the first mainstream African-American who is articulate and bright and clean and a nice-looking guy. I mean, that's a storybook, man," and quickly had to issue an apology for "any offense" he had caused. See, e.g., Thai and Barrett.

2 As Nicholas D. Kristof wrote at the time in an opinion piece in the *New York Times,* "The second most remarkable thing about [Obama's] election is that American voters have just picked a president who is an open, out-of-the-closet, practicing intellectual," pitting this against the view of Bush as

anti-intellectual. See Troy for a brief history of the presidency and public intellectuals, albeit one that is aimed primarily at the "conservative intellectual" market, and thus offering a more positive vision of George W. Bush's relationship with public intellectuals, even as it derides his father's anti-intellectual stance.

3 While too much has been made of the "twitter revolution" (as one Egyptian memorably tweeted, "hey frigging american analysts how about we let tunisians, who actually lived what happened decide how relevant twitter and wikileaks w[ ]ere?" [from the twitter feed of Egyptian blogger Alaa Abd El Fattah, @alaa, posted on 14 January 2011; also linked in York's article], it is true that, for example, cell-phone videos of the uprisings did make it to news organizations, and became a major source of firsthand information for those outside of such areas as Syria, which banned foreign media. See York for an analysis of the use of social media during the Tunisian Revolution.

4 Although there is an economic outcome to either scenario: just as Egyptians experienced the rather cynically ironic outcome of thinking out loud as a call for democratic reform in a global culture – the loss of vital tourist revenue – Americans are paying the price of not thinking (out loud) *enough* in the form of a persistence economic crisis plaguing one of the birthplaces of modern democracy and capitalism.

5 Polanyi's awards include the Royal Medal of the Royal Society of London and some thirty honorary degrees from six countries. Dr Polanyi is a Fellow of the Royal Societies of Canada, London, and Edinburgh, and of the American Academy of Arts and Sciences, the U.S. National Academy of Sciences, the Pontifical Academy of Rome, and the Russian Academy of Sciences. He is also a member of the Queen's Privy Council for Canada, and a Companion of the Order of Canada, and has served on the Prime Minister of Canada's Advisory Board on Science and Technology and the Premier's Council of Ontario. Polanyi has served as Foreign Honorary Advisor to the Institute for Molecular Sciences, Japan; as Honorary Advisor to the Max Planck Institute for Quantum Optics, Germany; and on the Board of the Steacie Institute for Molecular Sciences, Canada. He is a founding member of both the Committee on Scholarly Freedom of the Royal Society and the Canadian Committee for Scientists and Scholars, a human rights organization of which he is President. Dr Polanyi has been active for forty years in International Pugwash, a global movement of scientists and others with a professional concern about the social impact of science and seeking ways to prevent its misuse. He helped to found the Canadian Pugwash Group in 1960, serving as its first Chairman. Polanyi

has written extensively on science policy, the control of armaments, and peacekeeping. He coedited *The Dangers of Nuclear War*, and participated in the Canada 21 study of a 21st-century defence posture for Canada. He cochaired the Department of Foreign Affairs International Consultative Committee on a Rapid Response Capability for the United Nations.

6 In recent years, the role of the intellectual has been much debated in the media, and several scholarly monographs and essay collections have appeared on the subject. The recent U.S. presidential election, as we noted above, often pivoted around supposed divisions between intellectualism and "down to earth" values, elitism and populism, and so on. Each of these pairings separates the intellectual from the public, a divide that current scholarly works seem to complicate. Some of these take a wide historical and geographic approach (notably Posner, Small, Gattone, Melzer et al.), while others (Bender and Cummings) focus on one nation, one period – often our own – or even one individual. Some laud the intellectual who engages in public commentary, while others cast a more cynical eye on this figure and her or his effect (or lack thereof) on public life. Despite this contrast, however, these volumes tend to assume that the "public intellectual" is part of the public sphere (a rare occurrence) and thus different from the "non-public" intellectual or "non-intellectual public."

7 Here one thinks most obviously of Adorno and Horkheimer's famous indictment of American popular culture in "The Culture Industry: Enlightenment as Mass Deception," first published in 1944 as an essay in *Philosophische Fragmente*, published in 1947 as *Dialektik der Aufklärung*, and later translated as *Dialectic of Enlightenment*.

8 See Faflak's essay in this volume, Note 13.

WORKS CITED

Abrams, M.H. *The Mirror and the Lamp: Romantic Theory and the Critical Tradition*. Oxford: Oxford UP, 1953. Print.

Adorno, Theodor W., and Max Horkheimer. "The Culture Industry: Enlightenment as Mass Deception." *Dialectic of Enlightenment*. New York: Verso, 1997. 120–67. Print.

Barthes, Roland. *Mythologies*. Sel. and trans. Annette Lavers. London: Jonathan Cape, 1973. Print.

Baudrillard, Jean. *Simulacra and Simulation*. Trans. Sheila Faria Glaser. Ann Arbor: U of Michigan P, 1994. Print.

Bender, Thomas. *Intellect and Public Life: Essays on the Social History of Academic Intellectuals in the United States*. Cambridge, MA: Johns Hopkins UP, 1992.

Coleridge, Samuel Taylor. *Biographia Literaria*. 2 vols. Ed. James Engell and W. Jackson Bate. Princeton: Princeton UP, 1983. Print.

Coleridge, Samuel Taylor. *On the Constitution of Church and State*. Ed. John Colmer. 1976. *The Collected Works of Samuel Taylor Coleridge*. Ed. Kathleen Coburn et al. 16 vols. Princeton: Princeton UP, 1969–2003. Print.

Cummings, Dolan. *The Changing Role of the Public Intellectual*. New York: Routledge, 2005. Print.

Findlay, Len M. "Soft Sovereignties and Strokes of Genius: Situating the Indigenous Humanities within Canada." *Fedcan Blog* 6 July 2011. Web. 17 July 2011.

Gasché, Rodolphe. *The Tain of the Mirror: Derrida and the Philosophy of Reflection*. Cambridge, MA: Harvard UP, 1986. Print.

Gattone, Charles F. *Social Scientist as Public Intellectual: Reflections in a Changing World*. Lanham, MD: Rowman & Littlefield, 2006. Print.

Habermas, Jürgen. *The Structural Transformation of the Public Sphere: An Inquiry into a Category of Bourgeois Society*. Trans. Thomas Burger with the assistance of Frederick Lawrence. Cambridge, MA: MIT Press, 1991. Print.

Johnson, Samuel. "On Fiction [*The Rambler No. 4*]." *The Norton Anthology of Theory and Criticism*. 2nd ed. Gen ed. Vincent B. Leitch. New York: Norton, 2010. Print.

Kristof, Nicholas D. "Obama and the War on Brains." *New York Times* 9 Nov. 2008. Web. 16 July 2011.

McLaughlin, Neil. "Global Public Intellectuals, Autonomy, and Culture: Reflections Inspired by the Death of Edward Said." *Cultural Autonomy: Frictions and Connections*. Ed. Petra Rethmann, Imre Szeman, and William D. Coleman. Vancouver: U of British Columbia P, 2010. 111–31. Print.

Melzer, Arthur M., Jerry Weinberg, and M. Richard Zinman, eds. *The Public Intellectual: Between Philosophy and Politics*. Lanham, MD: Rowman & Littlefield, 2003. Print.

Plato. *The Collected Dialogues of Plato, Including the Letters*. Ed. Edith Hamilton and Huntington Cairns. Princeton: Princeton UP, 1961. Print.

Posner, Richard A. *Public Intellectuals: A Study of Decline*. Cambridge, MA: Harvard UP, 2001. Print.

Small, Helen, ed. *The Public Intellectual*. Malden, MA: Wiley-Blackwell, 2002. Print. http://dx.doi.org/10.1002/9780470775967.

Thai, Xuan, and Ted Barrett. "Biden's description of Obama draws scrutiny." *Politics*. 9 Feb. 2007. *CNN.com*. Web. 26 June 2011.

Troy, Tevi. "Bush, Obama, and the Intellectuals." *National Affairs* 3 (2010). Web. 16 July 2011.

Warner, Michael. *Publics and Counterpublics*. Brooklyn, NY: Zone, 2002. Print.

Wilde, Oscar. *Collins Complete Works of Oscar Wilde*. Centenary ed. Glasgow: HarperCollins, 1999. Print.

Wilde, Oscar. "The Decay of Lying." Wilde. *Collins Complete*. 1071–92. Print.

Wilde, Oscar. *The Importance of Being Earnest*. Wilde. *Collins Complete*. 357–419. Print.

Wunker, Erin. "Hopelessly Witty or Witless Hope: Notes from LTA Land." *English Studies in Canada* 35.4 (2009): 11–14. Print.

York, Jillian C. "Not Twitter, Not WikiLeaks: A Human Revolution." *Jilliancyork.com*. 14 Jan. 2011. Web. 16 July 2011.

"You're Getting Old." *South Park*. Writ. and dir. Trey Parker. Comedy Central. 8 June 2011. Television.

PART ONE

Public Readings

1 "Maga-scenes": Performing Periodical Literature in the 1820s

ANGELA ESTERHAMMER

Prologue: The Culture of Hope in a Transitional Age

A British middle-class reader of the 1820s perusing the periodical magazines, the most widely circulating reading material of the day, would have been informed again and again that the decade was characterized by "mediocrity" (Hazlitt 218). Judging from the general tenor of theatre reviews, the reader would have to conclude that the English stage was at a low ebb, and that amusement and instruction were more likely to be found in alternative media – public lectures or visual spectacles such as panoramas and exhibits of exotica. By the mid-1820s, the controversial celebrities who had dominated the Romantic landscape (Napoleon, Staël, Byron) were dead, as were its innovative young poets (Keats, Shelley, Byron). Book reviews assured readers that the copious productions issuing from the press now consisted overwhelmingly of second-rate imitations and immoral trash by "a host of writers, working for their bread on the spur of the occasion, and whose names are not known" (Hazlitt 222). At best, modern literature might be characterized as "a gay Coquette, fluttering, fickle, vain" who "renounces eternal fame for a newspaper puff; trifles with all sorts of arts and sciences [...] glitters, flutters, buzzes, spawns, dies, – and is forgotten!" (Hazlitt 219).

The above quotations from William Hazlitt's "The Periodical Press," an essay that appeared in the *Edinburgh Review* in May 1823, echo the remarkably widespread resignation perpetuated by 1820s print culture about the belated, imitative, mediocre quality of contemporary aesthetic production. Yet Hazlitt deliberately echoes the bad press his age was receiving in order to add an ironic turn: to suggest that a transitional age can actually give rise to a culture of hope. His article turns into an only slightly tongue-in-cheek celebration of periodical literature and its appeal to the reading public:

> We exist in the bustle of the world, and cannot escape from the notice of our contemporaries. We must please to live, and therefore should live to please. We must look to the public for support. [...] Therefore, let Reviews flourish – let Magazines increase and multiply – let the Daily and Weekly Newspapers live for ever! We are optimists in literature, and hold, with certain limitations, that, in this respect, whatever is, is right! (Hazlitt 220)

Despite the hyperbolic echoes of divine creation, monarchical ceremony, and Pope's *Essay on Man*, Hazlitt has a serious point: critical discussion and medial experimentation are healthy in a period of rapid change. In one of many notably gendered formulations, he implies that a period of splendid and consummate art gives rise to admiration, repose, and "effeminate delicacy" while a struggling and critical period calls forth "masculine boldness and creative vigour" (213). The paradox of Hazlitt's essay – that a deficient age can actually be superior to a literary golden age insofar as it encourages creative and critical boldness – reflects a far-reaching paradox in the self-image of the 1820s. For despite its self-deprecating rhetoric about mediocrity and cant, the post-Waterloo period in Britain is also an era of economic prosperity, public education, improvement, and progress – conditions encompassed in another phrase that appears constantly in periodical literature: "march of intellect" or "march of mind." Indeed, journalists often cite the increased number and circulation of periodicals themselves as evidence of the rapid improvement in philosophical, literary, and scientific knowledge. In addition to quantity, the pace at which information is being mobilized astounds readers and writers in the 1820s. Hazlitt marvels at the sheer speed of journalistic production – "The public read the next day at breakfast-time (perhaps), what would make a hundred octavo pages, every word of which has been spoken, written out, and printed within the last twelve or fourteen hours!" (224) – but he also remarks that the quality of "*extempore* writing" compares favourably with "more laboured compositions": "what is struck off at a blow, is in many respects better than what is produced on reflection, and at several heats" (222). Time pressure, information overload, the absence of dominant personalities, and the presence of a large anonymous reading public are factors that generate palpable anxiety, but they also call forth creative vigour.

Scene 1 Reviewing the Reviews

As Hazlitt realizes, the larger and more affluent reading public of the early nineteenth century makes new ventures in writing and publishing possible, but also creates a literary marketplace in which writers "cannot escape from the notice of [...] contemporaries" and "must look to the public for support" (220). The role of the public intellectual thus takes on an increasingly performative quality insofar as "performance" suggests action in the presence of an audience whose demands and responses the performer cannot ignore. But periodical writers also engage in performance in a more specific sense: they draw on forms of communication made popular by the embodied and experiential media that proliferated during the 1820s, from stage performance to public lectures to visual panoramas.

Recent studies in book, theatre, and media history have opened up new contexts for studying the performative strategies adopted by public intellectuals and by the periodical press. As the material and social conditions of early nineteenth-century print communication come into clearer focus, the pace of change in writing practices and in the concomitant evolution of reading publics is becoming ever more evident, as is the profound significance of these changes. Technological improvements such as steam printing and the machine manufacture of paper gradually brought down the price of printed matter over the course of the 1820s and had a demonstrable influence on literary form by making prose fiction and weekly or monthly periodicals more economically viable than they had ever been before.[1] The economic prosperity that followed within a few years of the end of the Napoleonic Wars increased the leisure time and disposable income of middle-class readers who turned in ever greater numbers to literary-cultural magazines that promised instruction, amusement, and access to a genteel lifestyle. A more specific account of the dynamics of periodical publishing in early nineteenth-century Britain might begin with the rivalry between the Tory *Edinburgh Review* (founded in 1802) and the London-based Whig *Quarterly Review* (founded in 1809) that was disrupted in 1817 by the appearance of the politically conservative but stylistically radical *Blackwood's Edinburgh Magazine*. Among the many influential innovations of *Blackwood's* was its change of format from a standard "review" into a "magazine" containing creative writing and coverage of metropolitan popular culture. Imitators and rivals of *Blackwood's*, notably the *London Magazine* (founded in 1820) and the *New Monthly Magazine* (relaunched in 1821), dominated the print culture of the following decade with their appeal to a broadly middle-class readership, although the groundwork was simultaneously being laid for the cheaper weekly "penny press" that would bring useful knowledge within reach of the working-class masses by the 1830s.[2] These developments in print culture took place against the colourful background provided by the visual and experiential media of metropolitan culture – melodrama, pantomime, panoramas, dioramas, lectures, exhibits, museums, sporting events – all of which played off and on one another. As Simon During has recently observed about Regency culture, "this market was characterized not so much by the specialization of its various sectors as by the interactions between them so as to animate activity across the whole" (346).[3]

One of the most obvious ways in which early nineteenth-century print culture draws strength from its own proliferation is with the "reviewers reviewed" genre. In addition to reviewing new books, plays, and concerts, by the 1820s periodicals avidly and sometimes obsessively review one another. Hazlitt's essay on "The Periodical Press" belongs to this genre: after a general overview of the state of the literary field, Hazlitt evaluates a dozen daily, weekly, and monthly publications in terms of their effect on contemporary literature, art, and public opinion. He thus participates in a feedback loop that developed together with the unprecedented expansion of the periodical press around 1820. New periodicals entering the market usually begin with a prospectus that takes stock of the existing field, and many magazines run regular articles that systematically evaluate the state of the periodical press at home and abroad. The *European Magazine*, for instance, had a recurring feature entitled "The Reviewers Reviewed" that its editor made use of for three consecutive months in 1824 to respond to Hazlitt's review of the reviews (*European Magazine* 85:129–38, 229–38, 336–8). Ridiculing and rebutting Hazlitt's "Periodical Press" essay almost sentence by sentence, the *European Magazine* argues *contra* Hazlitt that the age's proliferating "cant of criticism" (85:129) is not healthy, but instead exerts far too much influence on readers.

Cutting across the dialogue among periodicals is the explicit and implicit feedback between periodical writers and the reading public. Magazines relied for economic survival on their ability to appeal to the tastes of readers and respond nimbly to changes in public demand, and this immediate dependence on popular response is often cited by writers of the 1820s as a defining feature of periodical literature. Hazlitt's recognition that "We must look to the public for support" (220) becomes a still more prominent and more troubling theme in the contemporaneous survey of "Periodical Literature" by James Mill that appeared in the first issue of the *Westminster Review* (1824), where Mill tries and fails to reconcile the periodicals' beholdenness to readers' opinions and their need for "the applause of the moment" (Mill 207) with the traditional responsibility of literature to educate the public and correct its taste. What complicates the situation further is the unstable distinction between readers and writers. As the "reviewers-reviewed" genre makes evident, periodical writers are periodical readers; conversely, there are many ways for lay readers to become writers. Magazines generally devoted ample space to letters to the editor, and a significant number encouraged or even subsisted on reader contributions.

A more specific dialogue between magazine editors and reader-writers takes place in the "Notes (or Notices) to Contributors" pages at the beginnings or ends of issues – an intriguing, unstudied feature of many early nineteenth-century periodicals. These pages contain private communications between the editor and would-be contributors about the acceptance or rejection of their submissions. In the case of acceptance, the editor's note may give an indication of when the contribution will appear or encourage the writer to submit further material; in the case of rejection, brief reasons and serious or sarcastic suggestions for improvement are often included. Submissions might be praised as respectable, judicious, curious, clever, ingenious, or humorous; they might be criticized as too tame, too grave, too loosely and carelessly composed; they might be rejected as unsuited for the magazine or simply as "trash." While this public form of private correspondence is pragmatic, saving editors the time and expense of writing to contributors individually, it simultaneously serves to consolidate the magazine's editorial policy and advertise the contents of future issues. More elaborate versions of "Notes to Contributors," such as the editorial pages entitled "The Lion's Head" in the *London Magazine*, serve to provide entertainment to the entire readership, in part through the editor's performance as a witty connoisseur of the metropolis. These pages establish a model of dialogue between editors and reader-writers that can itself be subject to adaptation or parody in upstart magazines such as *Knight's Quarterly* (of which more below).

Against this vivid background of print and performance it is now possible to do finer-grained work by studying more experimental, ephemeral, and local phenomena. Short-lived ventures onto the periodical scene abounded during the unsettled 1820s, and magazines that survived for only a few issues can be revealing precisely because of their ephemerality. Taking advantage of opportunities and drawing inspiration from the practices of more-established magazines as well as from contemporary performance genres, these "indie" publications are a valuable gauge of the fashions, demands, communicative practices, and economic realities of the market. As the following examples will show, key figures of high-Romantic culture sought to reach a new public through the media provided by the 1820s marketplace, as did the university students and young entrepreneurs who would become leading public intellectuals of the Victorian era. Their creative productions draw on different types of communication – written and oral, print and performance – and demonstrate how the diversified cultural field of 1820s London builds on itself, generating reviews, imitations, and transmedial experiments that alter the relationship between producers and consumers of culture.

Scene 2 The Lecturer as Journalist: John Thelwall's *The Panoramic Miscellany*

The six-month, six-issue lifespan of *The Panoramic Miscellany* testifies to the challenge of surviving in the 1820s periodical market, but also to the hope it offered a Romantic-era intellectual that he might reach a new audience of middle-class and even working-class readers. John Thelwall had risen to prominence in the heady climate of the 1790s as a public lecturer, literary figure, and spokesperson for political reform. During the first three decades of the nineteenth century he devoted his attention to elocutionary training and speech therapy – subjects on which he lectured, wrote, and taught at the institute he established in London, where he also maintained close contacts with the city's scientific and medical institutions. Thelwall was thus one of the Romantic period's intensely interdisciplinary public intellectuals, a practitioner of interrelated arts and sciences whose strong commitment to public communication is evident in a lifelong career of lecturing at literary and philosophical institutes throughout Britain as well as in his writing and journalism. During the first six months of 1826, Thelwall attempted to harness his considerable experience as periodical writer and editor in order to launch an independent monthly magazine entitled *The Panoramic Miscellany*. Reflecting the rapid changes that had taken place in print culture since the time he began his journalistic and public-speaking career in the late eighteenth century, *The Panoramic Miscellany* reveals Thelwall's partial success but ultimate failure to adapt his long-standing ideological commitments to the new media context of the 1820s.

The Panoramic Miscellany arose out of Thelwall's traumatic break with the middle-class liberal *Monthly Magazine* to which he had contributed since its founding in 1796 and of which, in the mid-1820s, he briefly served as editor. When the new owners of the *Monthly Magazine* fired him in November 1825, Thelwall sought to perpetuate the commitments and ideals of the *Monthly* in an independent periodical. The *Panoramic*'s contents accordingly preserve the standard line-up of older monthly miscellanies such as the *Monthly Magazine*, including an editorial on the "Topic of the Month"; serialized feature articles on literary, scientific, historical, and political topics; original poetry and short fiction; coverage of current events in the scientific institutes, art galleries, theatres, and concert halls; reviews of new book publications; and routine sections containing parliamentary reports, weather statistics, agricultural reports, domestic news items, patents, bankruptcies, and obituaries. But the contents and editorial practice of *The Panoramic Miscellany* distinguish Thelwall's intervention into 1820s periodical culture as an attempt to encourage interdisciplinary and international dialogue, to promote public education, and above all to transfer his practice as lecturer and trainer in public speaking – thus, as a distinctive type of performer – into a print medium.

Like most editors of the day, Thelwall launches his periodical by reviewing the current state of print culture. The title of his leading article in the inaugural issue of *The Panoramic Miscellany* is a virtual thesis statement: "On the Connexion of Periodical Literature with the Moral and Intellectual Progress of Society" (*Panoramic* 1).[4] Thelwall's lengthy editorial echoes the main goals that publisher Richard Phillips and editor John Aikin had articulated in the editorial preface of the first issue of the *Monthly Magazine* thirty years earlier. In February 1796, the founders of the *Monthly* had promised to "open new sources of entertainment and instruction for their readers," to propagate liberal principles, to provide a forum for the "lighter exertions of learned and ingenious writers," and to publish genuinely good poetry – none of which was then being offered by other "Periodical Miscellanies" (*Monthly Magazine* 1:iii–iv). Thelwall's editorial statement of January 1826 reaffirms these goals while incorporating a retrospective analysis of the way periodicals like the *Monthly* have revolutionized print culture during the intervening thirty years. His defence of periodical literature links the proliferation of magazines during the 1820s to the "rapid march of mind" and to a notable increase in refinement, morality, intelligence, and taste, especially among the middle classes. By contrast, he claims, in the late eighteenth century middle-class tradesman had eschewed literature and book learning while they deemed card playing and drinking more useful and acceptable recreations, and the only "wretched flimsy and ill written sixpenny magazines" that were then available were read by young women (*Panoramic* 1). When periodicals such as the *Monthly Magazine* entered this unenlightened marketplace and addressed a large-scale, middle-class, predominantly male readership, they joined with newly formed public societies, mechanics' institutes, and middle-class universities in a grand mission of public improvement that, in 1826, still awaits appropriate recognition: "Of the powerful influence of periodical literature in forwarding the progress of general intellect, and the necessity of its agency to the end proposed, there are few, perhaps, who, even yet, have formed a proper estimate" (*Panoramic* 4). Thelwall refutes the idea that the brief information offered in miscellanies is superficial and displaces more profound scientific publications. Instead, he claims, accessible popular knowledge and serious research reciprocally support one another:

> It is the business of the periodical essayist to remove this veil of mystery from science, to translate its revelations into familiar language, and dispense to those who have more of thirst, than leisure, or opportunity for acquisition, so much as they have time to receive, or are prepared to comprehend. Is this a task for superficial minds? (*Panoramic* 5)

It is already evident from these opening pages of *The Panoramic Miscellany* why the aging Thelwall felt he had to find a way to continue the original mission of the *Monthly Magazine* – and why he hoped it was possible to do so in 1826 by founding a magazine of one's own. The responsibility of disseminating instructive and amusing information along with liberal principles has only gained in importance in the climate of heightened media awareness and optimistic "march of mind" that characterizes the 1820s, a climate that periodical literature itself has helped to form. Magazines are as important an organ for contributing to the improvement of society as the public lecturing and elocutionary training with which *The Panoramic Miscellany* goes hand in hand.

In accordance with the journalistic practice of the time, most of the articles in *The Panoramic Miscellany* are unsigned or signed with obvious pseudonyms. But Thelwall's deviations from this convention begin to demarcate his idiosyncratic use of the periodical medium, specifically the ways in which he adapts the magazine to accommodate his accustomed role as lecturer and the elements of performance involved in that role. Clear exceptions to the custom of anonymity are the lectures on elocution that form a centrepiece for most of the issues, each of which is identified in the title as "Mr Thelwall's Lecture." A good number of the articles contributed by other writers are conspicuously framed by headnotes and footnotes signed "Editor" or (occasionally) "J. Thelwall." Some of the "Original Poetry" is signed by Thelwall himself, and some of the regular pseudonyms used in the poetry department ("Ausonia," for instance) seem to belong to him as well. Other pieces that, judging by content and tone, are likely written by Thelwall are an enthusiastic multipart series on "The London University" (founded in 1826 as the first secular university in England), reports on public societies and educational institutions, articles on political economy, the three-part "Tour thro North Wales," some of the regular features including the agricultural reports, and the literary-critical articles. Foremost among his acknowledged contributions are the editorials that begin each issue, which are signed either with Thelwall's name or with a coded symbol consisting of a triangle followed by three dots in the shape of a second triangle (Δ ∴).[5]

A hallmark of *The Panoramic Miscellany* is the strong editorial presence with its sometimes personal, sometimes pedantic or patronizing tone. Like many magazine editors, Thelwall addresses contributors directly in the "Notices to Correspondents" pages at the end of each issue – apologizing, for instance, for having to print the article "On the Egyptian Zodiac" in "such small type" (*Panoramic* 146), welcoming submissions of poetry in Spanish, Portuguese, and Italian (298), or responding cordially to "our Correspondent T. P." who "hints" that Thelwall should include lighter and more humorous material (442). But he also carries on a running dialogue with contributors and readers throughout the *Panoramic* – for instance, by using headnotes to single out certain articles as outstanding or, conversely, by adding critical footnotes to distance himself from the claims made in other pieces. Thelwall treats his editorial role as a sustained conversation with contributors and readers, albeit one in which he claims the dominant voice. The dialogic tone of his editorial interventions suggests that he places the periodical miscellany on a continuum with oral media of communication such as public lectures, elocutionary training, and the educational institutions and debating clubs whose activities receive so much coverage in his magazine.

Several kinds and levels of dialogue take place in the pages of the *Panoramic*. One forum for dialogue is international, beginning with a steady partnership with the French *Revue Encyclopédique* that distributed Thelwall's magazine through its Paris office and from which the *Panoramic* draws several articles, reprinting them in English translation. In addition, the *Panoramic* pays special attention to the literature and science of Italy; reviews literature from across Europe; features articles on Spanish history and culture, Danish superstitions, the climate of France, and new developments in engineering and statistical surveys throughout the world; and devotes regular attention to India and Burma (presumably due to the ongoing Anglo-Burmese war). Interestingly, though, the *Panoramic* does not assume any knowledge of foreign languages on the part of its readers but conscientiously provides English translations of every non-English text or phrase, however brief, that appears in its pages. Insofar as this practice indicates a dedication to accessibility and a target audience among male middle- and working-class readers who are not expected to have an education in either modern or classical languages, it is a policy that subtly reveals how a magazine both selects and accommodates itself to a readership.

More than other magazines of the 1820s, though, *The Panoramic Miscellany* privileges the public lecture as a form of communication. In addition to Thelwall's own lectures on elocution, the *Panoramic* prints long excerpts from lectures delivered at scientific institutions, and the "Proceedings of Learned Societies" section contains eyewitness reports and précis of further lectures. Some of Thelwall's articles, particularly his continuing series on "The London University," include remarks on the practice of lecturing itself: "A lecturer should be plain, perspicuous and diffuse. The performance may be masterly, and throw great lustre upon the character of the lecturer [...]" (*Panoramic* 505). Indeed, the fundamental rhetorical orientation of *The Panoramic Miscellany* seems best described as the pedagogical mode of *lecture-discussion*. Thelwall as editor persistently gestures towards conversational exchange with contributors, correspondents, and readers, yet he maintains a controlling role in these conversations, initiating topics and framing the contributions of others by claiming the last word. His own articles often take the form of rebuttals to other men's lectures or speeches. In the May and June issues, for instance, Thelwall prints long excerpts from

"Mr Jacob's Report to the House of Commons, on the Trade in Foreign Corn" and develops his own counterposition in a passage-by-passage commentary. Similarly, February's leading article is a running commentary on a lecture recently delivered by Mr Banks at the City and Western Institutions, and in March, Thelwall follows the same practice with a lecture on "Geological Phenomena" that was delivered by Professor Brande at the Royal Institution. These editorials become dialogues between Thelwall and other public speakers who are thereby pulled, as it were, into the space of the magazine and challenged by Thelwall as if on the floor of the House or in the lecture hall. Their opinions are framed by Thelwall's commentary in much the same way that the articles by voluntary contributors are framed by his editorial interventions in footnotes or endnotes.

Thelwall resorts to a variety of tactics for trying to engage readers in intellectual debate. He includes brief queries on etymological questions – asking about the origin of the terms "Grub Street" or "John Bull," for instance – that solicit involvement from readers. Sometimes the interpolated questions are more philosophical: "What is eloquence?"; "What are metaphysics?"; "What is time?" (*Panoramic* 315, 374, 306). Another variant on the lecture-discussion mode, and another way in which *The Panoramic Miscellany* sets itself apart from rival magazines, appears in Thelwall's literary criticism and reviewing. The individual book reviews in the *Panoramic*'s notably long "Review of Literature" department are completely unsystematic, vary dramatically in length, and reflect Thelwall's personal interests in such topics as grammar and metrics. In contrast to the reviewing style that was nearly ubiquitous in periodicals from the *Edinburgh Review* to the *European Magazine*, where reviews included lengthy quotations from the book under discussion, Thelwall quotes minimally and instead offers his own evaluation. Also interesting is the gendered perspective of Thelwall's reviewing and literary criticism. Among the books he singles out for unusually lengthy treatment are publications by prominent women writers: Letitia Landon's *The Troubadour* (*Panoramic* 74–82); Mary Shelley's *The Last Man* (*Panoramic* 380–6); and Joanna Baillie's *The Martyr* (*Panoramic* 665–8). In addition to his characteristic mode of biased dialogue with male contributors, lecturers, or treatise-writers, Thelwall adopts a more hierarchical mentoring stance in relation to younger female writers, whom he nevertheless treats with notable seriousness and respect.

If Thelwall's editorial practice suggests an attempt to transfer his role as public speaker and educator into a print medium, the title of his magazine perhaps signals most vividly his awareness of the changing media field. The term "miscellany" has a well-established eighteenth-century genealogy, although it takes on a new currency in the mid-1820s when major publishers begin to market affordably priced "miscellanies" or anthologies in order to bring new and reprinted literature to a wide readership; the influential *Constable's Miscellany*, for instance, was in preparation at exactly this time. "Panoramic," on the other hand, is a brand-new nineteenth-century adjective, first recorded by the OED in 1813, that did not gain its abstract meaning of "universal" until after Thelwall's lifetime. In the minds of his readers in the 1820s, it might have conjured up recollections of another recently defunct publication, the *Literary Panorama* (1806–19), but its most immediate associations are with innovative visual media. Like other literary-cultural magazines, *The Panoramic Miscellany* contains reports about the new visual entertainments in London, including the Diorama (252, 396–7), the Cosmorama, and the proto-cinematic Poecilorama at the Egyptian Hall (397, 445). The link between these spectacles and the title of Thelwall's magazine is made explicit in the April issue when a correspondent writes in as "John Bull" expressing appreciation for the Poecilorama but ridiculing its pretentious Greek name. "John Bull" notes that Thelwall himself appears to share the "Greek mania" that led him to use the "scrap of every day Greek 'Panoramic'" on his title page rather than calling his journal, in plain English, "Thelwall's Monthly Magazine" (486). In a good-natured response, Thelwall concedes the point: booksellers, publishers, and readers will have no trouble recognizing that the *Panoramic* is *Thelwall's* magazine. Yet the title's significant gesture towards a new medium of visual representation seems indicative of Thelwall's awareness of technological innovation and his engagement with experiential media – above all with public speaking, which continues to stand at the centre of his commitment to rational communication and the march of mind.[6]

Scene 3 Improvising Editorship: *Knight's Quarterly Magazine*

Another sort of optimism about the potential of periodical culture in the 1820s is exemplified by *Knight's Quarterly Magazine*, six issues of which appeared in 1823–4. While *The Panoramic Miscellany*, as the 62-year-old Thelwall's first venture into independent editorship, seems at once enterprising and elegiac, *Knight's Quarterly*, as the product of a group of Cambridge scholars and young lawyers at the outset of their careers, points forward to the sociocultural work of the mid-nineteenth century. The magazine's leading lights were the future Victorian writers and politicians Thomas Babington Macaulay and Winthrop Mackworth Praed. Among their collaborators were Samuel Taylor Coleridge's son Derwent and his nephew Henry Nelson Coleridge, Thomas de Quincey, Edward Bulwer, William Maginn, and the barrister and Victorian penal reformer Matthew Davenport Hill. Principally, however, *Knight's Quarterly* was one of the earliest publishing and editorial ventures of Charles Knight, a key figure in nineteenth-century print culture and educational reform. Knight would soon take a central role in running the Society for the Diffusion of Useful Knowledge; in 1832 he would launch the Society's weekly *Penny Magazine,* the most important of the early Victorian periodicals that brought the "march of intellect" within reach of a mass middle- and working-class readership. Playful, performative, and experimental, *Knight's Quarterly Magazine* constitutes an ironic training ground in public communication and self-presentation for some of the key public intellectuals of the Victorian period.

Knight's Quarterly is a miscellany of prose and poetry that includes literary criticism, creative writing, and essays both serious and humorous. As Thelwall's *Panoramic Miscellany* adopted the format of the predecessor *Monthly Magazine, Knight's Quarterly* just as clearly models itself on *Blackwood's Edinburgh Magazine,* seeking to capitalize on the innovative style and tone of that recent and notorious entry into the literary market. *Knight's* offers its own versions of the pseudonymous editorial personalities made popular by *Blackwood's,* importing this format from the Edinburgh literary scene into the London one and taking it further in the direction of self-reflexive play with the boundaries of reality and fiction. Although other periodicals (including *Blackwood's*)[7] paid tribute to the quality of the writing in *Knight's,* the magazine folded within a year and a half due to a small readership, editorial conflicts, and the economic crisis of 1825–6. This short-lived periodical nevertheless deserves attention for its self-conscious performance of the process of editing a literary magazine. While the performative dimension of Hazlitt's journalism involves a heightened awareness of public response and that of Thelwall's *Panoramic Miscellany* entails the rhetorical gestures of a lecturer addressing an audience, in the case of *Knight's Quarterly* performance takes the form of ironic self-spectatorship: the writers and editors of *Knight's* are perpetually watching themselves act as writers and editors. Especially in the "Castle Vernon" scenes at the beginning of the 1823 issues, the recurring features entitled "The Editor" and "What You Will," and the miscellany "The Anniversary" that makes up most of the August 1824 issue, the magazine's writers theatricalize their own editorial activity, effectively staging the act of writing, assembling, and publishing each issue while they are actually doing so.

Thus "Castle Vernon, No. 1" – the piece that opens the first volume – performs the founding of the magazine by a group of young people in the drawing room of Lady Mary Vernon, fictional sister of Charles Knight's fictional editorial persona "Frederic Vernon." The scene is, on one level, a realistic depiction of the upper-middle-class social life of the magazine's actual writers, and the prose is thick with allusions to the real-life literary scene of 1820s London. On another level, the writers appear as caricatures of themselves, thereby introducing the pseudonymous personae they will adopt throughout the magazine's run. Yet another level of theatricality is added by the representation of the entire scene as a medieval court ruled by Lady Mary – a shared pretence that parodies Romantic medievalism and plays off the name of the magazine and its founder, Charles Knight. Within this multilayered scene of conviviality, the gentlemen critique the currently available literary magazines, resolve to launch "the most entertaining publication of the day" (*Knight's* 1:5),[8] and petition Lady Mary to be its patron. Lady Mary accepts, but only after holding a mock trial of the young men's sincerity and qualifications. As the medieval court morphs into a "high court of judicature" (1:4) for Lady Mary's investigation, the part-narrative, part-dialogue genre of "Castle Vernon" incorporates a plethora of text types: a formal pledge of devotion by the founders of *Knight's Quarterly* to Lady Mary (to add to the irony, it is a pledge to which they subscribe their *pseudonyms*), a declaration by which Lady Mary accepts the "rule and sovereignty" (1:12) of the magazine and appoints her brother Frederic its editor, and a formal account of the proceedings of the court signed by their duly elected secretary, "Peregrine Courtenay" (a.k.a. Winthrop Mackworth Praed).

Self-consciously layering real-life contexts and fictional allegories, mixing text types, and playing with actual, pseudonymous, and legal identities, the first instalment of "Castle Vernon" takes the place of the serious prospectus with which a new magazine normally entered the market. More precisely, "Castle Vernon" functions as an alternative, dramatized, ironic version of such a prospectus, foreshadowing the magazine's ironic tone and its often metafictional contents, incorporating a review of the existing periodical field, and showing potential readers what they themselves might look like: an elegant, literate, flirtatious, clever, and fun-loving group of young men and women. Thanks to a dense web of in-jokes and allusions to the clichéd contents of other periodicals, "Castle Vernon" also fulfils the function of the expected "review of the reviews" and thereby situates itself within the literary field.

Interspersing them with essays, book reviews, fiction, and poetry, *Knight's Quarterly* continues to include pieces that *perform* the usual contents and practices of a literary magazine. Charles Knight's recurring articles under the title "The Editor" are humorous dramatizations of the day-to-day realities of publishing the periodical. In the first instalment of "The Editor" (1:13–16), contributors keep proofs for too long or promise a "magnificent Essay" but deliver only an "Epigram"; star contributor "Vyvyan Joyeuse" fails to deliver anything at all; "Gerard Montgomery" has written something too risqué; other members of the coterie have submitted articles unacceptably coloured by political invective. Critiquing everything that his contributors have sent him and thereby sending up the regular contents of other literary magazines, the Editor produces a theatricalized version of the routine "Notes to Contributors" page. In later instalments the Editor appeals directly to "My dear Public" (2:1–11, 2:243–56) – a term that, by invoking a performative rather than conversational context and an anonymous "Public" rather than an intimate audience, contrasts interestingly with the more common address of 1820s journalists to the "(dear) reader." Asking the public to sympathize with his labours, he inserts the letters and notes his delinquent contributors have purportedly sent him in order to demonstrate what he as editor has to put up with in order to get the magazine into the public's hands.

At the end of each of the first four issues of *Knight's Quarterly*, a section entitled "What You Will" dramatizes the last-minute scramble to fill up pages and deliver the magazine to the printer. These sections foreground above all the improvised nature of periodical writing. In the October 1823 "What You Will" (1:443–57), a crisis caused by a delinquent contributor who doesn't even have anything in the "literary drawer, ready made" is resolved in deus-ex-machina style when a package from "Vyvyan Joyeuse" arrives with a few poems and riddles that can be strung together with interspersed commentary and ironic asides about the literary scene to complete the issue in the nick of time. In the January 1824 instalment (2:227–39), harried Sub-Editor "Paterson Aymer" (another of Charles Knight's pseudonymous personalities) finds himself with two blank pages left even after inserting all the poems and small pieces he has been handed by the regular contributors. He desperately fills the oppressive white space with an improvised review of the newly published novel he happens to be reading (Scott's *St Ronan's Well*) and an additional "*extempore* song" before signing off on 30 December at three o'clock in the morning.

Knight's Quarterly intervenes in the contemporary literary scene in a way that both enacts and parodies the determining factors of that scene. It uses wild experimentation with the boundaries of reality and fiction to foreground the improvised and haphazard nature of periodical literature. As in the more famous *Blackwood's*, its writers adopt pseudonymous personalities. Like the 1820s fiction of Scott and other contemporaries, *Knight's* layers heteroglossic text types and makes use of metafictional devices such as pseudo-editorial frames, found manuscripts, and "authentic" letters that are patently fake. Anxiety not just over the increasing speed and time pressure of writing for periodicals but about the resulting commodification of periodical literature is a running theme in most magazines of the 1820s, and *Knight's Quarterly* parodies these conditions in a characteristically metafictional item entitled "New Depository for Literary Manufactures" (1:96–103). This article takes the form of a letter to the editor of *Knight's Quarterly* from the proprietor of an establishment called "Paperstain and Co." "Paperstain" has discovered a business opportunity in the volatile periodical market by establishing "a factory for the exhibition and sale of original manuscripts, from the sermon to the sonnet" (1:96), and the company's letter quickly reveals itself to be an advertising flyer offering *Knight's Quarterly* the choice of its stock. By commenting on which genres are selling well, which periodicals are buying what, and what kinds of manuscripts are overstocked or remaindered, the "Paperstain" letter performs a send-up of the commodified contents of 1820s periodicals. Paperstain's sole sample in the category "Criticism in the Fine Arts" is from a "very impartial, and, if necessary, growling critic" who advertises his credentials to review panoramas as follows:

> On Panoramas. – Experienced as I have been, during the last thirty years, in every thing that pertains to Literature, Science, and Art; – honoured as I am by the acquaintance, by the patronage, by the friendship of so many distinguished persons in those branches; – having contributed in various ways to the illustration, to the decoration, and to the classification of many subjects of literary and artistical research; – being myself a member of several eminent societies in this metropolis; and holding an extensive

> correspondence in various parts of the United Kingdom, of Europe, of the world – I think myself qualified to write on Panoramas. (1:101)

Part of *Knight's* parody of the contemporary art scene lies in the fact that "On Panoramas" is the *only* manuscript Paperstain and Co. offer in the field of visual arts, as if to emphasize the clichéd fashionability of the new medium that has apparently displaced high art. The item's delineation of the qualifications and networks claimed by a typical writer and critic of the older generation ("during the last thirty years") is also incisive. While surely no specific reflection on John Thelwall is intended,[9] the parodic self-advertisement would not be an inaccurate description of Thelwall's activities as a Romantic-era public intellectual – one that sets the stage for his soon-to-be-launched *Panoramic Miscellany*.

Epilogue: Performative Communication

Knight's Quarterly Magazine memorably blends commentary on the contemporary media context and self-reflection on the processes of editing and publishing with clever creative writing. Making adept use of literary devices such as characterization, caricature, and irony, *Knight's* turns the periodical scene itself into literature. Thelwall's *Panoramic Miscellany*, on the contrary, draws largely on the models of communication familiar to a Romantic-era public intellectual conversant with literary and scientific institutions: lecturing, teaching, and the all-round perspective emblematized by the panorama. Both enterprises exemplify the ironically qualified optimism that Hazlitt, in his essay on "The Periodical Press," associates with a transitional age. *Knight's Quarterly Magazine* and *The Panoramic Miscellany* are neither commercial successes nor unacknowledged masterpieces. Insofar as both of them folded after six issues and have rarely been noticed since, they seem instead to affirm the accuracy of Hazlitt's observation that the literary production of the 1820s "glitters, flutters, buzzes, spawns, dies, – and is forgotten!". Yet Hazlitt's suggestion that even the ephemeral publications of the 1820s manage to "spawn" is borne out by *Knight's Quarterly*, which merits notice as an unexpected training ground in public communication for leading Victorian journalists and intellectuals.

Above all, the speculative and volatile climate of the 1820s provided scope for writers to experiment, to manifest the "creative vigour" (213) that Hazlitt dared to hope was possible in an era that was finding its way towards new forms of communication and expression. The relationship between writers and readers takes on a new urgency at a time when engaging a readership is a condition for the periodical's survival as well as for the fulfilment of its writers' ambitions to contribute to cultural critique and creative expression (in the case of *Knight's*) or to the march of intellect among the middle and working classes (in the case of the *Panoramic*). Thelwall's direct addresses to readers, contributors, politicians, public lecturers, and writers whose books he is reviewing constitute a late but optimistic attempt to disseminate reformist principles shaped during the 1790s and practiced in the course of a public-speaking career via a new medium of the 1820s, the independently published monthly miscellany. Meanwhile Charles Knight, Macaulay, the younger Coleridges, and others of their cohort seize on the timely model of *Blackwood's Edinburgh Magazine* in order to craft a youthful, playful, and insightful self-reflection on the London literary scene and thereby negotiate their places within it as public intellectuals of the rising generation. The effects of an evolving communicative context are evident in the extent to which these magazines draw on the conventions of performative media from public lectures and conversation to dramatic scenes, party games, courtroom trials, and advertising. If the coterie performances of the *Knight's Quarterly* group and the lecture-discussion mode of Thelwall's *Panoramic Miscellany* proved equally ephemeral, the very possibility of making these ventures shows that the periodical culture of the 1820s provided forward-looking (and hopeful) writers and thinkers with new opportunities to engage public opinion.

NOTES

1 Among the most relevant studies of these developments and the resulting climate of "information overload" are Altick, *English*; Erickson; and Siskin. For indicative surveys of production and circulation figures for periodicals, see Appendix C (391–6) of Altick, *English*; and Appendix 8 (572–7) of St Clair. For discussions of the ways in which other forms and transformations of media can have an effect on reading and the public, see Daniel Coleman's chapter in this volume on wampum as a communications medium.

2 For further interpretation of the developments alluded to in this very brief overview, see Klancher, Parker, Schoenfield, and Stewart.

3 During's essay on "Regency Culture" in the *Cambridge History of English Romantic Literature* provides a vivid survey of 1810s and 1820s life in London. See also Altick's classic study *The Shows of London,* to which recent research into late-Georgian theatre history is adding ever richer detail.

4 Since the single six-issue volume of *The Panoramic Miscellany* uses consecutive page numbering throughout, references in the present essay are given by page numbers only.

5 As elucidated in Thelwall's lecture on "Elements of Prosody" in the May issue, these two signs represent the "*Thesis* and *Arsis* of human speech" (*Panoramic* 636): a long/stressed syllable followed by a short/unstressed one. Rhythmically (as a trochaic foot) as well as phonetically (*TH*esis + *A*rsis), they stand for "Thelwall."

6 For a more extensive discussion of the *Panoramic,* see Esterhammer, "John Thelwall's *Panoramic Miscellany*" (originally published electronically on the University of Maryland's *Romantic Circles* Website).

7 Characteristically, *Blackwood's* expresses its approval of *Knight's Quarterly* with an ironic touch by introducing "Vyvyan Joyeuse," the fictional star writer of *Knight's,* into the convivial company of *Blackwoods'* fictional editorial coterie in No. 14 of the "Noctes Ambrosianae" series (*Blackwood's Edinburgh Magazine* 14 [July–December 1823]: 485–90).

8 References to *Knight's Quarterly Magazine* are given by volume and page number; pages are numbered consecutively in each of the three volumes, each of which comprises two quarterly issues.

9 On the contrary, David Stewart, who also remarks on the significance of the "New Depository for Literary Manufactures" piece, suggests that the intended target of the "Fine Arts" notice is "the brazen self-promotion engaged in by B. R. Haydon" (72).

WORKS CITED

Altick, Richard D. *The English Common Reader: A Social History of the Mass Reading Public, 1800–1900.* 2nd ed. Columbus: Ohio State UP, 1998. Print.

Altick, Richard D. *The Shows of London.* Cambridge, MA: Harvard UP, 1978. Print.

Blackwood's Edinburgh Magazine 14 (July–December 1823). Print.

During, Simon. "Regency London." *The Cambridge History of English Romantic Literature.* Ed. James Chandler. Cambridge: Cambridge UP, 2009. 335–54. Print. http://dx.doi.org/10.1017/CHOL9780521790079.016.

Erickson, Lee. *The Economy of Literary Form: English Literature and the Industrialization of Publishing, 1800–1850*. Baltimore: Johns Hopkins UP, 1996. Print.

Esterhammer, Angela. "John Thelwall's *Panoramic Miscellany*: The Lecturer as Journalist." *John Thelwall: Critical Reassessments*. Ed. Yasmin Solomonescu. *Romantic Circles Praxis* (September 2011). Web.

The European Magazine 85 (January–June 1824). Print.

Hazlitt, William. "The Periodical Press." *The Complete Works of William Hazlitt*. Ed. P.P. Howe. Vol. 16: *Contributions to the Edinburgh Review*. London: J. M. Dent and Sons, 1931. 211–39. Print.

Klancher, Jon P. *The Making of English Reading Audiences, 1790–1832*. Madison: U of Wisconsin P, 1987. Print.

Knight's Quarterly Magazine 1 (June and October 1823), 2 (January and April 1824), and 3 (August and November 1824). Print.

Mill, James. "Periodical Literature." *Westminster Review* 1 (1824): 206–49. Print.

The Monthly Magazine and British Register 1 (February–July 1796). Print.

The Panoramic Miscellany 1 (January–June 1826). Print.

Parker, Mark. *Literary Magazines and British Romanticism*. Cambridge: Cambridge UP, 2000. Print.

Schoenfield, Mark. *British Periodicals and Romantic Identity: The "Literary Lower Empire."* Houndmills: Palgrave Macmillan, 2009. Print.

Siskin, Clifford. *The Work of Writing: Literature and Social Change in Britain, 1700–1830*. Baltimore: Johns Hopkins UP, 1998. Print.

St Clair, William. *The Reading Nation in the Romantic Period*. Cambridge: Cambridge UP, 2004. Print.

Stewart, David. *Romantic Magazines and Metropolitan Literary Culture*. Houndsmills: Palgrave Macmillan, 2011. Print.

2 "A Wicked Whisper": Censorship, Affect, and Coleridge's "The Rime of the Ancient Mariner"

JULIA M. WRIGHT

Perhaps the most pernicious error that ever poisoned the happiness of mankind, has been the prejudice, that there is one sort of knowledge fit for the learned, and another adapted to the vulgar.

– William Drennan, *A Letter to his Excellency Earl Fitzwilliam, Lord Lieutenant, &c. of Ireland* (1795)

In this chapter, I wish to explore a gothic shadow of the public intellectual – the censor. Both censorship and the public intellectual posit the power of discourse to change hearts and minds; both posit a figure of higher intellectual and moral character to shape that discourse, and a larger population that is tacitly less educated or morally upstanding and will, in turn, be shaped by that controlled discourse; and, as I shall trace below, both figures in the Romantic period were wedded to ideas of sensibility and come together in the work of Samuel Taylor Coleridge. But one acts by withholding "dangerous" discourse, and the other acts by distributing educational or otherwise enlightening discourse.

Eighteenth-century Britain witnessed both the rise of sensibility as a model of textual affect, and the rise of censorship through the proliferation of legislation and officials to police discourse. British legislators worked hard to delineate and then suppress discourse they deemed dangerous, from the various stamp acts which controlled paper and print, to the Stage Licensing Act of 1737 which required that plays be passed by the Lord Chamberlain's office before being staged in a licensed theatre, to the so-called Gagging Acts of 1795, which included the requirement that two magistrates approve of any public lecture on a political subject. These legislative moves were buttressed by various prosecutions for publishing materials of various sorts, collapsing obscenity with sedition and critique with treason. This surge in censorship is contemporary with the rise of sensibility. Sensibility is an Enlightenment theory of emotional response as the foundation of morality: broadly speaking, sympathy, as an imaginative act, creates a sense of another's feelings (such as pain, happiness, embarrassment), which stimulates an emotional response (for instance, pity, joy, disappointment) and an ethical reaction (including benevolence, instruction, and condemnation). It was developed by such leading thinkers as Shaftesbury, David Hume, and Adam Smith: sympathy, as the universal capacity for "fellow-feeling," was understood to be the foundation of social cohesion and ideas of justice. According to sensibility, everyone has the capacity to imagine the sufferings of others, motivating benevolence to end suffering or justice to control those who cause suffering, and this imaginative capacity can be developed through print, spawning a literature of sensibility in which readers' emotional responses were solicited with the aim of moral instruction of some sort, as scholars such as Janet Todd have discussed – as in literature which detailed the abuses of slavery, for instance. But this capacity was also supposed to be modified by the moral judgment of the sympathizer and hence subject to distinctions of class and gender, distinctions related to but not fully governed by ideas of education. As George Haggerty notes, "'sensibility' is a symptom of the cultural ascendancy of the bourgeois individual" and that individual is tacitly male as well as middle class, so "Feeling as a culturally acceptable indulgence is masculine; feeling as a source of benevolence is masculine" (110). For many, sensibility in women and the lower classes is thus always at risk of tipping into excess (leading to illness, impropriety, the mob), and it is the educated, intellectual and therefore properly self-governing sensible subject – magistrates, the Lord Chamberlain – that must prevent such emotional excess by withholding, through censorship, the discursive spur to it.

Coleridge repeatedly demonstrates his keen awareness of the issues at stake in government censorship, though it took a while for him to come to the idea of a clerisy, a "trusteeship" as he puts it, "guardians of knowledge and culture who disseminate and maintain cultural values over time" (Barr, "Common" 124). In *The Plot Discovered* (1795), Coleridge not only complains about the Stage Licensing Act (19) but also warns that censoring political debate will pave the way for the censoring of all books: "He who prints and publishes against monarchy, as well as he who writes against it, is a traitor. The future editions will be treasonable. If the legislature can pass, if the people can endure such a law, it will soon pass, they will easily endure a domiciliary inquest, which will go through our private and our public libraries with the expurgatorial besom!" (10). These were his radical years, however. Post-1810, Coleridge became increasingly concerned with making discriminations between readers on the terms that Drennan, in my epigraph above, finds so "pernicious." In the *Statesman's Manual* (1816), Coleridge wrote, "But not even as a Sermon would I have addressed the present Discourse to a promiscuous audience; and for this reason I likewise announced it in the title-page, as exclusively *ad clerum*; i.e. [...] to men of *clerkly* acquirements, of whatever profession. I would that the greater part of our publications could be thus *directed*, each to its appropriate class of Readers" (35–6). By *On the Constitution of Church and State* (1829), his critique of a parliamentary act that would remedy the legislated political disenfranchisement of Catholics, Coleridge was imagining an institutionalization of this "clerkly" "class of Readers" as a "clerisy" that would supervise the nation's morality and, as a number of scholars have noted, a group akin to more recent ideas of the public intellectual.[1] But, more subtly than in these polemics, Coleridge's interest in controlling the reading of different "class[es] of Readers," I shall suggest here, emerges in his most famous work, "The Rime of the Ancient Mariner," particularly in the revisions he made to the poem, originally published in 1798, for its 1817 publication. Such interest perhaps reflects a rather more interventionist response than the self-fashioning matrix of 1820s periodical literature explored in Angela Esterhammer's opening essay for this volume – a public sphere whose autonomous formations Coleridge implicitly fears. The revisions of the "Rime" register not only Coleridge's developing ideas on "*directed*" reading but also a wider cultural interest in what we might term "hermeneutic censorship" – that is, reading that is framed by an authoritative voice, on terms consonant with Gramscian hegemony, in order to address the same anxieties about textual circulation as those reflected in legal censorship, particularly in their shared representation of dangerous discourse as a disease. The intellectual supplements the state censor for the sake of the public good, and both presume the need for reading to be "*directed* [...] to its appropriate class of Readers."

Elite Control over Affect: From Education to Censorship

Both censorship and "directed" reading assume the potential dangers of the freely circulating text, and in the eighteenth century and Romantic period drew their theoretical support from sensibility's ideas of affect. While Aristotelian catharsis imagines an audience unified in its emotional arousal and then cathartic release, sensibility, born of the Enlightenment, requires a level of judgment and reason. As Ann Jesse Van Sant argues of the late 1700s, "When sensibility became central to ethical and all other psychological aspects of human nature, investigative and rhetorical or dramatic methods overlapped, inviting observers to 'read' scenes of suffering with sympathetic identification and objective scrutiny" (59): sympathy, in other words, is a component of a hermeneutic process in which the intellectual activities of reason and discernment ("objective scrutiny") are crucial. In literary sensibility, moreover, the "reading" of such "scenes" also trains the readers' moral judgment and further enhances their capacity for sympathy. As Percy Bysshe Shelley puts it, "A man, to be greatly good, must imagine intensely and comprehensively; he must put himself in the place of another and many others; the pains and pleasures of his species must become his own" (517).

But what of readers who are not yet "greatly good"? If affect is modified by the competence of the reader, then affect can be unregulated (disorderly) where the readers are not so competent. Censorship is the most draconian response to this anxiety; efforts to direct readers' responses take a more moderate path by seeking to compensate for readers' lack of competence without withholding the text itself. This lack of competence can be a moral failure (in "sympathetic identification") as well as an intellectual one (of "objective scrutiny"), but in both cases, many texts suggest, can be ameliorated through the guidance of a superior. For instance, in Joanna Baillie's *De Monfort* (1798), Jane De Monfort tries to cure her educated brother's obsessive hatred:

> *(Pointing to the book.)*
> Thy willing mind has been right well employ'd.
> Did not thy heart warm at the fair display
> Of peace and concord and forgiving love[?] (3.1.2–4)

But De Monfort is so hardened to sympathy that he is unable to respond properly to "the book" even with his very moral sister's instruction to "warm at the fair display." Incompetence can also derive from a lack of education. In *Caleb Williams* (1794), William Godwin describes a public poetry reading:

> the hearers upon this occasion [...] were, for the most part, plain, unlettered, and of little refinement. Poetry in general they read, when read at all, from the mere force of imitation, and with few sensations of pleasure; but this poem had a particular vein of glowing inspiration. This very poem would probably have been seen by them with little effect; but the accents of Mr Clare carried it home to the heart. (84–5)

The performance and "accents" compensate for "little refinement" and so make possible the moral elevation of the illiterate audience through poetry that is otherwise, according to Godwin's text, beyond them. Another kind of assistance is provided by moralizing framing within the text. Hence, in the section on publishing in *The Detector of Quackery* (1802), John Corry suggests that moral framing can guide readers to the correct evaluation of immoral autobiographies (such as "the life of a military swindler" [142] and "Memoirs of a Demirep" [143]):

> Were such depraved mortals to publish their Memoirs as a demonstration of the fatal effects of vice, they might be considered as doing an act of justice in favour of public morals – similar to the dying declaration of criminals at the place of execution. But they not only endeavour to palliate their enormities, under the soft epithet of error, but in some instances they are abandoned enough to recommend similar practices; while an unprincipled publisher, for the sake of gain, circulates the mental cantharides which empoisons thousands! (142)

Corry's polemic also indicates the dangers of texts that are not framed to edify. Seduction escapes from textual representation to become a "recommend[ation]" from author to reader, and then a widespread contamination against which general readers have no defence, "empoison[ing] thousands!" In all three cases – the hateful but educated protagonist of Baillie's play, the "unlettered" audience in Godwin's novel, and the vulnerable readers in Corry's diatribe – reading must be guided by a more capable hand if it is to produce the proper response in incapable readers. Improper response is pathologized not only as a threat to the individual but also as a threat to the body politic through the proliferation of print, like spreading poison or disease.

But even capable readers are not entirely safe from "mental cantharides." In a letter to Mary Robinson (daughter of the author of the same name) dated 27 December 1802, Coleridge enacts a model of response that is resonant with the discussion here. As Michael Gamer suggests, this letter signals the "pornographic" reputation of Matthew G. Lewis's *The Monk* (1051). But the letter is centrally concerned not only with obscenity and the public reputation of authors but also with textual affect on terms resonant with Corry's contemporary *Detector*. Coleridge suggests, for instance, that encouraging his children to read Lewis or Thomas Moore would make him "an infamous Pander to the Devil in the seduction of [his] own offspring" (905). Coleridge is excessive – even gothic – in representing his terror of a lascivious textual energy, most strikingly when he mentions Peter Pindar, the pseudonym of a contemporary satirist, and declares, "I swear to you that my flesh creeps at his name!!" (905). While such authors seduce women, children, and "Debauchees" via print, they have a different, though no less intense, effect on Coleridge, who would later assume his place as a public intellectual through *The Statesman's Manual* and *On the Constitution of Church and State*. He suffers from an excess of tears (904, 905) and an array of physical symptoms: his "head turns giddy, [his] heart sickens," and his "flesh creeps" (905). Unseduced, Coleridge is yet awash in disgust and distress. To gain control over the affecting text, even the competent reader has to become something else, such as the "coproducer of the text" that Tilottama Rajan traces in Romantic hermeneutics (19); or a numbed consumer, as Steven Bruhm notes in his discussion of sensibility's reliance on "insensibility" as objective, safe distance, to protect the observing subject from feeling too much (17–20). Even the well-read, morally upstanding Coleridge, failing to exercise control over his reading, thus succumbs partly to the unhealthy effects of certain texts.

But Coleridge is using his own discomfort to justify his censorship of others – he can survive such distasteful reading with his morality intact, but his "offspring" are more vulnerable. As Donald Thomas notes, "Censorship [...] exists for the protection of the unsophisticated reader" (3). This concern with "the unsophisticated reader" was intense amidst the radical turmoil of the 1790s and closely connected to sailors, the central figures in Coleridge's "Rime." The 1789 mutiny on the Bounty has since become the more famous naval insurrection of the era, but the general mutiny at Spithead and the Nore in 1797 caused greater alarm at the time, and rapidly led to legislation barring communications that might sow dissent among the military. The mutiny began at Spithead on 15 April 1797, and in early May "the mutiny [...] was still increasing at Sheerness, the Nore, the Downs, and even to Yarmouth" (*Impartial History* 356). The leader of the mutiny surrendered on 14 June 1797, effectively ending the crisis.[2] But for two months, Britain, in the middle of a war with post-Revolutionary France and trying to quash growing revolutionary sentiments at home, was unable to control the fleet responsible for defending its southern and eastern coasts. Trials and executions of mutineers occupied most of the summer of 1797, and the press produced various pleas to sailors to remain loyal, from the lyric *Britain's Genius* to a pamphlet that pleaded, "Blot from the page of History the record of your shame [...] by a return to your duty" (*Address* 7). In the Committee of Secrecy's almost paranoid *Report* on secret societies and seditious threats in the British Isles during the 1790s, six of the twenty-eight appendices deal with naval courts martial in 1797 and 1798 – courts martial that, after the general mutiny in the spring of 1797, only involve the conviction of common sailors who professed radical principles while on their ships, not anyone who acted violently against any naval authority. The fear of mutiny, in other words, became a fear of the spread of seditious ideas that might lead to mutiny. The Committee of Secrecy invokes the spectre of a "systematic conspiracy," suggesting that

> The formation and structure of all these societies, in this country, in Ireland, and on the Continent, are similar; their views and principles are the same, as well as the means which they employ to extend their influence. A continued intercourse and concert has been maintained from the first origin to the present moment; sometimes between the societies themselves, sometimes between their leading members; and a frequent communication has been kept up with the government of France. (8)

In "continued" and "frequent communication," "these societies" create a web of seditious discourse through which they "extend their influence" even to His Majesty's navy – "mental cantharides," in Corry's phrase, which run through the vulnerable and poorly educated mass of common sailors. Coleridge's Mariner is no insurrectionist, though the role of the crew as his judges echoes the administration of justice reported on the mutinied ship, the Sandwich ("Rime" 89–98). But, in 1797–8, censorship and the concerns about the circulation of print to which it responds were very much focussed on precisely such low-ranking mariners as Coleridge represents in his "Rime."

Pathologizing and Remedying Popular Affect

The "Rime" changed a great deal between 1798 and 1817. The 658-line version of the poem published in 1798 relies heavily on pseudo-antique English and limits its paratextual material to a brief "Argument"; the 625-line text published in 1817 uses more modern English and greatly extends the paratextual material to include an epigraph as well as the familiar marginal gloss. It is not new to suggest that "The Rime of the Ancient Mariner" is concerned with the circuit between author, text, and reader. But critical emphasis to date has been on the construction of the authorial voices or the poem's handling of hermeneutics as a tacitly universal theory of interpretation.[3] However, Coleridge's text not only dramatizes scenes of reading – the Wedding Guest in the grip of the Mariner's narration, the gloss-author's redaction of the verse narrative – but also enacts a strategy for directing different "class[es] of readers" to different hermeneutic frameworks, refracting censorship through the kinds of direction already noted in Godwin, Baillie, and Corry. In his revisions to the poem after 1798, and especially in the addition of the marginal gloss and a Latin epigraph in 1817, Coleridge splinters his reading audience by creating different interpretive access points for the verse narrative: the gloss pitches the gothic tale into Christian allegory in straightforward English, a moral guide for readers of "less refinement" that transforms the tale of terror into parable; the Latin epigraph opens up a vista of unknown and unknowable "invisible" beings, encouraging men of "clerkly acquirements" to ponder the tale's supernatural machinery far from the confines of Anglican orthodoxy; and the verse narrative itself becomes a more conservatively gothic text in focussing the blame on the monstrous woman.

Across two decades of revision, however, the stanza from which my title is taken remained untouched except by the modernization of its orthography:

I look'd to Heav'n, and try'd to pray;
  But or ever a prayer had gusht,
A wicked whisper came and made
  My heart as dry as dust. (236–9)

In this distinction between "a prayer" and "A wicked whisper," Coleridge invokes the central premise of textual affect that undergirds both censorship and the public intellectual: some texts are good and invigorating, and others are "wicked" and detrimental in their effects. The "wicked whisper" is thus imaged as the opposite of prayer, where one parches and the other quenches. But there is another gothic pathology at work in the verse narrative that centers not on the "wicked whisper" but on the woman named "the Night-mare LIFE-IN-DEATH" in later versions of the poem (1817: 194), and that pathology unites the woman, the deaths of the crew, and the Mariner's symptoms from sea to land – a pathology that echoes what was then known of syphilis. The disease was not only redolent with connotations of obscenity and improper communications, but was also commonly termed in England "the French disease" and hence provided a ready metaphor for the circulation of revolutionary discourse associated with post-1789 France. One anti-reform pamphlet, for instance, explicitly invoked the disease in its title, *Free Communing; or A Last Attempt to Cure the Lunatics, Now Labouring under that Dreadful Malady, commonly called the French Disease* (1793).

In 1986, Nora Crook and Derek Guiton made a suggestive though very brief argument on this subject, one that has been widely overlooked in Coleridge criticism. They suggest that the shooting of the albatross owes a debt to Girolamo Fracastoro's Latin poem, *Syphilis* (1555), which Coleridge probably read in 1794 (121; 246n), and that the Nightmare Life-in-Death "comes in the shape of a harlot associated with a loathsome disease" (121).[4] The poem was not only available in Fracastoro's original Latin, however, but also through Nahum Tate's English translation, first published in 1686 and subsequently included in John Dryden's eclectic *Miscellany Poems*. This translation emphasizes and expands on elements of Fracastoro's poem that connect the problem of syphilis to sailors involved in imperial expansion and to fears of mutiny as a serious threat to empire.[5] Moreover, images of syphilis in Coleridge's narrative extend far beyond the figure of the woman – particularly in the 1798 version – and are specifically used to trope communication on terms that are consistent not with Fracastoro, but with eighteenth-century understandings of the disease as articulated, for instance, in the prefatory material appended to the Tate translation in Dryden's *Miscellany*. The Tate translation and paratextual material, in brief, firmly situate Coleridge's "Rime" within the late 1790s and specifically the era's interest in naval mutiny, empire, and the circulation of dangerous discourse.

In the 1798 "Rime," the as-yet-unnamed woman is introduced in the conventional blazon of a prostitute:

Her lips are red, *her* looks are free,
  Her locks are yellow as gold:
Her skin is as white as leprosy,
And she is far liker Death than he;
  Her flesh makes the still air cold. (186–90)

She has red lips, "looks" that are unrestrained rather than demure, and hair that suggests the commodification of her body. Moreover, as Crook and Guiton note of the 1817 version, she is represented as a diseased prostitute because "Her skin is as white as leprosy" (188), and "Her flesh makes the still air cold" (190): leprosy was believed to be a late stage of syphilis and, they add, "Syphilitics were renowned for feeling the cold more intensely than others" (91, 110). But the 1798 version, unlike the 1817 poem to which Crook and Guiton limit their discussion, also includes a verse that is devoted to the woman's companion, Death:

His bones were black with many a crack,
  All black and bare, I ween;
Jet-black and bare, save where the rust
Of mouldy damps and charnel crust
  They're patch'd with purple and green. (181–5)

Unlike the blazon of the wanton woman, this verse offers a close examination of diseased flesh and exposed bone on terms consistent with current representations of victims of syphilis. Early commentators refer to "bones which had swollen and suppurated to the very marrow" and a skin condition of which the "'crusts', or scabs, are black" (Cleugh 47, 48). Tate's translation relays similar details: "foul Botches o'er the Body spread," "and inmost Muscles to attack, / And pierce so deep, that the bare Bones have been / Betwixt the fleshy Breaches seen" (354). Coleridge's Death also exhibits another key symptom. While Fracastoro suggests that the loss of facial flesh causes "faint sounds" (Wynne-Finch 81) as the breath passes through the wounds, Tate is more suggestive: "When on the vocal Parts his Rage was spent, / Imperfect Sounds, for tuneful Speech was sent" (354). In the 1798 "Rime," Death's ravaged body similarly emits "Imperfect Sounds": "A gust of wind sterte up behind / And whistled thro' his bones [...] Half-whistles and half-groans" (195–8). Moreover, the tale of terror the Nightmare precipitates is told each time that the Mariner is in the grip of bodily pains: "Forthwith this frame of mine was wrench'd / With a woeful agony / Which forc'd me to begin my tale" (611–13), pain that first attacks the Mariner at night, and the Mariner then "pass[es], like night" (619) to tell the tale. Tate's translation laments that syphilis attacks at night the "Human Frame" (352): "when […] Night's ungrateful Shades and Vapours rise […] 'Tis then the Execrable Pains begin: / Arms, Shoulders, Legs, with restless Aches vext" (353). As in the description of Death, the language of the 1798 "Rime" echoes that of Tate's translation – "frame" (611), "night" (619) – and stresses key symptoms in that account. Made "restless" by syphilis-like skeletal pains, the Mariner travels from land to land with his nightly symptoms forcing him to seek relief in telling his tale once again. Syphilitic symptoms virally spiral outward from the Nightmare, to Death, to the Mariner himself.

Crook and Guiton argue that the 1817 poem is "a parable […] of the punishment inflicted on Europe for its rapacious exploitation of other continents" (121), anticipating a number of recent readings of the poem. Critics have convincingly connected the poem to various facets of the imperial project, from Alan Bewell's analysis of Life-in-Death as "the allegorical embodiment of colonial epidemiology" (105); to Debbie Lee's exploration of allusions to cholera in the context of the slave trade; to Sarah Moss's discussion of the impact of Coleridge's education in Christ's Hospital, a training school for imperial agents, on the poem's imagery and treatment of punishment. But Tate again provides a firmer basis for connecting the 1798 "Rime" to the concerns of the late 1790s. In Tate's liberal translation, the same passage that establishes the "parable" also prophesies imperial failure:

Know, you at last have reacht your promis'd Soil,
For this is *Ophyre*'s long expected Isle,
But destin'd Empire shall not yet obtain
Of Provinces beyond the western Main,
The Natives of long Liberty deprive,
Found Cities, and a New Religion give,
Till Toils by Earth and Sea are undergone
And many dreadful Battels lost and won;
For, most shall leave your Trunks on foreign Land […]
Your Foes o'er-come, your Fleet in Civil Rage
Shall disagree, and Ship with Ship engage.
Nor end your Sufferings here, a strange Disease,
And most obscene, shall on your Bodies seize. (373)

This is not just a moral condemnation of colonial expansion. It describes an imperial aspirant that will be defeated at every turn and on terms with an eerily prophetic ring for a British audience in 1798, evoking the loss of the American colonies; early failures to convert colonized peoples from their own religions; ongoing colonial difficulties in Ireland and India; the decimation of troops in India by cholera; and, of course, the mutiny at Spithead and the Nore the year before Coleridge published a poem rich in allusions to syphilis and this pseudo-myth of its origin: "your Fleet in Civil Rage / Shall disagree."

In the 1798 version, then, the figure of the woman and her mate have symptoms and features consistent with syphilitic infection that are duplicated in the Mariner, whose syphilitic symptoms "forced [him] to begin his tale" (613) – his gothic tale of the woman, her mate, and the deaths of the crew. The symptoms in these passages also reinforce the association, traced by Gamer, between the gothic and the obscene. The woman and her "fleshless Pheere" (180) appear at the moment in which Coleridge's narrative veers from travelogue to gothic tale of terror, from a ship stuck in the doldrums to a "naked Hulk" (191) that moves unnaturally "Withouten wind, withouten tide" (161). Syphilitic symptoms symbolically unite the gothic portions of the narrative – the spectre ship, the deaths of the crew, the animation of the crew's dead bodies, the ship's sinking – as well as the captivating moment of coerced narration.[6] Moreover, the extensive allusions to Tate's translation invite the (knowing) reader to grasp syphilis here as "the French disease," the political radicalism that censorship legislation in the 1790s sought to contain – radicalism that not only divided the English fleet at Spithead and the Nore, but also informed challenges to the costs and morality of empire.

If Coleridge's verse narrative renders the Mariner's tale pathologically, as both effect and medium of infection on a symbolic level, the prose gloss he first published in 1817 contains that pathology by turning gothic excess into religious mysticism, obscenity into the demonic, confession into moral exemplum, and imperialism into individual moral failure – and ambiguity into divinely sanctioned certainty. Like the poet's performance in *Caleb Williams*, it mediates the textual experience of readers to direct them towards a more beneficial goal than the surface of the text would allow The gloss's alternative narration – alternative in content as well as in "effect" (Wheeler 55) – walks the reader through a Christian reading of the Mariner's tale, conducting the reader to the safe conclusion that the Mariner will "teach, by his own example, love and reverence to all things that God made and loveth"

(1817: 209). The gloss, as John T. Netland argues, functions within a biblical hermeneutics in which "Reading is always morally purposive" (47), and it does so in the face of the verse narrative's semiotic richness and the ineffability of the Mariner's experience; as Netland puts it, the gloss "reflect[s] [...] a quasi-deistic reduction of religious experience to ethical principle" (52). The gloss is thus not only a site of interpretation, a framing moral guide like those which Corry encouraged, but also a means of deflecting attention away from the disruptive potential of the narrative.

The dominance of the moral narrative in the gloss is such that the gothic details, many of them grounded in Fracastoro and Tate's translation, become a kind of narrative excrescence – unnecessary to understand the basic plot and themes of the work. Gothic details are omitted in the gloss or put under partial erasure by similes or the word "seemeth": the woman's description is glossed "Like vessel, like crew!"; the ship's description is similarly rendered, as "It seemeth him but the skeleton of a ship. And its ribs are seen as bars on the face of the setting Sun" (1817: p. 193). The Mariner's self-vampirism – "I bit my arm, I sucked the blood, / And cried, A sail! a sail!" (1817: 160–1) – is euphemistically glossed, "at a dear ransom he freeth his speech from the bonds of thirst" (1817: p. 192). Nowhere is the elision of the gothic within the gloss clearer than in its termination three verses before the end of the poem. The gloss, which can be read seamlessly, grammatically, from beginning to end, concludes, "And ever and anon throughout his future life an agony constraineth him to travel from land to land; And to teach, by his own example, love and reverence to all things that God made and loveth" (1817: p. 208–9). This glosses over, so to speak, a much bleaker verse narrative in which the Wedding Guest, in the final, unglossed lines, "went like one that hath been stunned, / And is of sense forlorn. / A sadder and a wiser man, / He rose the morrow morn" (1817: 621–5). The gloss, in short, both censors the verse narrative by crossing out many of its gothic elements and "direct[s]" readers to draw from it not imperial anxiety or theological heterodoxy, but simple "love and reverence."

Elite Mysteries, Popular Lessons

But there is a further twist in this tale if we also consider the epigraph that was added in 1817. The epigraph, in Latin, is taken from Thomas Burnet's *Archaeologiae Philosophicae* (1692). While the gloss manages ambiguity and gothic excess through a coherent narrative of Christian causality and moral exempla, Burnet dwells on the possibility of the unknown. Translated, Coleridge's epigraph from the text reads,

> I can easily believe that there are more invisible than visible beings in the universe. But who will describe to us their families, ranks, affinities, differences, and functions? What do they do? Where do they live? The human mind has always sought knowledge of these things, but has never attained it. I admit that it is good sometimes to contemplate in thought, as in a picture, the image of a greater and better world; otherwise the mind, used to the minor concerns of daily life, may contract itself too much, and concentrate entirely on trivia. But meanwhile we must be ever vigilant for truth and moderation, that we may distinguish certainty from doubt, day from night. (Wu 528n)[7]

The content of the epigraph dwells on that which the gloss will not admit: doubt, the limits of human knowledge, and the false seductiveness of a coherent worldview. Moreover, the epigraph's author, Burnet, was involved in a key court case in the history of censorship: Burnet accused a publisher of translating and publishing one of his Latin works without permission, leading to the court case *Burnett v. Chetwood*. David Saunders has pointed out that the 1720 trial demonstrates the legal interest in "the variable abilities and susceptibilities of different contemporary readerships" (58) by addressing the appropriateness of making a religious text available in the vernacular. The judge in the case wrote that Burnet's text contained ideas to be "concealed from the vulgar in the Latin language, in which language it would not do much hurt, the learned being better able to judge of it" (qtd. in Saunders 58), bringing us back to the principle that Drennan found so "pernicious." The gloss, in distilling a Christian allegory from a gothic poem, also works to "conceal[ ] from the vulgar" ideas which, like the Latin epigraph that Coleridge selected, stray beyond the limits of Anglican dogma.

In his selection of epigraph, particularly given Burnet's place in the history of British censorship, Coleridge calls attention to the segregated hermeneutics by which interpretations are made available on different terms to different audiences. Urging caution in the imagining of a "greater and better world" beyond the mundane and trivial, as well as suggesting that human beings do not yet understand the nature of the invisible world, the epigraph supports a sceptical stance on the gloss's view of the Mariner's tale – especially such claims as "The Polar Spirit's fellow-dæmons, the invisible inhabitants of the element, take part in his wrong" (1817: p. 202). But the epigraph from "Coleridge's beloved Burnet" (Lowes 98) is in Latin, and Coleridge's audience had little hope of editions of poetry that would translate Latin passages for them (indeed, a number of twentieth-century editions of Coleridge's poetry, including the one used here, do not provide a translation of the epigraph). John Livingston Lowes suggests that the epigraph raises the question, "what, after all, *do* we readily believe, and what is the moderation that we keep, as we come under the compelling magic of the poem?" (239). That the epigraph remains in Latin suggests that these are questions for a very small ("clerkly," intellectual) readership – one that Coleridge, and some of his similarly educated contemporaries, assumed was capable of "moderation" when faced with the power of faith and "magic."

Scepticism and flirtations with gnosticism are the province of well-educated intellectuals – that is, those who can read Latin themselves. If prayer disappears into the ear of God, Latin disappears into the ear of the learned elite – Coleridge's "clerkly" readers of 1816 or "clerisy" of 1829. The paratextual material thus moves interpretation of the text in two directions. The original verse narrative establishes gothic narrative as pathological and proper religious confession as its only possible cure (though one that is withheld from the tale-telling, pain-wrenched Mariner), while the gloss transforms the pathology into an allegory in which the Mariner is cured and allowed to become a religious teacher himself, turning the tragic into the comic and the disruptive into strict orthodoxy. The epigraph from Burnet, however, finds a third way between the gothic and the pious through the unorthodox while preserving it from unwitting eyes, encouraging the knowing reader to consider the full resonances of the text and treat the gloss askance.

In his "Rime," then, Coleridge dramatizes the processes by which material could be "*directed*, each to its appropriate class of Readers." But he also dialectically stages their differences: the visible gaps in the gloss highlight its censoring of disruptive material in the verse narrative, and the untranslated Latin passage calls attention to its inaccessibility to readers who do not know Latin. Rather than an anticipation of Coleridge's most conservative articulation of a clerisy, then, in which an intellectual "trusteeship" supervises the national culture – echoing the role of the Lord Chamberlain in controlling material for the licensed theatres, and anticipating the role of the Motion Picture Association of America in rating film – the "Rime" calls attention to the elision of content, the censorship, that even such minimally intrusive "direction" demands. Consider an ethical debate in the environmentalist science-fiction series *SeaQuest DSV* (1993–6). The submarine's commander, Jonathan Ford (Don Franklin), is challenging the decision of Captain Bridger (Roy Scheider) to harbour a racist war criminal in order to achieve a peaceful resolution to a crisis:

> FORD: You well know, sir, there is always room to negotiate. To bring someone like this on board is a soulless choice. It's like inviting the Albatross of the Ancient Mariner [...]
>
> BRIDGER: All right, Commander. I'll enter all of this into the log. But before you go, I'd like to read you something:
>
> He prayeth best, who loveth best
> All things both great and small;
> For the dear God who loveth us,
> He made and loveth all.
>
> FORD: That's –
>
> BRIDGER: Yes, it is: "The Rime of the Ancient Mariner." ("Hide and Seek")

The scene ends with Ford's response to this: shocked, he puts his hand over his mouth and appears to rethink his position. That Ford's African Americanness is represented as contributing to his revulsion at the war criminal adds to the resonances of this scene. The white captain silences the black commander's argument both for the existence of evil ("soulless") and the imperative "to negotiate" – both gothic excess and ambiguity. Like Baillie's De Monfort, Ford is to find his "heart warm at the fair display," the four lines of verse transforming his moral insistence that his objections be recorded in the captain's log into a silence reinforced by his hand over his mouth. This exchange also registers the survival of Coleridge's text as a moral text and specifically for the moral it takes from Fracastoro on the needless slaughter of wildlife. Moreover, the series enacts the moral framing of Coleridge's "Rime," and not only this scene: most episodes were followed by short educational pieces, at first a naval officer commenting on the science and technology issues raised by the preceding episode; and later, in season two, the actors introducing ocean wildlife.

Through the "Rime," then, from Coleridge's time to ours, we can trace an interest in directed reading as a form of hermeneutic censorship, in which less capable readers are guided to the correct moral view by an intellectual elite – but it is a model in which readers remain less capable and the elite remains firmly in place. Seaquest's Commander is to change his mind not because the Captain has offered a reasoned reply to his moral objections that causes him to reevaluate his position, but because he has quoted a piece of canonical poetry – a passage given the cultural weight of a proverb. The passage is offered as self-evident truth, wielded by the Captain, with all of his moral, intellectual, and military authority, to instantly reverse the Commander's position; it is revelation from on high, not intellectual education or debate. And this is the risk posed by the public intellectual's conceptual overlap with the censor; insofar as both figures posit a more capable intellectual and a less capable public, they buttress hegemonic claims to superior knowledge of what is "right" and "best." The public intellectual occludes the idea of an intellectual public, able to read and interpret for themselves in the clerisy "Nightmare" of freely circulating discourse – or Drennan's ideal in which there is "one sort of knowledge" for all.

NOTES

I am grateful to the Canada Research Chairs Program and Social Sciences and Humanities Research Council of Canada for their generous support of my research, and to Tilottama Rajan (in whose graduate class on Romantic hermeneutics this paper had its origin), Joel Faflak, Jason Haslam, Daniel Wilson, and Arnd Bohm for their helpful comments as I developed this essay. I would also like to thank Susan Henry for her research assistance.

1 For discussions of Coleridge's concept of a clerisy, see, for instance, Barr ("Common"); Klancher; White; and Prickett.

2 Mutinies continued, including one on a ship in the Downs on 24 June 1797, an extension of the general mutiny, and another on the Lady Shore off the coast of Brazil in August 1797.

3 See, for example, Bohm, Heise, Hess, and Netland. For an excellent discussion of traditional hermeneutics and the "Rime," see McGann, *Beauty* 135-72. My argument builds on such readings of the poem as concerned with the "the process of interpretation itself" (Harding 59), but also considers biblical hermeneutics and its scholarly cognates as theories of interpretation for "men of clerkly acquirements" (in Coleridge's phrase), not for "unsophisticated readers." Very recently, and late in this volume's progress through the reviewing process, Mark L. Barr has situated the gloss in the

context of legal concerns about controlling radical discourse in general (rather than concerns about sailors in particular, as is my interest here) ("Forms"). All references to the poem are to the 1798 version unless otherwise indicated.

4 As Crook and Guiton note, "Wordsworth said he gave Coleridge the idea of shooting the albatross. Perhaps Coleridge adopted the suggestion because he saw possibilities of combining the motif with Fracastoro's allegory" (246n).

5 For a suggestive reading of Fracastoro's *De Syphilis* as an early, complex (even contradictory) response to the colonial project, see Campbell.

6 His tale is also a confession of his killing of the albatross. In a discussion of De Quincey's *Confessions*, Jacobus suggests, "Autobiography is the French disease [...] De Quincey identifies confession not only with the 'demirep' or prostitute, but with the effeminate foreignness that infects his own 'English' confessions from within" (224).

7 On Coleridge's reading of Burnet's larger corpus, see Lowes. Wu notes that "Coleridge entered Burnet's remarks in his notebook, 1801 or 1802" (528n).

WORKS CITED

An Address to the Seamen in the British Navy. London: W. Richardson, 1797. Print.

Baillie, Joanna. *De Monfort: A Tragedy. Plays on the Passions*. 1798. Ed. Peter Duthie. Peterborough, Ont.: Broadview P, 2001. 299–387. Print.

Barr, Mark L. "The Common Law Illusion: Literary Justice in Coleridge's *On the Constitution of the Church and State*." *College Literature* 35.3 (2008): 120–41. Print. http://dx.doi.org/10.1353/lit.0.0010.

Barr, Mark L. "The Forms of Justice: Precedent and Gloss in *The Rime of the Ancient Mariner*." *ELH* 78.4 (2011): 863–91. Print. http://dx.doi.org/10.1353/elh.2011.0034.

Bohm, Arnd. "Text and Technology in Coleridge's *The Rime of the Ancient Mariner*." *English Studies in Canada* 15 (1989): 35–47. Print.

Britain's Genius; A Song: To the Tune of "Come and Listen to my Ditty," – Occasioned by the Late Mutiny on Board His Majesty's Ships at the Nore. London: T. Cadell Jr. and W. Davies, 1797. Print.

Bruhm, Steven. *Gothic Bodies: The Politics of Pain in Romantic Fiction*. Philadelphia: U of Pennsylvania P, 1994. Print.

Campbell, Mary B. "Carnal Knowledge: Fracastoro's *De Syphilis* and the Discovery of the New World." *Crossing Cultures: Essays in the Displacement of Western Civilization*. Ed. Daniel Segal. Tucson: U of Arizona P, 1992. 3–32. Print.

Cleugh, James. *The Secret Enemy: The Story of a Disease*. New York: Thames and Hudson, 1954. Print. http://dx.doi.org/10.1097/00000441-195708000-00019.

Coleridge, Samuel Taylor. *Collected Letters of Samuel Taylor Coleridge*. 4 vols. Ed. Earl Leslie Griggs. Vol 2. Oxford: Clarendon P, 1956. Print.

Coleridge, Samuel Taylor. *The Plot Discovered; Or An Address to the People, Against Ministerial Treason*. Bristol: n.p., 1795. Print.

Coleridge, Samuel Taylor. "The Rime of the Ancyent Marinere." 1798. *The Complete Poetical Works of Samuel Taylor Coleridge*. 2 vols. Ed. Ernest Hartley Coleridge. Oxford: Clarendon P, 1912, 1975. 2: 1030–48. Print.

Coleridge, Samuel Taylor. "The Rime of the Ancient Mariner." 1817. *The Complete Poetical Works of Samuel Taylor Coleridge*. 1: 186–209. Print.

Coleridge, Samuel Taylor. *The Statesman's Manual*. 1816. *Lay Sermons*. Vol. 6 of *The Collected Works of Samuel Taylor Coleridge*. Princeton: Princeton UP, 1972. 1–52. Print.

Committee of Secrecy of the House of Commons. *Report*. London: J. Plymsell at the Anti-Jacobin P, 1799. Print.

Corry, John. *The Detector of Quackery; or, Analyser of Medical, Philosophical, Political, Dramatic, and Literary Imposture*. London: T. Hurst, 1802. Print.

Crook, Nora, and Derek Guiton. *Shelley's Venomed Melody*. New York: Cambridge UP, 1986. Print.

Drennan, William. *A Letter to his Excellency Earl Fitzwilliam, Lord Lieutenant, &c. of Ireland*. 3rd ed. Dublin: J. Chambers, 1795. Print.

Free Communing; or A Last Attempt to Cure the Lunatics, Now Labouring under that Dreadful Malady, commonly called the French Disease. Edinburgh: Fairbairn, 1793. Print.

Gamer, Michael. "Genres for the Prosecution: Pornography and the Gothic." *PMLA* 1141.5 (1999): 1043–54. Print. http://dx.doi.org/10.2307/463463.

Godwin, William. *Caleb Williams; Or, Things as They Are*. 1794. Ed. Gary Handwerk and A.A. Markley. Peterborough, Ont.: Broadview P, 2000. Print.

Harding, Anthony John. *The Reception of Myth in English Romanticism*. Columbia: U of Missouri P, 1995. Print.

Heise, Ursula K. "The Never-Ending Tale: Narrative and Lyric in Coleridge's 'Rime of the Ancient Mariner.'" *Colby Library Quarterly* 24 (1988): 116–32. Print.

"Hide and Seek." Writ. Robert Engels. *SeaQuest DSV*. Created by Rockne S. O'Bannon. NBC, 1993–96. Television.

Herzog, Scott. *Poisoning the Minds of the Lower Orders*. Princeton: Princeton UP, 1998. Print.

Hess, Scott. "The Wedding Guest as Reader: 'The Rime of the Ancient Marinere' as a Dramatization of Print Circulation and the Construction of the Authorial Self." *Nineteenth-Century Studies* 15 (2001): 19–36. Print.

Impartial History of the War, from the Commencement of the Revolution in France, [...] Including an Account of the General Mutiny among the Seamen at Spithead and the Nore. Manchester: Sowler and Russell, 1799. Print.

Jacobus, Mary. *Romanticism, Writing and Sexual Difference: Essays on* The Prelude. Oxford: Clarendon P, 1989. Print. http://dx.doi.org/10.1093/acprof:oso/9780198129691.001.0001.

Klancher, Jon. *The Making of English Reading Audiences, 1790–1832*. Madison: U of Wisconsin P, 1987. Print.

Lee, Debbie. "Yellow Fever and the Slave Trade: Coleridge's *The Rime of the Ancient Mariner*." *ELH* 65.3 (1998): 675–700. Print. http://dx.doi.org/10.1353/elh.1998.0026.

Lowes, John Livingston. *The Road to Xanadu: A Study in the Ways of the Imagination*. Boston: Houghton Mifflin, 1930. Print. http://dx.doi.org/10.2307/40217885.

McGann, Jerome. *The Beauty of Inflections: Literary Investigations in Historical Method and Theory*. Oxford: Clarendon P, 1985. Print.

Moss, Sarah. "'The Bounds of His Great Empire': The Ancient Mariner and Coleridge at Christ's Hospital." *Romanticism* 8.1 (2002): 49–61. Print. http://dx.doi.org/10.3366/rom.2002.8.1.49.

Netland, John T. "Reading and Resistance: The Hermeneutic Subtext of *The Rime of the Ancient Mariner*." *Christianity and Literature* 43 (1993): 37–58. Print.

Prickett, Stephen. "Coleridge and the Idea of the Clerisy." *Reading Coleridge: Approaches and Applications*. Ed. Walter B. Crawford. Ithaca: Cornell UP, 1979. 252–73. Print.

Rajan, Tilottama. *The Supplement of Reading: Figures of Understanding in Romantic Theory and Practice*. Ithaca: Cornell UP, 1990. Print.

Saunders, David. *Authorship and Copyright*. New York: Routledge, 1992. Print.

Shelley, Percy Bysshe. "A Defence of Poetry." *Shelley's Poetry and Prose*. 2nd ed. Ed. Donald H. Reiman and Neil Fraistat. New York: Norton, 2002. 509-35. Print.

Tate, N[ahum], trans. *Syphilis: Or, a Poetical History of the French Disease*. 1686. By Girolamo Fracastoro. *Miscellany Poems*. Ed. John Dryden. London: Jacob Tonson, 1713. 5: 333–81. Print.

Thomas, Donald. *A Long Time Burning: The History of Literary Censorship in England*. London: Routledge & Kegan Paul, 1969. Print.

Todd, Janet. *Sensibility: An Introduction*. London: Methuen, 1986. Print.

Van Sant, Ann Jessie. *Eighteenth-Century Sensibility and the Novel: The Senses in Social Context*. Cambridge: Cambridge UP, 1993. Print.

Wheeler, K.M. *The Creative Mind in Coleridge's Poetry*. Cambridge, MA: Harvard UP, 1981. Print.

White, Deborah Elise. "Introduction: Irony and Clerisy." *Irony and Clerisy*. Ed. Deborah Elise White. *Romantic Circles Praxis Series* 1999 (July 2004): 25. Web.

Wu, Duncan, ed. *Romanticism: An Anthology*. 2nd ed. Oxford: Blackwell, 1998. Print.

Wynne-Finch, Heneage. *Fracastor: Syphilis or the French Disease. By Girolamo Fracastoro*. London: William Heineman Medical Books, 1935. Print.

3 Sense and Sensibility: Anatomies of Hope in Romantic-Century Medical Pedagogy

JAMES ROBERT ALLARD

In the opening lines of his "Introductory Lecture" to incoming surgical students at the famous Guy's and St Thomas's Schools in London, a lecture he gave almost yearly from the mid-1790s to the 1830s and published in *Lectures on the Principles and Practices of Surgery* in 1824, Sir Astley Cooper states that "neatness," "gentleness of manner," and "self-possession" are the most vital qualities of a successful surgeon, qualities that "forward the interests of professional men, whilst they diminish the sufferings of human nature" (2). To illustrate his point, Cooper offers this brief anecdote in the early moments of the lecture:

> I was invited by a surgeon, some years since, to see a patient who had a compound dislocation of the ankle joint: there existed a considerable degree of pain and inflammation; the surgeon at once suddenly introduced a probe, raised some of the parts by it, and, his Latin being as bad as his surgery, said with utmost coolness, *Dedenda est Carthago*, "Carthage must fall!" thereby implying that amputation must be performed; indeed, from the rough manner in which he treated his patient, there seemed no other chance for the poor fellow's recovery. In this case, gentleness might have prevented the necessity for amputation. (2)

Cooper points to a lack of "gentleness" in this encounter, manifested both in how the surgeon "suddenly introduced the probe" and in how he spoke to the patient: coupled with the rough and, perhaps worse, haphazard way in which he handled the instruments and tissues, his tone of "utmost coolness" bespeaks a sense of careless detachment, rather than the controlled professionalism and easy confidence that the situation demanded. Furthermore, Cooper's evident concern for the patient, revealed not just in the criticism of the surgeon's technique and behaviour but also in the loaded observation that there "seemed" no alternative, which suggests that the *optics* of the encounter are as vital to its outcome as is surgical skill, underlines the growing importance of learning the perhaps more abstract, discursive elements of being a surgeon. While subsequent lectures detail the specifics of the physical skills, practical knowledge, and general wisdom that surgeons need to develop, hone, and embody, this early, foundational emphasis on certain personal characteristics that we might associate with that crucial, if curious, phenomenon of "bedside manner," is telling. Simple professionalization is surely part of the reason for this emphasis, but such professionalizing gestures are also part of an ongoing effort to establish the surgeon, as one species of professional medical practitioner (and at this particular historical moment, an increasingly important one),[1] as an authority to be heeded.

Such a goal faced numerous obstacles, not least the always problematic winning of "hearts and minds": in an 1825 essay entitled "Medical Students," published in the *European Magazine*, the anonymous author opines, "Taken in the aggregate, your medical students are a sad wild and harum-scarum set, addicted furiously enough to all the licentious pastimes of this most mighty metropolis, and by no means overburthened with prudence and circumspection" (276). Cooper's enumeration of important personality traits that young surgeons must develop effectively links their professional fortunes with not just a record of success but also a capacity to inspire the confidence and command the respect of patients, fellow practitioners, and the public at large, a claim made with growing frequency and urgency in many of the period's most important teaching texts. Since the late decades of the twentieth century, we have become accustomed to the notion that the sick or injured are overseen by a health care *team*, consisting, on the one hand, of a highly trained group of medical specialists that may include, depending on the nature of the problem, EMTs and paramedics; emergency and trauma specialists; any one of a number of surgical or internal medical specialists and his or her dedicated teams; critical care and recovery staff; physical and rehabilitation therapists; and, of course, nurses, assistants, and sometimes students at every stage,[2] while, on the other hand, the team is also considered to include spiritual advisors; friends; family members; and a wide and varied "social support" network, sometimes professional, oftentimes not. The implication is that one's prognosis involves reading the combination of the potential for a sound body and "good spirits," and patients are told repeatedly that a positive attitude – in other words, an unfailing sense of hope – is a vital component of healing and recovery. But for Cooper and many of his contemporaries, the burden of managing all aspects of the process, including bolstering the sense of hope and optimism in both patients and their families, lies entirely with the surgeon, even more than it might with any other medical professional.[3] Fears of quackery; resistance to the sense of "submission" that attends putting oneself under the care of another; and, in the case of surgery in particular, the nature of the procedures themselves – for so many amplified by the workings of the imagination – among a host of other concerns, fostered a sense of anxiety in the general population that ranged from paralysing fear to open hostility.[4] The process of training surgeons in this era worked to counter this anxiety by emphasizing the burden of responsibility and the capacity of the surgeon to carry it, for while "history" may tell of "civil discords and fearful atrocities, those crimes and disorders which [...] stamp man, created in the image of his maker, with the visage of a fiend and the heart of a brute," the history of medicine, especially from the latter half of the eighteenth century when surgery is on the rise,

> is the history of peace and goodwill, of endless harmony, and unceasing philanthropy. Instead of recording the desolations of war, and the growth of immorality – the deadly effects of human passions, and the bloody triumphs of senseless ambition – her province is to note the diminution of mortal suffering; and the only triumphs which she records are those obtained over sickness, death, and sorrow. (Hamilton 1:v)

More than a healer, the surgeon is the hero of a story told in the pages of the textbooks and lectures absorbed by trainees and lived in the surgical encounters they are training to manage.

Reading a variety of such texts, I contend that there is a significant shift in how the key teaching texts and various pedagogical gestures framed the raw anatomical and procedural information in terms of the proper management of the surgeon-patient encounter, a shift that both speaks to continuing changes in medical theory and pedagogy and responds to growing public concern about those very changes. Focussing specifically on a selection of key "introductory" moments – from the prefatory gestures in textbooks to transcripts and notes detailing preliminary lectures and other initiatory activities and rituals (and especially on the work of Cooper, as we will see below) – I suggest that every moment of a surgical student's training was marked by an acute awareness of such a shift and its accompanying anxieties. Moreover, those responsible for training the next generation were not simply working to show them how to become surgeons; they were anxiously engaged in the project of convincing the public of the very necessity of the entire enterprise: the training of surgeons to both manifest and enable a sense of "hope" was itself marked by a sincere hope, in all concerned, that the process itself was, perhaps paradoxically, worth the anxiety and the extraordinary efforts to alleviate it. Just as surgery has a history, both as part of a larger history of medicine and as a discipline unto itself, so, too, do the popular attitudes that, for better or worse, mark its place in the public sphere – attitudes many people would likely recognize, if only through their various pop culture, usually film and television, manifestations. As Rachel Prentice, an anthropologist who studies surgeons in training, suggests, "a full understanding of how a resident [whether at the turn of the nineteenth century or the twenty-first] comes to embody the knowledge, skills, and values of a surgeon requires understanding how social milieu and guided practice interact" (535).[5] I would add that a full understanding of how surgeons come to occupy the exalted place they do, within the profession and without, requires an understanding of how an emerging awareness of that very interaction becomes part of the training itself. In terms of the Romantic medical pedagogy explored in this chapter, this awareness reflects a productive response to the kind of burgeoning media culture explored by Angela Esterhammer in her chapter for this volume. At the same time, it indicates this response's more opportunistic side: the medical profession's ability to (self-)censor, to paraphrase Julia Wright's chapter for this volume, in the name of shoring up the profession's public as well as clinical authority. While there should be no question that the training was and is prompted and underscored by an altruistic desire to produce the most effective healers, we should take seriously the degree to which (the still) hotly contested definitions of "most" "effective" "healers" served (and still serve) to frame that sense of altruism, and we must therefore attend to the histories and underlying ideologies of medical practice and pedagogy, not in an effort to attack or diminish any sense of medical authority, but to help to create the conditions whereby *all* parties in medical encounters are best able to be part of the efforts to foster and bolster the sense of hope that has always been such a fundamental part of the healing process. Ultimately, attending to the process by which young surgeons in training were taught not just how to perform but how to serve as effective mediators – between health and sickness, between patient and medical establishment, even between one's own "professional" and "private" identity – and how they were taught to embody, manifest, and nurture hope, at this crucial time in the history of Western medicine, is still very much of the moment, as we continue to wrestle with such complex issues as private versus public health care, seemingly ever-increasing burdens on an overtaxed medical system (from the oft-discussed "doctor shortage" to the changing needs of an aging but longer-living population), and still-evolving popular perceptions of those professionals to whom we often instinctively entrust the management of our health and well-being.

Teacher, Heal Thyself

Before turning to Cooper, I want first to offer a brief (and admittedly interested) sketch of the medical pedagogical scene of the late eighteenth and early nineteenth centuries by attending to the ways in which some of the period's important texts and figures point to the changing perception of the figure of the surgeon himself and his place not just in "health care" but in the popular imagination. John Hunter, perhaps more than any other single figure, is celebrated as the father of modern, scientific surgery; contemporary histories of surgery, and often still those in our day, observing that the claim "[t]hat surgery was coeval with the other branches of medicine, or perhaps antecedent to any of them, will not admit of a doubt" (*Edinburgh Practice* 635), nevertheless point to Hunter's work as crucial and definitive. Usually Hunter's unmatched efforts to establish surgery and anatomy as proper sciences, as opposed to "crafts" or "trades," by devoting himself to exhaustive laboratory study, obsessive and countless dissections, and herculean efforts to teach his methods more than his theories to several generations of surgeons serve to justify the celebration.[6] Pauline Mazumdar suggests, however, that, beyond his numerous scientific advances, Hunter, "hero of the College of Surgeons, had left to his successors a philosophy of surgery that contributed to their clinical confidence, their self-respect, and to their status within the medical profession" (126),[7] and thus was as interested (if only implicitly) in the public *image* and professional status of the surgeon. Such efforts, if not initiated by Hunter then certainly magnified by him, had the effect of prompting his contemporaries to produce a host of surgical instruction manuals that devote at least some space to providing a history of surgery that stresses its recent, epoch-making advances. Samuel Sharpe, for example, in *A Treatise on the Operations of Surgery*, published in at least eleven editions from the 1730s to the mid-1780s, argues that "the Methods of operating in Surgery have of late Years been exceedingly improved in *England*, and there is no Treatise of Character on that Subject written in our Language [that] it is not necessary to apologize for this Undertaking" (1); that (non)apology alludes to the numerous other such texts then in circulation and to the belief that many *should* be in circulation is an indication of the interest in and importance of the subject. William Bromfield, likewise feting the "late improvements in surgery," observes that

> What was formerly pursued only by a few, and that with languor and disgust, is now sought after by most with vigour and curiosity. What most surgeons were contented to believe upon the credit of books, is now learned from the inspection of dissected bodies; and there is scarce a man in *England*, who thinks himself qualified to practise surgery, (even in those parts of the country most remote from *London*, and the observation of skilful men) till he has by hearing anatomical lectures, and attending dissections, gained a competent knowledge of the structure of the human body. (2–3)

Bromfield's emphasis on the figure of the highly trained and specialized surgeon here is the crucial point, for while he seems to suggest that many may practice various and valuable healing arts, only the properly "qualified" will practice surgery – particularly important since these improvements have "diffused the knowledge of surgery through the kingdom, opening, as it were, so many schools, in which that art is taught by the best instructors, Nature and Example" (3). Nominating "Nature and Example" as the best instructors of the surgical sciences foregrounds, first, their status as "science," in that they are the result of systematic study of observable phenomena; and, second, their status as uniquely demanding and therefore highly regulated disciplines – hence the need for "schools" both to teach and police its practices.

But lest the "diffusion" of knowledge give rise to the perception that learning surgery is somehow easy, less laudable, or open to any but the most gifted and qualified because of its apparent omnipresence, we are continually reminded that the work of surgery and, of course, surgeons themselves are extraordinary instances of already uncommon talents. After devoting several pages to a history of surgery from Æsculapius in

Ancient Greece to the present in Great Britain, *The Edinburgh Practice of Physic and Surgery*, first published in 1800 and one of the more important teaching texts of the period, notes that "Since the commencement of the present century, surgery has been enlarged with many valuable and important improvements, of the greatest part of which we have availed ourselves in the course of the following treatise [that] it would far exceed the limits of a work of this nature to enumerate the names and writings of such authors as have lived within the above period" (640–1). In effect, establishing itself as a compendium of medical and surgical knowledge, so comprehensive that it absorbs all other texts, this text also suggests that the names and accomplishments of contemporary surgeons are, at least among the intended (professional) readers, so well-known, numerous, and deserving of approbation, more so than ever before, that the need to continue the process of enumeration is not only impossible but unnecessary. Such a gesture, I would argue, is a continuation of the effort to demonstrate the properly professional and thoroughly documented authority of surgeons. By 1825 (interestingly, the same year as the anxious "Medical Students" essay), Charles Averill could confidently say in the opening sentence of his *A Short Treatise on Operative Surgery*, a text dedicated to Cooper, that "The most cursory description of the operations of Surgery, is more than sufficient to demonstrate, that the art of performing them, *with a proper regard to the lives and necessities of patients*, can neither be learned by a spectator, nor taught by any prescribed rules, without actual and frequent practice" (1; emphasis added). Surgery is, now, a proper scientific discipline that requires extraordinary time and effort to learn, let alone master, and only those most engaged in the process have earned the right to practice and call themselves surgeons.

Operating Theatre

In all of these instances, we can see a growing insistence that being a surgeon is about *being* a surgeon, not just about "doing" surgery, and teaching the process of becoming a surgeon was Astley Cooper's primary task for over forty years at a number of London's premier medical institutions. In other words, Cooper is of particular interest here not just because of his well-established (and by all accounts well-earned) status as one of the leading surgeons of the day, but also, and perhaps more importantly, because he was one of the most well-respected and practised teachers of the day, as well: a man whose expertise and philosophies were shaped in part at the lectures and operating tables of both Hunter and preeminent surgeon Henry Cline, himself one of Hunter's disciples, Cooper, in turn, shaped several generations of surgical students, helping to establish "scientific surgery" as the ultimate expression of Western medical theory and practice. In the preface to one of the many editions of the lectures of Cooper, his one-time pupil Frederick Tyrell notes that the principles' "excellence and accuracy have been proved, not only by the extensive and successful practice of Sir Astley himself, but by the experience of several thousands of medical men who have received them from him, and by whom they have been propagated through all parts of the world in which surgery is practised as a science" (iii). Important to note here is that the basis for Tyrell's claim is not the numbers of successful surgeries or the recovery rates of numerous patients (though, surely, such things are implied) but the initiation of "thousands of medical men" into the fold in which – and this is key – "surgery is practised as a science" and, in turn, their initiation of thousands more. When presented with a copy of this edition, Cooper observed that the text "contains a faithful account of the principles of Surgery, which, for forty years, I have been endeavouring to learn, and of the practice which, for thirty-two years, I have been in the habit of teaching, in that school which is proud to rank amongst its Lecturers in Surgery the names Cheselden, Sharp, Warner, Else, and last, although not least, of my most able and judicious preceptor and predecessor, Mr Cline" (iv). Here, too, Cooper's own claims for the strength of the principles is not solely the sound science upon which they are based but also the stamp of approval granted by the roster of masters and celebrities, a roster that now includes his own name. Thus, medicine (at least in the Romantic Century 1750–1850) is as much about the larger-than-life characters and their stories, about heroes who embody vast expertise and experience and thus personify hope itself, as it is about the legacy of the theories and advances that have continuing relevance in medicine today.

As we have already seen, Cooper liberally adorns his lectures with a variety of (often disturbingly funny) illustrative anecdotes. The simple fact of the presence of the stories is itself interesting: as Prentice points out, "Story-telling is an important part of medical teaching, conveying social information about medical practice and social structures," as well as being "Intimately connected to the narrative art of case presentation" (548). In Cooper's case, the stories tend to feature an almost Gothic spectacle of ineptitude. In one such story, a young but eager dresser (an apprentice position) tells a surgery boy (a kind of general helper, not necessarily a student of any kind) who happened to have a bad leg, "I should like to cut off your leg," and the boy responds, "Indeed! ... I should not like it" (*Lectures* 3). But upon being convinced that the leg would never be of any use to him and told that he would be paid for the chance to allow the dresser to practice, the boy submits. During the procedure, the boy began to bleed somewhat more than the dresser anticipated, and when the tourniquet broke, the dresser "jumped about the room" and failed to stop the bleeding until "a pupil accidentally called, who had the presence of mind to apply the key of the door to the femoral artery [and] gained time for the application of another tourniquet" (4). The point, for Cooper, is not that the dresser should never have performed the procedure in the first place – in fact, I would argue that mastering the tactics to convince the boy to allow the procedure is precisely what Cooper is after – but that his lack of the self-possession demonstrated by the second pupil almost led to disaster. Of course, self-possession goes beyond keeping cool in an emergency:

> I caution the pupils from speaking unguardedly before the patients; it can do no good to let them know what is intended for their cure, which it very often prevents. Some time ago, a man came into Guy's Hospital, having a disease that required an operation, and by no means a dangerous one. A pupil, when conversing with him, asked him where he came from: the man replied, "From Cornwall." "O did you?" said the pupil; "Well, I can tell you, you will never see Cornwall again." The patient became alarmed, and immediately left the hospital. (6)

In addition to the obvious purpose of materializing the abstract principles he's working to drill into the students, Cooper is also continuing the process of manifesting his own authority – a gesture, perhaps, many of us can recognize from our own experiences in the lecture hall – for in telling these stories, he offers himself as one who has seen it all and therefore has a seemingly endless supply of wide-ranging expertise to offer student and patient alike – precisely the message at the core of his lecture and the overarching theme of the pedagogy he personifies.

There are, Copper suggests, a variety of sources for such authority and expertise, but perhaps the most important is in the character of the surgeon himself. Demonstrate the necessary self-possession, say, and others are less likely to question one's authority; or, even better, others will simply grant it without even the shadow of a question: "Patients generally form an opinion of a surgeon's ability by his manner: if he be of a dry, morose turn, he is apt to alarm not only the patient, but his whole family; whereas, he who speaks kindly to them, and asks for particular information, is supposed to have more knowledge, and receives more respect" (2). Embodying the professional competence necessary to complete the task at hand, making patients and their families see and respond to it is fundamental to the successful operation. But, of course, successful operations require more than the right attitude. Encouraging the students to take their studies seriously, to entirely devote themselves to acquiring all of the skills and knowledge they possibly can (so as not, he says to "be exposed to ridicule, and perhaps worse"), Cooper says, simply, "You should know the nature of the human machine well" (4). But even here, in perhaps the most basic lesson of any such introductory lecture, the "you-get-out-what-you-put-in" moment, Cooper's mind is always on the issues emanating from popular perception and the necessities of establishing and maintaining professional authority. He states: "If you have a watch injured, you will not give it to a tinker to repair – you will get the best watchmaker you can to set it right. How, then, can it be supposed, that the finest and most perfect organization we know of, when out of order, should be consigned to the hands of unlearned persons? Mistakes of this kind do, it is true, sometimes happen, but much less often now than formerly" (4). Perhaps we can hear an echo of the familiar metaphor of God as Watchmaker here, made particularly relevant to Cooper and his contemporaries by William Paley, whose popular and controversial *Natural Theology; or, Evidences of the Existence and Attributes of the Deity*, published in 1802, sought to prove the existence of God by grounding its arguments in anatomy and other physical sciences.[8] If we do hear such an echo, then Cooper's collocation of the surgeon with the watchmaker speaks volumes, for the surgeon emerges here not just as a master craftsman with unique, highly specialized, and highly prized talents moulded by years spent honing the craft, but as *the* Master Craftsman, the Maker of All Things. In any event, Cooper's conviction that consigning "the finest and most perfect organization" in an injured state to any but the most qualified of experts is a mistake, and that such a mistake is less likely to happen now than in the past, takes as given two important, if still contentious, points: first, that surgeons are or should be the *only* experts to be trusted when the body is injured; and, second, that the stakes for those who engage in the study and practice of surgery are higher now than ever before. The point of one's time as a surgical trainee (and in the period that time was becoming steadily longer and more regimented[9]) was not only to learn surgery, but to *become a surgeon*, and the one does not always guarantee the other.

For this reason, Cooper is not at all shy about broadcasting his own status as a surgeon by wielding *his* authority in such a way that ensures he is clearly seen and unquestioningly accepted as the "master" to the "apprentices" assembled in the lecture – a group seeking initiation into a community of experts that to a degree demands the rejection of allegiance to other communities and at least a partial abandonment of their codes and prejudices. At the lecture's close, for example, Cooper takes a moment to address discipline and decorum, both in their studies in general and in lecture attendance in particular. His admonition is prompted by an awareness of the lingering conceptions of class that attend: first, the slowly eroding physician/surgeon distinction and, second, the emerging sense (however attenuated or naive it may be) that it is the "best and brightest" who study surgery, regardless of their class or economic background. "Some," he notes, "will be fluttering in the boxes of another theatre, or come here only to interrupt their more steady fellow-students." Worse,

> Perhaps some who are fashionably dressed may think proper to look down with contempt upon the students whose attire is plain and more modest; but should such a feeling exist, I would advise such persons to pause a while, and consider what it is that makes one man superior to another in this profession. When they commence their career of public life, the plain, industrious, intelligent young man goes slowly but steadily in the right track of his profession, and rises to respectability, perhaps even to a high rank; on the other hand, the fashionable lounger, who neglects to improve himself, finds his want of knowledge and his bad habits equally retard him: instead of rising, he sinks lower; his friends disappear, and at last he falls into obscurity, reduced to a pitiable state, blaming and abusing his more fortunate rivals. (7)

In the world of surgery, Cooper would have the students believe, the choice is between "great genius" that's the product of "uncommon industry and assiduity" (5), to adapt his description of John Hunter, or pitiable obscurity.

The Anatomy of Hope

One of Cooper's tactics to hammer this lesson home – though perhaps it is more fair to see it simply as one of his core beliefs than as any kind of pedagogical gesture – is repeatedly to emphasize the extraordinary and extraordinarily important profession the students are seeking to enter by stressing its very public nature. Surgeons are not ordinary people, is the implicit message in every line of the lecture; they are not even ordinary medical practitioners. The perhaps intimidating presence of *Astley Cooper*, the name as much as the person, at their introductory lecture is proof enough that ordinary is not an option, and that being a surgeon is as much an exercise in identity politics as it is an embodiment of specific skills. Cooper urges:

> the head must always direct the hand, or otherwise the operator is unfit to discover an effectual remedy for the unforeseen accidents which may occur in his practice. Without this quality a man may do well enough in ordinary cases, but can do little on sudden emergencies; it inspires confidence, and almost insures the success of the operation. These qualities forward the interests of professional men, whilst they diminish the sufferings of human. (2)

Similarly, believing in one's own skills and committing to the absolute necessity of greatness – developing, that is, the ego associated with surgeons in popular culture, publicly performing the heroic acts that support that ego, and willing a sense of hope into even the most desperate encounter – is likewise crucial. As Cooper points out in the introduction to *Surgical Essays*, published in 1818 with his colleague Benjamin Travers:

> The variety which of necessity occurs in the practice of the Surgeons – the facility afforded to them in their respective plans of treatment – the opportunities of improving the practice of Medical Surgery – of observing the results, general and comparative, of Operations of every description – and especially of prosecuting inquiries into Morbid Anatomy, by prompt examination of the dead body, and of parts removed by operation – are advantages which while they afford ample compensation for the labours of clinical research, would allow no pretext for indifference in those, who, conscious of their value, were not influenced by an ardent desire to improve and impart them. (ix–x)

Successful surgical outcomes for patients and, in some ways apparently more importantly, the advancement of surgical science are about the *will* of the surgeon. In such passages we can perhaps see early examples of the encoding of behaviours that manifest as ego, hubris, and arrogance (key elements of the "God Complex") that are so often a part of popular depictions of medical professionals, especially surgeons – evidence, I would argue, of the complexity of the continuing efforts to negotiate the surgeon-patient encounter, but also, in an important sense, evidence of the *success* of the early moments of the history of those negotiations, for only those who occupy a central place in the pantheon of "most effective healers," no matter how contested that place might be, would register either the promise or the anxiety that such character traits evince. More to the point, while the task of the surgeon may be to will patients back to health by, in part, willing them to maintain an unflagging sense of hope and belief in the surgeon's skills, his ultimate task is to work to ensure the continuing dominance of his science and art: advancing the "interests of professional men" and engaging in the "labours of clinical research" will serve not only to make surgeons the most effective healers but will also help to further solidify their image as such, creating a kind of feedback loop powered by hope but centred on the surgeon, the ultimate embodiment of Western medicine. And the "professional men" in this equation are not only the students, but their masters, as well. Cooper and his contemporaries were not working simply to share their knowledge and train a new generation of surgeons to carry the torch; they were deeply, zealously invested in the process of ensuring that there was a torch, a beacon of hope, to be lit in the first place.

The "Medical Students" essay, which takes great joy in exaggerating (if in some cases only just) the popular perception of medicine and its, at best, most junior and, at worst, most incompetent, personnel, takes equal pains to announce the names of the most celebrated practitioners and engages in the kind of hero worship that is so frequently associated with this most spectacular of medical sciences:

> Notwithstanding, however, the general heedlessness of our medical students, there always have been, and always will be, some choice and eager spirits, whose whole hearts and minds are absorbed in the study of a science than which none can be more interesting, more important, or more beneficial to mankind. Hence it is that England can proudly boast of a COOPER, a BRODIE, an ABERNETHY, a HORNE, a LAWRENCE [...] The success

> and fame of these "master spirits" will stimulate others to the achievement of a similar elevation. (280)

In addition to occupying such a prominent place in this list of "master spirits," Cooper played a key role in the process by which medicine, and surgery specifically, could be seen to produce such figures in an age when a "Romantic subjectivity" and celebrity culture collided in the terrain prepared by the explosion of print culture. At the same time, Cooper's influence, evident in his writings and in the generations of practitioners who learned from his example, serves to illustrate the early history of the ways and means of the rhetoric of hope that continues to play such a key role in medical encounters in our own day. Cooper's introductory lecture, attendance at which became a sort of initiation rite on its own, is thus a crucial instantiation of that process in action: at once a key document in medical history and a critical moment in the still-reverberating Romantic legacy.

NOTES

I gratefully acknowledge the financial support of the Canadian Institute for Health Research and Brock University's Humanities Research Institute, and I thank Ann Howey, Sherryl Vint, and Adriana Pagnotta-Allard for their comments on earlier drafts.

1 Numerous histories of medicine, particularly of the period between 1750 and 1850, treat the role and rise of surgery and the figure of the surgeon; for brief surveys see Rosen; Temkin; Mazumdar; Porter, *Greatest* 360–74; and Allard 38–42.

2 See Hirschauer for a discussion of the notion of the "surgeon-body," a shifting and modular group of experts that, in the operating room alone, can consist of "between five and nine [people], not counting mere onlookers attracted to spectacular operations" (293). If we take into account the "team" beyond the operating room, this aggregate body can number several dozen or more.

3 To be sure, Cooper and other contemporary surgeons had "teams" of various sizes as well, but the emphasis in much of their training, as we will see, is on the surgeon as "hero" who is (or should be) perceived to hold both the burden of care and the "fate" of the profession solely in his (always, of course, *his*) hands. Traces of this kind of emphasis on the individual are

still visible in the notion of a "primary care provider" or "chief surgeon," and in the clear definition of and strict adherence to hierarchies of various kinds, but my point is that we see a shift in emphasis, at least in practice in most instances, away from the stress on the "surgeon-hero" and toward the smooth functioning of a "team."

4 Roy Porter's work is especially useful for understanding the shifting popular perception of medical practice, institutions, and practitioners in the late eighteenth and early nineteenth centuries. See, for example, *Patients and Practitioners*, *Patient's Progress* (with Dorothy Porter), *Health for Sale*, and *Quacks*.

5 My thanks to T. Kenny Fountain for introducing me to Prentice's work.

6 Scholarly work on Hunter (and on his equally notable brother William) and his legacy is immense, but see Jacyna for an excellent account of his status in the Romantic period and immediately following and Moore for a recent biography of Hunter (and, by extension, "Modern Surgery").

7 Mazumdar continues: "The immense, even religious, veneration in which the College of Surgeons held Hunter in the early part of the nineteenth century is expressed in the series of Hunterian Orations held every year in the 14th of February, Hunter's birthday, an arrangement which clearly reflects that of the Harveian Orations of the Royal College of Physicians" (126–7). The "Harveian Orations," of course, are named for William Harvey, the early seventeenth-century English physician credited with the discovery of the circulatory system.

8 Paley's ideas continue to provoke reaction and to be invoked in the "intelligent design" conversation; Richard Dawkins, for example, famously attacks Paley's work in *The Blind Watchmaker* (1986).

9 See Mazumdar 122 (Table 3) for a table detailing what a surgical student's eight or so years of training, including six years as an apprentice, might have looked like.

WORKS CITED

Allard, James Robert. *Romanticism, Medicine, and the Poet's Body*. Burlington, Vt.: Ashgate, 2007. Print.

Averill, Charles. *A Short Treatise on Operative Surgery, Describing the Principal Operations as They are Practised in England and France; Designed for the Use of Students in Operating on the Dead Body*. 2nd ed. London, 1825. Print.

Bromfield, William. *Chirurgical Observations and Cases*. 2 vols. London, 1773. Print.

Cooper, Astley. *Lectures on the Principles and Practices of Surgery; As Delivered at the Theatre of St Thomas's Hospital*. 4th ed. London, 1835. Print.

Cooper, Astley, and Benjamin Travers. *Surgical Essays*. 2nd ed. London, 1818. Print.

The Edinburgh Practice of Physic and Surgery; Preceded by an Abstract of the Theory of Medicine and the Nosology of Dr Cullen: And Including Upwards of Six Hundred Authentic Formulæ, From the Books of St Bartholomew's, St George's, St Thomas's, Guy's, and Other Hospitals in London, and From the Lectures and Writings of the Most Eminent Public Teachers. London, 1800. *ECCO*. Web. 7 July 2010.

Haley, William. *Natural Theology; or, Evidences of the Existence and Attributes of the Deity*. London, 1802. Print.

Hamilton, William. *The History of Medicine, Surgery, and Anatomy, From the Creation of the World, to the Commencement of the Nineteenth Century*. 2 vols. London, 1831. Print.

Hirschauer, Stefan. "The Manufacture of Bodies in Surgery." *Social Studies of Science* 21.2 (1991): 279–319. Print. http://dx.doi.org/10.1177/030631291021002005.

Jacyna, L. S. "Images of John Hunter in the Nineteenth Century." *History of Science* 21 (1983): 85–108. Print.

Mazumdar, Pauline M.H. "Anatomy, Physiology, and Surgery: Physiology Teaching in Early Nineteenth-Century London." *Canadian Bulletin of the History of Medicine* 4 (1987): 119–43. Print.

"Medical Students." *European Magazine* 86 (1825–26): 276–80. Print.

Moore, Wendy. *The Knife Man: Blood, Body-Snatching and the Birth of Modern Surgery*. Toronto: Bantam, 2005. Print.

Porter, Roy. *The Greatest Benefit to Mankind: A Medical History of Humanity*. New York: Norton, 1997. Print.

Porter, Roy. *Health for Sale: Quackery in England 1660–1850*. Manchester: Manchester UP, 1989. Print.

Porter, Roy, ed. *Patients and Practitioners: Lay Perceptions of Medicine in Pre-Industrial Society*. Cambridge: Cambridge UP, 1985. Print.

Porter, Roy. *Quacks: Fakers and Charlatans in English Medicine*. Stroud: Tempus, 2000. Print.

Porter, Roy, and Dorothy Porter. *Patient's Progress: Doctors and Doctoring in Eighteenth-Century England*. Cambridge: Polity, 1989. Print.

Prentice, Rachel. "Drilling Surgeons: Social Lessons of Embodied Surgical Learning." *Science, Technology & Human Values* 32.5 (2007): 534–53. Print. http://dx.doi.org/10.1177/0895904805303201.

Rosen, George. "Romantic Medicine: A Problem in Historical Periodization." *Bulletin of the History of Medicine* 25 (1951): 149–58. Print.

Sharpe, Samuel. *A Treatise on the Operations of Surgery, With a Description and Representation of the Instruments Used in Performing Them: To Which Is Prefaced an Introduction on the Nature and Treatment of Wounds, Abcesses and Ulcers*. 9th ed. London: 1769. Print.

Temkin, O. "The Role of Surgery in the Rise of Modern Medical Thought." *Bulletin of the History of Medicine* 21 (1951): 248–59. Print.

Tyrell, Frederick. Preface. *The Lectures of Sir Astley Cooper on the Principles and Practices of Surgery, With Additional Notes and Cases*. By Cooper. N.p., 1826. iii–iv. Print.

4 "I know the difference between what I see and what I only want to see": Remembering India's Partition through Children in *Cracking India*[1]

NANDI BHATIA

In critical discussions of the 1947 Partition of India – a moment of rupture that caused the largest forced migration of the twentieth century and led to unprecedented violence, the horror of which is lodged in the collective memory of the generation that survived its brutality and trauma – the writer's role becomes especially significant.[2] Literary creations, which made "the very first step to engage this nightmarish moment, outside of journalism" (Kamra 99), serve as memorials to this event. Even though, in terms of the scale that ravaged humanity, the Partition was similar to the two world wars and the Holocaust, governments believed it was best left forgotten in the interest of celebrating independence and postcolonial nation building. In India, therefore, says Urvashi Butalia, "there is no institutional memory of Partition." Because of its own complicity, "the State has not seen fit to construct any memorials, to mark any particular places – as has been done, say, in the case of holocaust memorials or memorials for the Vietnam war" (272). And no notable commemorative site at places where people camped, crossed borders, and lost lives have been marked (Butalia 272).[3] Simultaneously, the Partition has been subjected to a haunting silence by survivors too traumatized or faced with "collective guilt" to talk about it publicly.[4] And as such historians as Gyan Pandey (2001) and Ravinder Kaur have pointed out, the official history of the Partition has focussed primarily on the achievements of leaders at the expense of obscuring the story of individual loss – material, psychic, territorial, familial – and the trauma that dominates individual and collective memory. Along with the work of these historians, Urvashi Butalia, Ritu Menon, and Kamala Bhasin's alternative histories, which analyse testimonies of survivors in tandem with historical documents, newspaper reports, and state archives, present a picture of Partition in which stories of brutality, death, abduction, rape, victimization, and loss of home, family members, and property take centre stage.[5]

Several Indian and Pakistani creative writers, intellectuals, and scholars who witnessed the event as adults or as children have re-created these accounts in the form of "autobiographically-infused scholarship and literary expression," accounts which work "against the repressive silence and forgetting that pervaded survivors' homes" (Greenberg 262). In addition, those who were born after Partition but grew up listening to stories of mass atrocity, have written about the event through what Marianne Hirsch, writing in the context of the Holocaust, calls "*postmemory*," or the articulation of "the aesthetic strategies of tragic identification, projection, and mourning" that characterize "second generation" memory (8; emphasis in original). Thus, the literary writer aids the project of generating a culture of public awareness and consciousness about the Partition to work "against [the] silence and forgetting"[6] of a painful moment, which, until the recent assembling of the testimonies of the abducted, was largely consigned to whispers. By presenting fictionalized accounts of experiences that have remained "unspeakable" or obscured in official records, literary texts offer strategies for counteracting official histories, and in so doing, offer some semblance of hope in filling the gaps in a historiography that has largely overlooked the human consequences of Partition.[7]

This function is especially crucial because traditional historical methodologies are dismissive of personal recollections, which are seen as being prone to bias, distortion, and exaggeration, as opposed to "authentic," reliable, or factual accounts that can be used as evidence in historical discourse (Pandey, "Prose" 214). This kind of history has little use for personal narratives, even though the latter provide important insights into violence, sectarian strife, and trauma, as Butalia, Menon, Bhasin, and Kaur have demonstrated through the personal testimonies they have recorded. However, when testimonial access is also limited by survivors' reluctance to confront the past and share their experiences publicly, literary texts' presentation of fictionalized stories and characters that engage the subjects of violence, trauma, and silence through such devices as flashback, dialogue, storytelling, and irony (for example), enable the production of cultural memory that resonates with the individual memories of those who actually witnessed the Partition. In this, the voices of children, which remain largely absent from actual testimonial accounts collected by historians, acquire especial significance.

Confronting the violence from the position of not being fully indoctrinated into ideologies of class or religion, children can enable a radical questioning of adult versions of history.

To amplify my claim, I turn to an analysis of Bapsi Sidhwa's novel, *Cracking India* (1991). Sidhwa is a creative writer who lives in the United States and has authored a number of novels, and *Cracking India* is her most acclaimed work. Set in the city of Lahore, it recovers the story of the Partition through Lenny, a young girl whose age ranges from about five until ten in the course of the novel, and who observes the scattering of neighbours, servants, and all those who work for her family in the wake of impending Partition, news about which comes only in snatches and fragments. Like Lenny, Sidhwa was a child when India was partitioned into two nations – India and Pakistan. Hence, Lenny's act of remembering Partition and telling the story of her family, neighbours, and changes in the city may be read as a fictionalized autobiographical rendering in which the adult narrator frequently interjects through introspection and commentary on Lenny's observations. However, the autobiographical voice, while placing the author in the text and simultaneously distancing her from Lenny, imparts narratorial authority to Lenny so that the voice of the child can emerge and render visible aspects that perhaps adults cannot see. Because it is a fictional text, I do not treat *Cracking India* as simply "documenting" an alternative account, a critical strategy that risks overlooking "the interpretive function of reading and writing about the Partition, the discursive construction of subjectivity, agency, nationalism, and history that are involved in its narrativization" (Didur 5). Instead, my interest in analysing *Cracking India* is to see how the narrative strategies of fiction and the evocation of memory in writing the story of Partition several decades later enable the characters' – and in particular children's – negotiation with a troubled past and with a triumphalist historiography that either avoids the subject by maintaining a silence about it or talks about it primarily in terms of the government's achievements in rescuing and resettling refugees as people moved across borders to their new homelands.[8]

In India, the subject of Partition to this day remains a matter of public concern, interest, and discussion. Often prompted by the ongoing strained relationship with Pakistan, a relationship that occupies the public domain of news, the subject jogs memories of the tangible effects of Partition felt by the vast majority of the populace in the north and suffuses conversations in the private sphere. If literary narratives are public sites that have the potential to shape cultural opinion and render visible the dynamics, competing agendas, dissenting voices and gaps which exist in neat explanations that serve the public domain of politics – an assertion made and complicated time and again across a range of periods, as the chapters in the present volume attest – then *Cracking India*'s oscillation between hopefulness and hopelessness exposes the nationalistic reincarnations of Partition. Even though the hope expressed in the novel is marked by contradictions since, as the editors point out in the introduction to this volume, "hope cannot be sentimentalized or simplified as a derivatively utopian concept" (19), Sidhwa's novel is exemplary of what Faflak and Haslam identify as the "capacity for culture to function as a mode of (hopeful) intellectual expression and critique" (18), one that insists upon the child's opinion as having an important place in what constitutes "public opinion." The novel's publication and circulation in the West and its inclusion in university curricula gives it multiple audiences and an expanded readership, which in turn amplifies the scope for public discussion. This possibility itself offers hopes for new insights at a time when efforts are being made globally to understand the politics and effects of genocides and their implications for children. How might children aid the production of the history of Partition, testimonies, eyewitness accounts, and its terror and brutality? And what kinds of issues would their feelings and questions – often ignored or dismissed by adults – open up for discussion? These are some questions that this chapter attempts to answer.

I flirt, briefly, with hope

At the beginning of the novel, Lenny makes the statement, "I flirt, briefly, with hope" (Sidwha 19), as she attempts to come to terms with her polio-stricken leg. Lenny, "unable to bear the thought of an able-bodied future" (23) transforms her world into a hopeful one by playing around in school and doing things that able-bodied children do. Yet her own flirtation with hope for a reformed foot transposes into a larger narrative as she, her family, and everyone she loves are confronted with the brutal violence that explodes before and during the Partition. Hope is all that sustains Lenny and her family as the forced migration of neighbours and deaths of such family friends as Inspector Rodgers culminate in Lenny's beloved Ayah Shanta's abduction by her friend and admirer Ice-Candy Man. Right until the end of the novel, the readers, like Lenny and her family, are left on tenterhooks as they wait for any leads about Ayah. Finally, Lenny, on a tip-off from her cousin – who has heard whispers that Ayah now resides in Hira Mandi (Diamond Market), where Ice-Candy Man has forced her to become a dancing girl against her will – learns about her and urges Godmother to seek her out. After visiting Ayah, Godmother ensures her safe passage to her family in Amritsar, which, after the Partition, falls under India.[9] Since the novel ends with Ayah's return to her family and with Ice-Candy Man's disappearance across the Wagah Border into Amritsar, Ayah's afterlife is not known to the readers. The novel thus leaves gaping holes and questions about the afterlives of survivors, many of whom belonged to lower-caste and working-class groups. This lack of closure is all the more important given that several refugee colonies still exist in India, despite the government's closure of the Ministry of Rehabilitation and Resettlement in 1965, by which it signalled the end of the refugee crisis and the integration of refugees into new places of relocation.[10]

Most critical work on *Cracking India*, while acknowledging that the story is told from the perspective of a young girl, has paid attention primarily to (the Hindu) Ayah's abduction by (Muslim) men in an attempt to foreground the religious-cum-nationalist divisions for which Ayah's abduction became a signifier, a signifier that, further, points to notions of nationalist belonging or unbelonging.[11] Yet Lenny places Ayah's abduction not in the narrative of communal divisions that characterizes most analysis, but rather in terms of her own innocent betrayal of Ayah and also the betrayal by those who, in her memory, loved her. This narrative of "betrayal" is of acute importance, for it foregrounds a story of secular and peaceful interpersonal relations amongst different religious communities in Panjab before the division of the subcontinent. For what Lenny remembers are relations and friendships amongst Ayah's Hindu, Muslim, and Sikh friends and the coexistence of these communities in Imam Din's village Pir Pindo when she visits with him, and where she first meets his great grandson Ranna, a boy her own age. In fact, before the outbreak of violence, the religion or ethnicity of the characters Lenny hangs out with, especially of those who eventually become Ayah's abductors, is not emphasized. Rather, Lenny's recollections of the conversations amongst the villagers, as troubles begin to break out in the city of Lahore, are recorded in terms of their pledging to forge a united front against the perpetrators of violence, and Muslim and Sikh neighbours making promises of "neighbourly brotherliness." This is not to say that there was no sectarian violence in the subcontinent's history before 1947. Yet what Lenny notes is equally relevant in highlighting the principles of peace and mutual respect that communities often practiced, principles which get obscured in histories of sectarian violence. Her recollection of interreligious and interethnic camaraderie before Partition thus provides a social and cultural history of Panjab that undermines the communal narrative that many histories of Partition are prone to produce.[12] Indeed, Lenny's remembrance of the shifting demographics as people begin to migrate, and of the altered relations among communities in the park, along with the disappearance of Queen Victoria's statue from it, speaks to the destruction of personal relationships when Partition becomes a reality. Recorded without judgment, Lenny's commentary, on both interpersonal relations and the violence that she witnesses, functions as an acknowledgment of the contradictions produced by Partition, as friends turn on each other in the name of community and religion. If she initially notices any identitarian concerns, it is in the fragments of conversations amongst adult members of the Parsee community, who, as a minority of 200 in Lahore, are struck by insecurity about the possible outcome of Partition for them. A Parsee by birth, Lenny renders visible the fact that while the Parsees constitute a community that is ostensibly left out of the perils of sectarian violence, it is not one that remains unaffected by Partition, especially as emphasized by Colonel Bharucha, the community's president, during a gathering.

Because of Lenny's initial inability to see the people around her in terms of their religious and ethnic identities (Lenny does not notice that Ice-Candy Man is Muslim, but the adult narrator does), she links her own polio-stricken body, as Daiya argues, to that of the cracking national body, rather than provide an analysis of Ayah's body as a site upon which her Muslim abductors exact revenge against the Indian (read Hindu) nation. Lenny's birthday "falls on the day India is partitioned, and her disability due to polio (blamed by Dr Bharucha on the British who brought polio to India) is a metaphor for the birth of the two nations as disabled by the British partitioning of the subcontinent. Thus, the child Lenny's minoritized, female, disabled body materially represents the legacy of British colonialism: disease and a disabled South Asia" (Daiya 78). This conflation of Lenny's disabled body with the national body works as a metaphor for challenging triumphant accounts that announce the new and momentous beginnings of an independent nation, as in Jawaharlal Nehru's powerfully celebratory speech about the fulfilment of India's "tryst with destiny."[13] Instead, Lenny's pained body, subjected to several surgical procedures, suggests the fault lines of the nation and its failed promises of citizenship that become evident in the imperilled state of the people.

By linking her own body to the terror that she witnesses, Lenny forces the reader to find an explanation for her nightmares. An early nightmare is connected to the "caterpillar" (English men and women marching in a band) coming out of the Salvation Army compound and transposing into "a single German soldier on a motorcycle," accompanied by a siren, which for her is the sound of "brutality," and hints at the savagery to come through a reference to the Holocaust: "No one had taught me to fear an immaculate Nazi soldier. Yet here he was, in nightmare after nightmare, coming to me on his motorcycle," she says (Sidhwa 31).[14] On one level, Lenny's nightmares connect the child's personal trauma to the public event of Partition. On another, from the adult narrator's perspective, the nightmares suggest the politicization of the child and her growing awareness of her location in a world where her identity, too, is vulnerable, and is inevitably linked to the horrors of world events in which political leaders have a role to play. Since it is not fully comprehensible to Lenny *how* they are linked, the final rupture – the splitting of the nation, which assigns new identities to its newly formed citizens – is interrogated by Lenny through the metaphor of a simple card game:

> Playing British gods under the ceiling fans of the Faletti's hotel – behind Queen Victoria's gardened skirt –the Radcliff Commission deals out Indian cities like a pack of cards. Lahore is dealt to Pakistan, Amritsar to India. Sialkot to Pakistan. Pathankot to India.
>
> I am Pakistani. Just like that. (Sidhwa 150)

The imagery of the "game" – which foregrounds the presence of British officials such as Cyril Radcliffe, who chaired the commission that decided the boundaries of the two new nations[15] – suggests the arbitrariness in the colonial rulers' method of defining new national boundaries in ways that created cartographic instabilities and, with excessively damaging outcomes, sealed the fate of millions. While the game itself suggests a gamble in which there are winners and losers, the fact that the players are far removed, literally, from the cities the colonial rulers dole out to the colonized suggests that the risk is not theirs but that of the hordes of (absent) people who populate these cities. Highlighting the irony of the decisions made by those "British gods," decisions that result in the formation of new national and community subjects so that Lenny becomes a "Pakistani. Just like that," she foregrounds the power that the colonial regime exercised up until the very last moment of the onset of independence and the simultaneous subcontinental division, which assigned people new identities in a matter of days.

At the same time, Lenny's apathy towards nationalist leaders also extends to the ineffectiveness of the process of refugee resettlement. Thus, the appearance of the state through its Rehabilitation Mission for abducted women is not celebrated; rather, the abducted women's camp behind her house, which she calls the "women's jail" (Sidhwa 201) – the place from which her new Ayah, Hamida comes – emerges in her memory as a site of confinement for the "fallen women" (226). Lenny remembers it as a zone of harassment from where she hears the haunting cries of wailing women, cries "verging on the inhuman" (224). Such a depiction negates the optimism that is provided in official accounts of refugee camps.[16]

Focussing on her own "deformed" foot also makes Lenny alert to other bodies in pain, bodies of those who experience the horror of the Partition from the social margins. To this end, Lenny brings attention to stories of the dhoti-clad gardener, Hari, who is forcibly circumcised and whose name is changed to Himat Ali, pointing, through this transformation, to the ways in which personal ties were severed and new identities forced and created as the decisions made by colonial and national leaders split the subcontinent. Readers also learn of the dalit sweeper, Moti, who, to avoid persecution, converts to Christianity and is renamed David Masih. These snapshots of Lenny's memory are moments that quickly recede from the narrative as Ayah's story takes centre stage. Yet they are reminders of the importance of the fragments that remained etched in the child's memory – fragments about the physical, ideological, and psychic ramifications of Partition violence.

A deeply personal narrative that captures the anguish of children like herself, Lenny's stories thus recast the division of Panjab through a child's eyewitness account that turns minor characters, including servants, students, and the inhabitants of the villages of Pir Pindo and Dera Tek Singh, into subjects of history. Sidhwa's investment in Lenny as the primary storyteller is, then, particularly important for examining classed and localized narratives of Partition – of dalits, working-class men and women, and the rural poor. To this end, the inclusion in the story of Ranna, who sustains unbearable scars when his village is attacked by Sikhs, acquires special importance. Ranna's story further expands the meanings of Partition and the disciplinary mechanisms, punishments, and revenge tactics perpetrated on those whose bodies came to be conflated with religious communities and nations as news of the Partition began to spread.

No one noticed Ranna as he wandered in the burning city.[17]

As a child from the same village as that of the family cook, Imam Din, Ranna does not have the privileges and protection of class that are available to Lenny. And though close in age, Lenny and Ranna are also set apart by their religion: Ranna is a Muslim and Lenny is Parsee. Thus, while no one notices Ranna in the "burning city" where he wanders about as a refugee after his village is attacked and many of his kith and kin are killed, he is subjected to the most horrific form of violence. As his aunt, Noni *chachi*, says, it's a wonder that he survives. Even though Lenny is the primary storyteller, it is significant that "Ranna's story" receives a separate space in the text under this heading. This is the intervention of the adult narrator and author, who strategically give space to Ranna's story in order to emphasize that it needs to be listened to and understood on its own terms. Because Ranna's story differs quite significantly from Lenny's own story of witnessing violence, which is always told from a distance and usually occurs when she is in the company of her Ayah or other adults, the adult narrator forces Lenny to become a listener of Ranna's story, which, narrated in bits and pieces, makes clear the impossibility of retrieving the whole "truth" about the attacks.

It is possible that Sidhwa's telling of Ranna's story is based on the testimony of Rana Khan, whom she thanks in her acknowledgments with the following words: "I thank Rana Khan for sharing with me his childhood experiences at the time of Partition. He lives in Houston, and still bears the deep crescent-shaped scar on the back of his head, and innumerable other scars" (Sidhwa 9). Since the publication of Butalia's *The Other Side of Silence* and Menon and Bhasin's *Borders and Boundaries*, personal testimonies have become an important method of telling stories about the Partition. Bringing a personal testimony into the space of a literary text, however, enables new forms of interpretation that recognize the interruptions and fractures of memory, and also raises questions about how the writer herself is implicated in this retelling. If, indeed, Rana Khan in Sidhwa's acknowledgment is the child Ranna whose story she assembles in the novel, for the adult narrator, the overlapping memories of Sidhwa and Khan when they were children offers an experience of remembering the history of Partition collectively through the spaces accorded to Lenny's and Ranna's memories in the novel. Re-created from the space of the United States (Houston, Texas) where both Khan and Sidhwa reside, the representation of their intertwining stories (of Sidhwa and Khan and the fictional characters, Lenny and Ranna) once again negates the vocabulary of communal separatism by emphasizing the bonds of affiliation that are forged through the recognition of a shared history, and enables a memorialization of the children's experiences of Partition's atrocities, cataclysms, and survival mechanisms.

After surviving the attacks on his village, Pir Pindo, attacks that result in the killing of his family members and leave him for dead, Ranna, along with his aunt and uncle, takes refuge in Imam Din's quarters behind Lenny's house. Lenny's narration of how she hears Ranna's tale of survival, when she visits Imam Din's quarters, reminds readers that it can only be recovered as a patchwork of memories. Lenny says,

> I almost live in the quarters. Hamida sits with us for short periods and when she pulls Ranna to her lap and he presses against her, her disorderly hands grow tranquil. I only go to the house to sleep. I eat my meals in Imam Din's quarters, relishing everything Ranna's Noni *chachi* cooks. That's when they talk – using plain Punjabi words and graphic peasant gestures – Ranna, bit by bit, describing the attack on Pir Pindo, Noni *chachi* recounting her part in the story, and Iqbal *chacha* intervening with clarification, conjecture and comment. (Sidhwa 206)

The significance of this narration lies in the ways in which specific instances are described and also serves as a reminder of the fragmentary nature of Ranna's recollection and the importance of multiple mediations of other affected voices – Ranna's uncle's and aunt's – before it registers to Lenny that "like Ranna, Pir Pindo is brutally altered [...] that his family" as she "knew it, has ceased to exist [...]" (206).

In "Mediated Lives: Oral Histories and Cultural Memory," Roxanne Rimstead brings to attention the ethical concerns that underlie the "erasure of oral histories in the academic discussion of Canadian autobiography and Canadian Culture" and argues for the need to consider these:

> Because oral histories democratize the subject of history and culture by providing a public forum in which the silenced people can speak, I argue that we should interrogate our critical practices by asking if we reinscribe

> cultural muting in our interpretation or lack of interpretation of the genre, or conversely, if we idealize the role of intellectuals and their power to intervene in lived reality. (140)

Ranna's story, an oral history that is carefully narrated in a different register (by according a separate space in Lenny's fictionalized autobiographical account) can be read as an ethical strategy that represents for readers an aesthetic through which it can be heard so that it neither escapes attention nor is muted or blurred in Lenny's own remembrance. This is crucial because, as Jonathan Crew points out (by way of Maurice Halbwach's work on social and collective memory), memory is also "linked to social forgetting; any act of recall entails an act of oblivion" (75). Giving a separate space to Ranna's story through the generic convention of a story within a story enables the foregrounding of his memories of the literal scars on his body and on other bodies whose annihilation he witnessed.

That the author is fully cognizant of the possibility of "social forgetting" is made clear in the novel when Lenny reminds the reader of her own fragmented memory:

> How long does Lahore Burn? Weeks? Months?
>
> We climb to the roof of the Daulatrams' two-story house to watch. The Daulatrams flee.
>
> The Shankars, too, go …
>
> Still we go to the Daulatrams' abandoned house to see Mozang Chawk burn. How long does Mozang Chawk burn …?
>
> Mozang Chawk burns for months … and months …
>
> …the buildings could not have burned for months. Despite the residue of passion and regret, and loss of those who have in panic fled – the fire could not have burned for … Despite all the ruptured dreams, broken lives, buried gold, bricked-in-rupees, secreted jewelry, lingering hopes … the fire could not have burned for months and months …
>
> But in my memory it is branded over an inordinate length of time: memory demands poetic license. (Sidhwa 148–9)

It is notable that even though *Cracking India* has a child as its protagonist/narrator and there are several other children, it is not a children's book. Indeed, the representation of the horrific violence that one encounters in the text may also seem shocking to adult readers of the novel. The novel then seems to signal the need to pay attention to children's accounts because they can tell us what adults, who have been already imbued with class, caste, and religious positions, may not see. To this end, also important is Lenny's recollection of Papoo, the child of a sweeper, who faces a form of violence that does not seem connected to the Partition when she is drugged and married off to a man substantially older than her. Bringing in her story proposes a rethinking of the ways in which the dominant story of Partition, one that is invested in the ideology of nationhood, obscures other kinds of ongoing local and intracommunity violence against children.

Conclusion

To sum up, it is arguable that novels such as *Cracking India* force a remembering of the Partition by engaging in compelling acts of memory which crack open the silences and whispers surrounding the Partition and expose, in the process, the elisions and erasures that went into the process of nation building. "I've noticed a lot of hushed talk recently. In bazaars, restaurants and littered alleys men huddle around bicycles or squat against walls in whispering groups" (Sidhwa 110), says Lenny, as she attempts to understand the transformations caused by Partition; she further begins to ask questions that reflect the innocence of a child being inducted as a witness to a harrowing history: "Will the earth bleed? And what about the sundered rivers? Won't their water drain into the jagged cracks?" (124). While the subject matter of the novel resonates with those who were born into this history, for readers (especially those born after the Partition but who grew up listening to distressing tales through family whispers) the graphic images of violence in the novel and the details of victimization, witnessing and survival enter into what Hirsch calls the "space of postmemory" (7). Hirsch uses the term "postmemory" "to describe the relationship of children of survivors of cultural or collective trauma to the experiences of their parents, experiences that they 'remember' only as the stories and images with which they grew up, but that are so powerful, so monumental, as to constitute memories in their own right" (8). *Cracking India* offers the potential for turning such readers, along with other readers, into listeners of the children's version of an event that oscillates between trauma and loss, and hope and survival. Like Lenny, for those who survive Partition in the novel, it was hope that sustained them. Hamida – who is no longer accepted by her family because she is abducted, and is unable to see her children as a result of the apparent dishonour this act has bestowed on her – turns to Lenny for hope, once she becomes her new Ayah. While taking care of Lenny, she tells her stories of her forced separation from her children after she became a "fallen woman" as if the curious Lenny's capacity to listen might offer a talking cure. The realism of Hamida's story suggests how she attempts to come to terms with her situation. To this end, the text reminds us that hope works out differently for the various characters. For the middle-class Parsee community, hope lies in assimilation with the dominant groups in power. For Ranna, hope is mediated by the intervention of Lenny's family as he is sent off to a convent school to acquire an education. As for Ayah (Shanta) and Papoo, we do not know. Suggesting the lack of an easy resolution regarding the Partition, Lenny leaves it up to the readers to look for answers about their lives.

The circulation of such literary texts beyond the borders of nation-states also enables the global dissemination of knowledge about the Partition. *Cracking India,* which is now taught in several courses in North American universities, was made into a film in 1998, by Indian Canadian filmmaker Deepa Mehta, titled *Earth.* The film not only gives the novel an extended shelf life; it also extends the connections of Partition to diasporic communities. As Prabhjot Parmar has argued, the South Asian diaspora, which, in Canada, celebrated its 100th year in 1997, has also "contributed to the evocation of the forgotten experience of millions" (194). Mehta's adaptation of *Cracking India,* which commemorated fifty years of Partition, serves as a statement against sectarian violence in postindependence India, violence which reproduces memories of Partition through repetition of the carnage that marked Partition (Parmar 201). In situations when minorities become targets of communal attacks and are treated as antinational, or when neighbourhoods, which started out as refugee colonies, are declared illegal and the living arrangements of residents threatened (as happened during the 2002 demolition of homes in Delhi's Lajpat Nagar area, which started out as a colony for Partition refugees), the past of the Partition resurfaces and begins to shape "people's strategies and responses to their present in ordinary and extraordinary circumstances" (Kaur 4). Beyond this, Mehta also establishes the global relevance of Partition, and the lessons to be learnt from it, by connecting the subject of her film to "events that dominated the world political spectrum of the 1990s: ethnic cleansing in Kosovo and its surrounding regions, the Rawandan massacres, and the remerging possibility of Quebec's separation from Canada."[18] For the South Asian diaspora in Canada, says Parmar, "the issue of Quebec's sovereignty, the demand for a Quebec independent of Canada serves as a reminder [...] of the traumatic division of India and Pakistan" (203). Texts such as *Cracking India* and its cinematic depiction in *Earth* are reminders, therefore, that the issues thrown up by Partition – about identity politics, political mobilization, and state practices – "define not only our past but, in crucial ways, our collective future" (Kaul 4). At a time of increasing cynicism about the relevance of the humanities, the corpus of Partition literature establishes the importance of literary representations that reveal the instability of borders and boundaries, as well as the intellectual necessity of engaging with fragments and localities that may belong to the realm of "Other" worlds but which nonetheless provide compelling reasons for searching out the interconnections of the world – both historically and in the present.

NOTES

I gratefully thank Teresa Hubel and Preet Aulakh for reading this essay with great interest and providing engaged critical input, Prabhjot Parmar for our ongoing conversations on this subject, and Joel Faflak and Jason Haslam for inviting me to contribute to the volume and for asking probing and important questions. In addition, I want to thank my parents, Shyama Bhatia and Harbans Singh Bhatia, and family members of their generation, for sharing their memories about the Partition, memories that compel me to return to this topic.

1 Lenny in Bapsi Sidhwa, *Cracking India* 250.
2 According to Kavita Daiya, "In the nine months between August 1947 and the Spring of the following year, by unofficial counts, at least sixteen million people – Hindus, Sikhs and Muslims – were forced to flee their homes and become refugees; at least two million were killed in ethnic violence" (6). See Yusin and Bahri for a reading of the novel through the lens of trauma theory.
3 Ravinder Kaur suggests that it was only in 1997 that "the Indian government established a nondescript five-metre-tall structure at the India-Pakistan border at Attari in Punjab [...] to mark fifty years of independence. The structure is paved with shiny black granite stone, a kind often used in modernized kitchens of middle class Indian homes, with an inscription in bold letters: 'Dedicated to 10 Lakh Punjabis who died unsung in 1947.' The monument does not attract much attention among the thousands of Indian and foreign tourists who visit the border

every evening to witness the dramatic flag exchanging ceremony between the Indian and Pakistani border police" (10).

4 Parmar, for example, cites Amarjit Chandan, a Panjabi poet living in Britain, who attributes the paucity of Partition narratives in Panjabi poetry and folk songs to a possible "collective sense of guilt or failure" (194).

5 See Gyan Pandey, *Remembering Partition*; Kaur; Butalia; and Menon and Bhasin.

6 See Greenberg.

7 Some of the best-known collections include Alok Bhalla's three-volume *Stories about the Partition of India* (1994), Muhamad Umar Memon's *An Epic Unwritten: The Penguin Book of Partition Stories* (1998), Mushirul Hasan's *India Partitioned: The Other Face of Freedom* (1995), and Saros Cowasjee and K.S. Duggal's *Orphans in the Storm: Stories on the Partition of India* (1995). After several decades of critical silence, the subject of Partition has now begun to receive critical attention, and much of this literature has been brought to attention. Aside from the above-mentioned anthologies, since 2000 the following critical works, which analyze heterogeneous literary texts, testimonials, personal narratives, films, short stories, and art, in order to understand the complexities of Partition, have emerged: Didur; Kaul; Settar and Gupta; Ravikant and Saint; Datta; Pandey *Remembering*; Daiya; Gera Roy and Bhatia; Kaur; and Sarkar.

8 In *Since 1947*, Kaur provides an analysis of the government's role in the resettlement of refugees.

9 For an analysis of the destruction and demographic transformation of Amritsar and Lahore in the wake of the 1947 division, see Talbot.

10 For information on the Ministry of Rehabilitation and Resettlement, see Kaur.

11 See, for example, Daiya. It is estimated that about 75,000 women, such as Ayah, were abducted during the Partition (Butalia 3). Butalia's work on the recovery operations initiated by the governments of India and Pakistan for finding the missing women and reinstating them into their families and her own conversations with women who were "recovered" or still live as refugees sketches out the physical and psychic traumas that accompanied the Partition – and the survivors' attempts to deal with this trauma. Butalia points out the limitations of the accounts given by these women, mediated, as they are, by fragmented memories, and also by the presence of family members, including men, that interfered with the women's disclosures of their experiences. She also examines the state's role in the recovery of these women as one that turned into a nationalistic mission of rescue through which the state presented itself as the saviour of these women. Taking

their cues from the pioneering research undertaken by Butalia, and Menon and Bhasin, who, in Suvir Kaul's words, established how "sexuality and gender have a constitutive centrality" (10) in forcing an interrogation of the orthodox histories of the Partition, critics have read the abduction of Ayah as an instance that renders visible the links between the "public and the private" (Didur 7), "patriarchal power relations" and the conflation of the "sacredness of the nation and the sacredness of Woman, making women both an object of protection and target of violence – both physical and discursive – in the struggle for independence" (7). Such analysis is both important and necessary in that it provides a critical vocabulary for exploring the consequences of Partition for women, sexuality and gender relations, and explores how these are defined in terms of nation, community, and religion.

12 See Pandey, *Construction.*

13 For a text of the speech, see http://www.guardian.co.uk/theguardian/2007/may/01/greatspeeches (accessed 20 December 2010).

14 The reference to the "immaculate Nazi soldier" may be read as the author's intervention, mobilized by what Hirsch identifies in the context of the Holocaust as "images that have become generally familiar, perhaps even pervasive, in contemporary memory and discussion of the Holocaust" (4). While the two moments – Partition and Holocaust – are not to be collapsed, evocation of the latter suggests the gravity and the scale of Partition violence through an event that has a strong resonance with the Western reader. For another reading of this scene, see Yusin and Bahri (89–90).

15 The Boundary Commission, which comprised four Indian High Court Judges and was chaired by Sir Cyril Radcliffe, delayed publishing the Boundary Award until 16 August 1947, and thus contributed to "the massacres which swept the Punjab region" (Talbot xviii).

16 For a discussion of governmental policies of resettlement, see Kaur 84–120.

17 Sidhwa 218.

18 Parmar cites the following statement that Mehta made in an interview: "The reason I wanted to do a film about the partition of India into India and Pakistan was that also it is an exploration about what happens with sectarian war, whether it's Rwanda or Kosovo or which ever country has been colonized and where the colonizers left, the way the French left Vietnam, they've always left a country divided. Fifty-two years later, for us, we are still struggling with the same boundary issues. As is Ireland or Kosovo" (202).

WORKS CITED

Butalia, Urvashi. *The Other Side of Silence: Voices from the Partition of India.* New Delhi: Viking, 1998. Print.

Jonathan, Crew. "Recalling Adamastor: Literature as Cultural Memory in 'White' South Africa." *Acts of Memory: Cultural Recall in the Present.* Ed. Mieke Bal, Jonathan Crew, and Leo Spitzer. Hanover: UP of New England. 1999. 75–86. Print.

Daiya, Kavita. *Violent Belongings: Partition, Gender and National Culture in Postcolonial India.* Philadelphia: Temple UP, 2008. Print.

Datta, Nonica. *Violence, Martyrdom and Partition: A Daughter's Testimony.* New Delhi: Oxford UP, 2009. Print.

Didur, Jill. *Unsettling Partition: Literature, Gender, Memory.* Toronto: U of Toronto P, 2006. Print.

Faflak, Joel and Jason Haslam, eds. "Introduction: Public Hopes." *The Public Intellectual and the Culture of Hope.* Toronto: U of Toronto P, 2013. 3-28.

Gera Roy, Anjali, and Nandi Bhatia, eds. *Partitioned Live: Narratives of Home, Displacement, and Resettlement.* India: Pearson-Longman, 2008. Print.

Greenberg, Jonathan D. "Against Silence and Forgetting." *Partitioned Lives: Narratives of Home, Displacement, and Resettlement.* Ed. Anjali Gera Roy and Nandi Bhatia. India: Pearson-Longman, 2008. 255–73. Print.

Hirsch, Marianne. "Projected Memory: Holocaust Photographs in Personal and Public Fantasy." *Acts of Memory: Cultural Recall in the Present.* Ed. Mieke Bal, Jonathan Crew, and Leo Spitzer. Hanover: UP of New England, 1999. 3–23. Print.

Kamra, Sukeshi. *Bearing Witness: Partition, Independence, End of the Raj.* Calgary: U of Calgary P, 2002. Print.

Kamra, Sukeshi. "Partition and Post-Partition Acts of Fiction: Narrating Painful Histories." *Partitioned Lives: Narratives of Home, Displacement and Resettlement.* Ed. Anjali Gera Roy and Nandi Bhatia. India: Pearson-Longman, 2008. 99–115. Print.

Kaul, Suvir, ed. *The Partitions of Memory: The Afterlife of the Division of India.* Bloomington: Indiana UP, 2001. Print.

Kaur, Ravinder. *Since 1947: Partition Narratives among Panjabi Migrants of Delhi.* New Delhi: Oxford UP, 2007. Print.

Menon, Ritu, and Kamla Bhasin. *Borders and Boundaries: Women in India's Partition.* Delhi: Kali for Women, 1998. Print.

Pandey, Gyan. "The Prose of Otherness." *Subaltern Studies VIII.* Ed. David Arnold and David Hardiman. Delhi: Oxford UP, 1994. Print.

Pandey, Gyan. *Remembering Partition: Violence, Nationalism and History in India*. Cambridge: Cambridge UP, 2001. Print. http://dx.doi.org/10.1017/CBO9780511613173.

Pandey, Gyan. *The Construction of Communalism in Colonial North India*. Delhi: Oxford UP, 2006. Print.

Parmar, Prabhjot. "'Moving Forward Though Still Facing Back': Partition and the South Asian Diaspora in Canada." *Partitioned Lives: Narratives of Home, Displacement and Resettlement*. Ed. Anjali Gera Roy and Nandi Bhatia. India: Pearson-Longman, 2008. 192–213. Print.

Rimstead, Roxanne. "Mediated Lives: Oral Histories and Cultural Memory." *Essays on Canadian Writing* 60 (1996): 139–65. Print.

Ravikant and Tarun K. Saint, ed. *Translating Partition*. New Delhi: Katha, 2001. Print.

Rawat, Ramnarayan S. "Partition Politics and Achhut Identity: A Study of the Scheduled Castes Federation and Dalit Politics in UP, 1946–48." *Partitions of Memory: The Afterlife of the Division of India*. Ed. Suvir Kaul. Bloomington: Indiana UP, 2001. 111–39. Print.

Sarkar, Bhaskar. *Mourning the Nation: Indian Cinema in the Wake of Partition*. Durham, NC: Duke UP, 2009. Print.

Settar, S., and B. Indira Gupta, eds. *Pangs of Partition. Vol. II. The Human Dimension*. Delhi: Manohar, 2002. Print.

Sidhwa, Bapsi. *Cracking India*. Minneapolis: Milkweed Editions, 1991. Print.

Talbot, Ian. *Divided Cities: Partition and its Aftermath in Lahore and Amritsar 1947–1957*. Karachi: Oxford UP, 2006. Print.

Yusin, Jennifer, and Deepika Bahri. "Writing Partition: Trauma and Testimony in Bapsi Sidwha's *Cracking India*." *Partitioned Lives: Narratives of Home, Displacement and Resettlement*. Ed. Anjali Gera Roy and Nandi Bhatia. India: Pearson-Longman, 2008. 82–93. Print.

PART TWO

Public Performances

5 Margaret Cavendish's Civilizing Songs

KATHERINE R. LARSON

In what ways can Margaret Cavendish, a woman of the seventeenth century, contribute to our contemporary understanding of the role of the public intellectual in shaping a culture of hope? Writing in the aftermath of the English Civil Wars, the Duchess of Newcastle would not have characterized herself as a "public intellectual." Nor, of course, would she have recognized the phrase as it has evolved in critical debates since the watershed moment of the Dreyfus Affair (see, for example, Jennings and Kemp-Welch). In his 1993 Reith Lectures, Edward Said – whose own public intellectualism is discussed briefly in Imre Szeman's contribution to this volume – memorably described the intellectual as a committed truth teller prepared to defy "all sorts of barriers" to communicate with and educate his or her society (*Representations* 10). For a woman to claim such a role was highly problematic in a period when public social performance was typically the preserve of men and when the public circulation of a woman's words risked signalling an unchecked sexual appetite. The shaming and silencing mechanisms that worked to restrict women's linguistic interventions in early modern culture testify to the challenges inherent in negotiating a position that might facilitate public self-expression without compromising sexual reputation.[1]

Despite prescriptive injunctions, women across social classes were engaged in a rich spectrum of rhetorical practices in sixteenth- and seventeenth-century England. As petitioners, patrons, letter writers, translators, and creators of poems, pamphlets, and plays, they made vital contributions to early modern intellectual culture and succeeded in carving out alternative communicative spaces for themselves that enabled them actively to engage with and to transform restrictive contexts of utterance.[2] Said's rendering of the intellectual as a committed truth teller, however, provides a particularly rich framework for assessing Margaret Cavendish's wide-ranging intellectual interventions. An audaciously public and prolific writer – she published fourteen volumes between 1653 and 1671, all lavishly produced in folio – Cavendish positioned herself as a self-professed "Servant to Truth" (*Sociable* 135) whose writings were designed to teach and, ultimately, to "civilize" her audience.[3]

Music – especially vocal music – constitutes a crucial didactic medium for Cavendish in this regard. This essay will explore the rhetorical function of song in Cavendish's writings in terms of what Said has described as the "intellectual performances [...] both in the sense of opposition and the sense of engaged participation" ("Writers" 36) that can be facilitated by the arts. Song and the spaces within which songs were circulated and performed were deeply politicized during the Civil Wars and the Interregnum, constituting important channels for intellectual intervention and sociopolitical commentary. Cavendish probes the acoustic potency of the speaking and singing voice, seeking to harness the "natural" and "civilizing" eloquence that she associates with singers. By deploying implicitly royalist musical genres and creating alternative performance spaces within her writings, Cavendish establishes a viable rhetorical position for herself that enables her to critique the devastating upheavals of the Civil Wars even as this position works to justify her transgressive authorial stance.

An Early Modern Public Intellectual

In reading Cavendish as a public intellectual who claims the authority to edify her readers and to enact cultural change, my argument builds on recent work that has compellingly "elasticate[d]" the historical boundaries framing contemporary discussions concerning the intellectual, thereby "uncover[ing] much deeper roots to our ways of thinking about how intellectuals have historically been defined and redefined in public consciousness" (Small 12). Critics have traditionally dismissed the controversial Cavendish, with her propensity for outlandish dress and her obsession with social status and lasting fame, as an eccentric anomaly and, at best, a marginal intellectual figure; Virginia Woolf perhaps most famously characterized her in *A Room of One's Own* as a "giant cucumber" (62) choking the roses and carnations in the garden of English literature. Woolf's scathing depiction has elicited much laughter from scholars and students over the years, but, as Said reminds us, the intellectual "is supposed to be heard from, and in practice ought to be stirring up debate and if possible controversy" (*Representations* 52). The image of Cavendish as a colossal cucumber certainly helps to underscore the "boldness and vulnerability" (Said, *Representations* 10) of her claim to a public vocation as a writer in a period that too often suffocated women's literary innovations. Woolf's image, however, also unwittingly attests to Cavendish's mark on her cultural landscape. In recent years, as critical interest in her prolific writings has exploded, scholars have begun to recognize the significance of her contributions to seventeenth-century cultural, political, philosophical, scientific, and literary debates.[4] Perhaps all public intellectuals, regardless of historical context, need to be willing to be "giant cucumbers" speaking out within otherwise docile gardens.

Cavendish was, nevertheless, a marginalized figure in many respects, "triply exiled" (Rees 27) by virtue of her gender and, during the Civil Wars and the years of the English Republic, her staunch royalism and resultant geographical dislocation.[5] Far from dissuading her from intellectual engagement, however, it is precisely this marginal status that seems to have motivated her aggressively public authorial stance (as suggested by Larson and Rees). For Said, the experience of exile, whether actual or metaphorical, can play a profound role in shaping a public intellectual voice. Exile, he argues, fosters "eccentric angles of vision" (*Representations* 39) that can prompt more objective, probing, and fundamentally didactic critique. This certainly seems to have been the case for Cavendish. Her political conservatism makes her an unusual exilic figure; many of her most poignant assessments of the Civil War conflicts advocate a return to the status quo. Within her historical context, however, her determination to wrestle with seminal political and cultural questions in her literary, philosophical, and scientific texts – and, as a woman, to publicize those interventions – is remarkable. Moreover, she uses her writings to generate a radical defence of women's rhetorical and even political authority. Many of Cavendish's works confront the educational and social restrictions that prevented women from contributing in a meaningful way to seventeenth-century public discourse and imagine spaces that create opportunities for such engagement. Read in these terms, Cavendish emerges as a compelling example of an early modern public intellectual whose prolific writings exhibit her determination publicly to position herself as an effective and powerful truth teller for her society.

"Nature's Musicians": The Rhetoric of Song

In *Bell in Campo* (1662), a play set in a fictionalized version of the Civil Wars, Cavendish's heroine Lady Victoria follows her husband to the front only to be confined within a garrison town. In response, she rallies a formidable female army. In an impassioned speech to her "heroickesses," she laments the social restrictions that have resulted in women's subjection: "had our educations been answerable to theirs, we might have proved as good soldiers and privy counselors, rulers and commanders, navigators and architects, and as learned scholars both in arts and sciences, as men are." She encourages her female army to make the most of their "schools of martial arts and sciences" so that they might persuade men that women are "fit to be copartners in their governments, and to help to rule the world" (47–9). It is not a coincidence that Lady Victoria is a formidable orator. Rhetorical ability was integral to public life in early modern England, and Cavendish's writings testify to her longing for the skill and the opportunity to emulate men who can speak publicly "on a Sudden and Extempore upon any Subject" (*Sociable* 74). Indeed, her plays regularly juxtapose female rhetorical virtuosi like Lady Victoria and Lady Sanspareille with shy recluses like Lady Bashfull and Lady Contemplation in what Sara Mendelson has called a strategy of "anti-autobiography" ("Playing" 195–212).

Thanks to her literary collaborations with her husband and the scientific and philosophical salons that he hosted both in England and on the Continent, the aristocratic Cavendish would have been accustomed to an atmosphere of intellectual encounter. Yet she was notoriously bashful and claimed to be a poor speaker, insisting that she preferred retirement and solitude to the torments of "Mode" (*Sociable* 116–18) society.[6] Cavendish's preoccupation with eloquence in her works as well as her portrayals of herself in *Sociable Letters* (1664) conversing confidently with other women, learned natural philosophers, and her beloved Sir W.N. can in large part be attributed to her failure to amass "symbolic capital" (Bourdieu 646) in oral contexts. Unable "to Speak in a Friend's behalf" or successfully "to Plead for [her] own Right" (*Sociable* 74) as a result of her gender, political disfavour, and her bashfulness, Cavendish opted for textual intervention instead, using her printed works to engage with and confront a wide range of her contemporaries (Larson 138–65).

Music, song in particular, plays a crucial rhetorical role in Cavendish's writings. Music's affective power was widely recognized in early modern England. John Calvin declares in the Preface to the *Geneva Psalter*

(1543) that "there is hardly anything in the world with more power to turn or bend [...] the morals of men [...] And in fact we find by experience that [music] has a secret and almost incredible power to move our hearts in one way or another" (157). Three quarters of a century later, in *The Compleat Gentleman* (1622), Henry Peacham underscored the affinities between rhetoric and music more explicitly in a passage that also anticipates rhetorical analyses of musical form: "Yea," he writes, "in my opinion, no Rhetoricke more perswadeth, or hath greater power ouer the mind; nay, hath not Musicke her figures, the same which Rhetorique? What is a *Reuert* but her *Antistrophe*? her reports, but sweete *Anaphora's*? her counterchange of points, *Antimetabole's*? her passionate Aires, but *Prosopopoea's*?" (103). Music was, of course, a valued skill for the well-educated individual; Castiglione's Count Ludovico declares music to be "not only an ornament but a necessity to the Courtier" (57). But music also emerges in early modern literary and cultural texts as a powerful rhetorical practice. In moderation, Peacham declares, music could assuage "melancholy and deiection of the mind" and "the heate and furie of our anger" (98). At the other extreme lie the "disordered delights" of what Calvin calls "dishonest and shameless songs," which, he argues, breed "poison for the corruption of the world" (157).

If the musician shared the rhetorician's ability to move and persuade a listener, then music that incorporated or relied on text – the song – became doubly powerful. As Calvin anxiously notes, "when [the evil word] has the melody with it, it pierces the heart much more strongly and enters within; as wine is poured into the cask with a funnel, so venom and corruption are distilled to the very depths of the heart by melody" (157). The question of how best to instil a text's meaning, imagery, and (ideally edifying) moral in a listener through musical setting strongly influenced the development of early modern English vocal repertoire. Secular song shifted from carols and imitations of French *chansons* to encompass the intricate word painting of late sixteenth-century madrigals and the solo *ayre* or lute song, which made lyrics more audible to listeners. These changes culminated in the declamatory vocal style of early seventeenth-century opera and monody. Concerns about the relationship between text and musical setting assumed particular ramifications for church music, as Calvin's strong defence of "honest" and "holy" songs suggests (157). Tapping into the heart of Reformation debates, Protestant writers argued that, when a sacred text is intelligible and well matched to a melody, music could unite an auditor or a singer with God.

The affective spectrum associated with song composition and performance assumed particular discursive significance for women in early modern England. If music was believed to hold the capacity to incite Alexander, as Castiglione puts it, to "rush off to arms" (55) or, in Calvin's words, to "move and inflame the hearts of men to invoke and praise God with a more vehement and ardent zeal" (156), it was also widely associated with emasculating desire and passion; the figure of the siren encapsulates song's seductive potential (Austern). Not surprisingly, the excess of affect associated with music became especially problematic when attributed to female musicians, and especially the female singer, whose body – open mouthed, breathing, emoting, on full display – is her instrument. Early modern accounts of women playing and singing teeter anxiously between commendations of the pleasure derived from hearing a talented performer and concerns about sexual impropriety.

Cavendish stands as a fascinating case study for considering this relationship between music and rhetoric and the potential impact of songs produced or invoked by women as "intellectual performances" (Said, "Writers" 36). Faced with a political situation very much beyond her control, her wide-ranging writings are consistently preoccupied with the power language holds to enact cultural change. Even as Cavendish confides to Madam in *Sociable Letters* her "Envy" and "Emulation" of eloquent men (74), she blames the misuse of words for the outbreak of the Civil Wars. In *Loves Adventures* (1662), she contrasts Sir Serious Dumb's "civil words" that promote a "sweet society" that is "void of strife" with the potency of Sir Timothy Complement's studied and artificial eloquence (73). The latter assumes dangerous and even magical dimensions in Cavendish's writing. Declaring that orators should either be advanced within society or utterly banished, Cavendish muses in *Sociable Letters*: "you cannot chuse but Admire, and Wonder at the Power of Eloquence, [...] for it Charms the Senses, and Inchants the Mind [...] and makes the Souls of men the Tongue's Slaves" (75). Above all, Cavendish lauds "Natural Orators" (75) whose decorous, civil, and implicitly upper-class speech practices help to maintain social order.

Cavendish returns repeatedly to music in these descriptions of rhetorical potency. Like Francis Bacon and Thomas Hobbes, she is very interested in what she calls in *Philosophical Letters* (1664) the "Generation of sound" (72), exploring the acoustic effects that music has on "the spirits of men" (*Worlds* 24). "A timely, kind, and discreet Discourse from a Friend, will compose or quiet his troubled Mind," she writes in *Grounds of Natural Philosophy* (1668). "Likewise, an untimely, unkind, hasty, malicious, false, or sudden Discourse, will often disorder a well-temper'd, or Regular Mind [. . .] and the same Effects hath Musick, on the Minds of many Human Creatures" (159–60). As this example suggests, Cavendish holds the musician in the same anxious esteem as the orator. The civilizing "Natural Orators" she admires are, she declares, "Nature's Musicians, moving the Passions to Harmony, making Concords out of Discords, Playing on the Soul with Delight" (*Sociable* 74). She eschews "Artificial Singing" in the same breath as she dismisses "Artificial Speaking," lumping both together as examples of "Enticing Arts" (*Natures* 314). Cavendish's concern here with music's seductive potential is telling. Just as she seeks to assure her readers of her virtue in their encounters with her published writings, her insistence on the "civil" and "civilizing" aspects of song performance stems from a related need to mitigate the sexual threat that her representations of the singing body might signify.

Cavendish regularly characterizes intellectual interaction in terms of musical performance. In *Sociable Letters*, she likens a recent visit to a "Consort of Learning and Wit": "This Consort was Natural Philosophers, Theological Scholars, and Poets, and their Discourse was their Musick, the Philosophers were the Bass, the Theologers the Tenor, and the Poets the Treble, all which made an Harmony wherein was Variety and Delight" (128–9). Music functions in her writings, however, at once as a metaphor for productive social exchange and as a rhetorical tool in its own right. Drawing on imagery reminiscent of Calvin's funnel, in *Natures Pictures* (1656, 1671) she goes so far as to describe music as a "Syringe" through which the "Liquor" of good conversation is "squirt[ed] [...] into the Ears of the Mind, and this will bring a perfect Cure" (239). In such moments, Cavendish's musical metaphors tap into royalist representations of musical harmony as a civilizing discourse even as it resonates with broader cultural conceptions in the period of musical consonance as reflective of divine and social order.[7] Music constitutes for Cavendish an idealized eloquence and a potentially harmonizing agent for a society that has been turned upside down by war.

Plain Old Ballads: Song and Truth Telling

Given Cavendish's insistent blurring of the boundaries between language and music, it is perhaps not surprising that she returns again and again in her writings to the voice, which she terms a "natural" musical instrument (*Worlds* 24). In the sections on music included in *The Worlds Olio* (1655), she devotes considerable attention to the singing voice. She worries about its vulnerability: "there is no prevention against the breaking of the voice, for old age will come and destroy that sound, and though it doth not break the strings of the voice, yet time dryes and shrivels them so short, that they cannot be stretched out to any note or strain" (24). In the chapter entitled "Of Voices," she ponders the physical attributes that impact vocal potential. Fat people cannot possibly be good singers, she declares, because "the fat hath straightned their passages, so to the making of a good voice, there must be a wide throat, and clear winde pipes, and strong lungs" (25).[8] She combines this exploration of the physiology of the voice with careful attention to the oral performance of her writings.[9] One of the epistles prefacing *The Worlds Olio*, for example, instructs her readers "*that every Chapter may be read clearly, without long stops and staies.*" Warning her audience that "*the very sound of the Voice will seem to alter the sense of the Theme,*" Cavendish likens the "*whine or squeal*" of a bad reader to the "*ill Musician* [...] *who instead of playing he puts the Fiddle out of tune, and causeth a Discord*" (sig. A6r). While such moments underscore her fascination with vocal production, whether spoken or sung, they also serve as important reminders of the elusiveness of the early modern voice.[10]

Song, the product of the human body as instrument, encapsulates the ephemerality of the vocal soundscapes of early modern England. Songs are preserved in traces that include musical notation, texts that circulated to well-known tunes, and in the positioning of vocal and instrumental parts in scores that facilitated impromptu musical gatherings. They are also evoked through descriptions – like Cavendish's – of the singing body and related physiological accounts of the movement of breath and the production of sound, examples of what Bruce Smith has compellingly termed "*somatic* notation" (*Acoustic* 112). Songs feature prominently throughout Cavendish's plays: some pieces authored by her and others by her husband. She displays familiarity with popular vocal repertoire, recalling in *Sociable Letters* that Mrs F.W. sang "a line of an old Song, Oh the Lovely Brown, as 'tis, how it Shames the Lilies" (159) and inserting allusions to popular ballads in plays like *The Comical Hash* (1662). Song was clearly a regular pastime in the Cavendish household. Cavendish lists it in the *Worlds Olio* among her favourite entertainments (16), while in *Blazing-World* (1668) song is one of the "harmless sports" (111) with which the Duke's soul entertains the Empress's soul. Song seems to have become particularly important for Cavendish when she and her husband were living in exile on the Continent. She befriended Utricia Swann, who studied music with Constantijn Huygens and who was well known as a talented singer (Whitaker 118), and she and her husband enjoyed many visits in Antwerp with the Duartes, a family of singers "all very skilful in the Art of Musick" (*Life* 87; Hulse).

Despite her clear interest in the voice and in vocal music, Cavendish's reticence in oral contexts extended to musical performance. In Letter 202 of *Sociable Letters*, which offers the most extensive treatment of song in Cavendish's writings, she describes a musical evening with the Duarte sisters. The letter, addressed to Eleanora Duarte, devotes considerable space to Cavendish's performance anxiety. She agrees to sing "some Pieces of Old Ballads" for Katherine and Frances Duarte because their company puts her into a "Frolick Humour," but when she is asked to sing "one of the Songs my Lord made, your Brother Set, and you were pleased to Sing," she balks, pleading lack of vocal skill (274). At first glance, her self-effacing excuses position her as the antithesis of the "natural" musicians glorified elsewhere in her work: "nay," she worries, "instead of Musick, I should make Discord, and instead of Wit, sing Nonsense" (274). Part of the goal of the letter is undoubtedly to flatter Eleanora, who, like her sisters, has a "Harmonious Voice" (274). Yet there is more to this letter, I think, than an excessive humility topos. Despite her insistence on the contrast between the "Tone" of her voice and Eleanora's "Clear Singing," Cavendish returns repeatedly to her own voice and her willingness "to Sing an Old Ballad" (274) for Katherine and Frances. Far from excusing herself from the invitation to perform, Cavendish goes so far as to insist that her voice is particularly well suited to the ballad genre: "the Vulgar and Plainer a Voice is, the Better it is for an Old Ballad" (274).

Cavendish's choice of vocal genre is ideally suited to public intellectual performance. Natascha Würzbach and Bruce Smith have productively read the early modern ballad in performative terms, as a "communication act" that enabled a writer or singer to claim a position of authority relative to his or her audience on a range of topics (Würzbach 28, 65–6). Ultimately, as Smith has argued, the "intense first-personhood of ballads" offered a singer – and especially a female singer – access to unlimited "fantasies of identity" ("Female" 296; *Acoustic* 201). This feature would undoubtedly have appealed to an autobiographically inclined writer like Cavendish seeking to negotiate an authoritative subject position at the boundaries between oral and print culture. Cavendish's writings attest to her recognition of the importance of the ballad genre in the period as a strategic and potentially distancing mode of self-expression, particularly for women.[11] In *The Publick Wooing* (1662), for example, Mistress Fondly, Mistress Vanity, Mistress Trifle, and Mistress Parle confide their longing to marry by singing snatches of "old Ballad[s]" (400) that encapsulate their individual perspectives. Yet ballads, circulated orally by singers across social classes and printed on broadside sheets, were also recognized as a public and deeply politicized form of communication.

In the seventeenth century, the ballad can best be understood as a mode of "affective" journalism (McShane Jones 144) and "public action" (Trull 135) designed to provoke and to shape audience response to contemporary events, particularly at times of acute political uncertainty.[12] Produced with increasing frequency in the years surrounding King Charles's execution in 1649 and again leading up to the Restoration, ballads functioned as a crucial vehicle for sociopolitical commentary and satire. As Parliament began to crack down on royalist textual production during the late 1640s, ballad *singing* became increasingly difficult. Even after the public performance of ballads was banned in 1649, however, ballads continued to flourish in print. Perhaps because they were able to elude parliamentarian censorship more easily than other genres, ballads became an important propaganda tool and source of entertainment for royalists, keeping morale high and paving the way for the Restoration.[13] Read within this context, the "Old Ballads" that Cavendish sings in Letter 202 not only situate Cavendish in nostalgically English terms vis-à-vis the continental musical style of the Duartes, but also constitute a strong royalist statement and an oblique challenge to the reversal of political fortunes that she and Newcastle were facing living in exile in Antwerp: "I am willing to Sing an Old Ballad," she declares, "yet not to Dwell in Oblivion" (274–5).[14] It is telling that the news of the collapse of the Republic in 1659 prompted a flurry of broadside ballads, many of which were produced by exiled royalists (McShane Jones 138). The ballad's currency in the period was thus not so much as musical newsbook, as critics like Hyder Rollins have influentially suggested, but rather as a didactic and often moralizing source of "truth concern[ing] the ideal political world" (McShane Jones 144). For a royalist woman seeking to claim a position as a public truth teller, the choice of the ballad genre could not be more fitting.

As Lady Solitary notes in *The Comical Hash*, the pleasure of a "plain old Song" derives precisely from the ballad's function as a conveyer of truth: "there were more that could have taken more delight to hear an old Ballad sung, which Ballads are true stories put into verses and set to a Tune, than in all there *Italian* and *French* Love whining Songs, and languishing tunes" (574).[15] The rhetorical potency that Cavendish attributes to her "Old Ballads" in Letter 202 stems from a related contrast between her "Plain" performance and the artful songs composed by Eleanora's brother. In the midst of the praise she lavishes on Eleanora's "Sweet Voice," Cavendish distances herself from her addressee's extensive musical training, manifested in Eleanora's "Quavers, and Trilloes, and the like," ornaments that "would be as Improper for an Old Ballad, as Golden Laces on a Thrum Suit of Cloth" (274).[16] As the letter evolves, Cavendish seems to be associating her own "Vulgar and Plainer Voice" and resultant choice of the ballad genre with a more "natural," and implicitly more truthful, approach to singing.

Throughout her writings, Cavendish situates herself as a committed truth teller whose knowledge stems from "natural" reason rather than formal training. She grounds her philosophical and scientific writings on the premise that truth can never fully be known; at best, natural philosophers strive to express probabilities. Accordingly, she derides the experiments promulgated by the Royal Society and, in particular, Robert Hooke's defence of the microscope in *Micrographia* (1665), arguing that such supposed forays into knowledge hinder true rational inquiry: "The truth is, most of these Arts are Fallacies, rather than Discoveries of Truth; for Sense deludes more than it gives a true Information, and an exterior Inspection through an Optick-glass, is so deceiving, that it cannot be relied upon." Cavendish rather embraces "Regular Reason" as "the best guide to all Arts" and defends her philosophical projects as a campaign "to find out truth, or at least the probability of truth" (*Observations* sig. b3r). Her argument strategically helps to bolster the authority of her own opinions: since God obscures the truth of nature, all hypotheses, including hers, must command respect.[17] If her philosophical and scientific writings seek truth in the natural world, her dramatic and poetic works strive to reveal the truths of human society. "*I would have my Playes to be like the Natural course of all things in the World*," she declares in an epistle prefacing her first volume of plays (*Playes* sig. A4r). The stories in *Natures Pictures* are similarly advertised as "many sorts of Passions, Humours, Behaviours, Actions, Accidents, Governments, Laws, Customs, Peace, Warrs, Climates, Arts and Sciences" (sig. b2r) for her readers' benefit and instruction.

Far from seeing her supposed lack of education as an impediment, therefore, Cavendish paradoxically uses it to validate her claim to a more "natural" rhetorical and implicitly "civilizing" potency. In an epistle appended to *Philosophical and Physical Opinions* (1655), she writes: *"nature is Prevalent in all qualities and conditions; And since nature is so generous to distribute to those that fortune hath cast out, and education hath neglected, why should my readers mistrust nature should be sparing to me"* (sig. A4v). Accordingly, she reminds her readers not to expect her writings to conform to conventional rhetorical rules that "fetter" (*Natures Pictures* sig. cr) nature and prompt a slavish form of writing.[18] Her self-portrayal as a "natural" orator freed from the constraints of rhetorical convention validates her transgressive authorial voice and enables her to justify her experimental style as a decision that is at once unconventional, didactic, and civilizing. "I hope," she declares in *Natures Pictures*, "that this Work will rather quench Passion, than enflame it; will beget chast Thoughts, nourish the love of Virtue, [...] encrease Civility, strengthen fainting Patience, encourage noble Industry, crown Merit, and instruct Life: will damn Vices, kill Follies, prevent Errors, forewarn Youth, and arm the Mind against Misfortunes; and in a word, will admonish, direct, and perswade to that which is best in all kinds" (sigs. bv–cr).[19]

The distinction that Cavendish develops in Letter 202 between ballad singing and the elegant performance of the Duarte sisters picks up on these arguments in a number of important ways. Given Cavendish's recurring insistence on the civilizing potential of her work and her depiction of "natural" oratory in musical terms, it is difficult not to read her association of "Old Ballads" with a "Plainer" style in Letter 202 as another example of the "natural" and truthful eloquence that she believes holds the capacity to challenge and mitigate the political upheavals of the Civil Wars. Significantly, it is only when Cavendish contemplates shifting away from her favoured "Plainer" musical genre to tackle Eleanora's brother's compositions that she worries about creating musical "Discord": "my Voice and those Songs, would be as Disagreeing as your Voice and Old Ballads" (274).

Cavendish is certainly attuned to the affective power that song holds, particularly within the intimate environment of the Rubenshuis, where she and her husband lived in Antwerp and where she hosted the Duartes. She marvels at the ecstasy prompted by Eleanora's "Harmonious Voice [...] [that] Invites and Draws the Soul from all other Parts of the Body [...] to sit in the Hollow Cavern of the Ear, as in a Vaulted Room, wherein it Listens with Delight" (*Sociable* 274). As a "Ballad-Singer" (274), however, Cavendish does not seem to harbour any doubts concerning her own ability to persuade her audience. Nowhere in the letter does she allude to the text of the ballads that she sings. We are left only with an intimation of an acoustic experience, a tantalizing instance of what Christopher Marsh has brilliantly called "the sound of print" (175). Yet Cavendish's account of her performance suggests a declamatory vocal style that would have ably transmitted the ballad's narrative core: "neither should Old Ballads be Sung so much in a Tune as in a Tone, which Tone is betwixt Speaking and Singing" (*Sociable* 274).[20] The resultant sound may not, she admits, exactly evoke the "Musick of the Spheres" (274), but her determination to create a sound that is "more than Plain Speaking, and less than Clear Singing" underscores her attention to the ballad's performative function, particularly within the sociopolitical context of the Interregnum. Lady Examination acknowledges the ballad's communicative force in *The Comical Hash*: "The truth is, I have observed that when an old Ballad is plainly sung, most hearers will lissen with more delight, than to *Italian* and *French* Singers, although they sing with art and skill" (574). Cavendish's self-representation as a singer of "Old Ballads" in Letter 202 elides her contributions to the evening's entertainment with the affective – and implicitly royalist – potency of her beloved "Nature's Musicians." If, in Said's words, the public intellectual is above all "a being set apart, someone able to speak the truth to power" and "endowed with a faculty for representing, embodying, articulating a message, a view, an attitude, philosophy or opinion to, as well as for, a public" (*Representations* 7, 9), ballad singing emerges in Cavendish's writings and within the early modern context as a particularly potent intellectual medium.

Singing in "Vaulted Room[s]": Politicized Spaces of Song Performance

Cavendish's intellectual performance in this letter has a decidedly public impact. Her decision to locate the representation of her singing body within a published text immediately opens her seemingly private letter – and her ballad singing – to a public audience. She reinforces this public stance by associating her ballad performance with the implicitly royalist space of the musical and conversational salon. Although Cavendish dismisses her speaking and singing abilities and looks to her writings to create a rhetorically viable subject position for herself, she was, like many royalists, an active participant in exclusive salon gatherings during the Interregnum. We know that she benefited from the scientific and philosophical gatherings hosted by her husband and brother-in-law. Katie Whitaker has convincingly argued that she likely also visited the salon of Béatrix, Duchess of Lorraine, at Beersal, which featured music, conversation, and courtly games (118–24). Moreover, as Letter 202 demonstrates, Cavendish attests to her enjoyment of her literary and musical evenings in Antwerp with the Duarte family, which undoubtedly recalled the centrality of the salon within the Caroline court. As a lady-in-waiting to Henrietta Maria, Cavendish would have been familiar with the queen's fostering of salon culture, whereby witty conversation and theatrical and musical performance became politicized markers of class and courtliness for women.[21] By positioning herself as a singer of old ballads within the space of the miniature salon she shares with the Duartes, Cavendish aligns herself with this tradition.

We also know that Cavendish was associated with another royalist salon: the musical evenings hosted in London during the Interregnum by the composer Henry Lawes.[22] Cavendish visited Lawes when she was in London in the early 1650s with her brother-in-law, attempting to plead for her husband's compounded estates. Lawes's relationship to the Cavendish family dates back at least twenty years prior to these encounters; this connection likely factored into Cavendish's decision to visit the composer.[23] That Cavendish should choose to frequent the home of a prominent royalist who was also an acquaintance of her husband is not in itself surprising. Given her sensitivity to the affective power of language and music, coupled with her failure successfully to petition the parliamentary committees for her share of her husband's estates during her stay in London, however, her choice of host seems especially fitting. Lawes was a composer and a musical collaborator whose works attest to his commitment to communicating the "sense" of language through musical setting; Ian Spink has emphasized the major contribution that his musical treatments of Cavalier poetry made to the development of the declamatory vocal style in England. Over and over again, Lawes's contemporaries praise him for his detailed attention to the nuances of English poetry. John Milton famously commemorated the composer in a 1646 sonnet that celebrated his unprecedented skill in creating music that "tun'st [the] happiest lines in hymn, or story" and for "First [teaching] our English music how to span / Words with just note and accent" (294–5).[24] These are features that Lawes himself highlights as musical aims in his *Second Book of Ayres, and Dialogues* (1655): "the way of *Composition* I chiefly profess [...] is to shape *Notes* to the *Words* and *Sense*" (sig. av). Lawes's reputation for "sensitive" musical setting would have resonated strongly with Cavendish. As she confides to Madam in *Sociable Letters,* it is not simply a matter of "prefer[ring] Eloquence [per se] before all other Musick," but rather its "Sense, Reason, and Wit" (75). Lawes's strong connection with the royalist cause would only have reinforced this appeal. Within the royalist space created by the semipublic musical gatherings at Rutland House, Lawes's home constituted an alternative court, where music and poetry held the power nostalgically to re-create Caroline culture and to critique Cromwell and Parliament.

Recalling the salon environment that Queen Henrietta Maria fostered at court, Lawes's gatherings welcomed and validated women's conversational and musical contributions. Lady Mary Dering, Alice Egerton, by then Countess of Carbery, her sister Lady Mary Herbert, and Lady Elizabeth Brackley were regular guests, and the meetings also featured the poetry of royalists like Katherine Philips and the performances of talented singers like Mary Knight. In a dedicatory poem prefacing Lawes's first book of *Ayres and Dialogues* (1653), the "*brightest* Dames, *the splendour of the Court*" who frequented Lawes's salon dazzle Milton's nephew Edward Phillips. While Phillips describes these women in terms of their beauty, "*a silent* Musick *to the Eye*" that creates a "*double Harmony*" (sig. Av) with the airs they came to hear, it is becoming increasingly clear that these women (several of whom studied and performed with Lawes in other contexts) were actively involved in these gatherings as audience members, as poets, and as performers.[25] As Hero Chalmers has convincingly argued, given the feminized depictions of music in the period, women's musical involvement within Lawes's circle would have figured as a particularly important "symbolic political force," situating women as "consummate agents" of the musical harmony commonly used by Royalists to signify "proper political order" (80). The prominence accorded to the Egerton sisters, Lady Mary Dering, Katherine Philips, and Mary Knight in the dedications and commendatory verses included in *Ayres and Dialogues,* together with Lawes's insistence in the 1655 collection that his printed works are intended for "Musicians of both Sexes" (sig. av) further reinforce the significance of women within Lawes's musical circles.

Cavendish alludes only briefly in her autobiography to her attendance at Lawes's meetings: "I had been in England a year and a half, in which time I gave some half a score visits, and went with my Lords Brother to hear Musick in one Mr *Lawes* his House, three or four times"

(*True Relation* 53–4). This tantalizing reference, however, appears in close proximity to her detailed account of her frustrating experience as a hesitant – and ultimately unsuccessful – petitioner before the parliamentary committee at Goldsmiths' Hall, which leads directly into a bitter castigation of "words rushing against words" (52) and an apology for her own bashfulness that has "many times obstructed the passage of [her] speech" (53). The "perfect cure" for these ills, she argues, will only come about once "Nature as well as Human governments [are] civilized" (53). Her allusion to Lawes occurs eight lines later. Lawes's musical gatherings, featuring talented female performers and poets and musical settings of Cavalier poems exhibiting all the qualities that Cavendish associates with "Nature's Musicians," would have been particularly inviting and, as Katie Whitaker suggests, "[i]nspiring" (136) for a royalist woman acutely conscious of her own sense of rhetorical and political impotence. Indeed, it was during this time that Cavendish published her first volume, *Poems and Fancies* (released in 1653, the same year as Lawes's first instalment of *Ayres and Dialogues*). The collection includes a series of verses lamenting the ruin of the wars that links her with the harmonizing and civilizing "royalist polemic" (Whitaker 146) being performed and published by Henry Lawes and his circle.[26]

The importance for Cavendish of an alternative social space dedicated to "civilizing" rhetoric and music and that sanctioned women's verbal and musical agency cannot be overstated. Her writings overflow with spaces (however temporary) such as Lady Victoria's army camp, Lady Happy's convent of pleasure, the female academy, and the "Conventicles" (*Orations* sig. a4r) of her female orators, which are dedicated to the development of women's rhetorical prowess, often within unstable political contexts. Cavendish herself uses her paratext to create fantasy social spaces within which she can converse with her readers in an atmosphere of exclusive hospitality that enables her to compensate for her own personal and political vulnerability.[27] Positioning herself within her writings in the role of textual host, she welcomes noble readers to her "feast" (*Worlds* sig. A3v) or, in the case of the *Orations* (1662), to "the Chief Market-place" (sig. a3v), and portrays her works in architectural and proprietary terms: "*[T]hose that do not like my Book, which is my House, I pray them to pass by, for I have not any entertainment fit for their Palats*" (*Worlds* sig. A3v). The pattern of exclusive hospitality that emerges in such moments is inextricably linked to Cavendish's longing for discursive authority relative to her audience and testifies to her determination to create spaces within her texts that make possible meaningful intellectual interventions denied to her in oral settings.

When Cavendish pens her letter to Eleanora Duarte, she not only invites her readers across the textual threshold of the published letter into a seemingly private salon space, but she also plays host to Katherine and Frances as they perform for each other within the "Vaulted Room[s]" (*Sociable* 274) of the Rubenshuis. The letter positions Cavendish as a committed ballad singer whose "Plainer" musical style suggestively aligns her with the "natural" eloquence she so admires and strives to emulate elsewhere in her writings. While Cavendish seemingly defers to Eleanora's vocal training in Letter 202, she nonetheless dominates the account with an extensive description of her own voice. Indeed, the letter relies on the same strategies of textual control that characterize the rest of Cavendish's epistolary essays. Her decision to publish the letter is itself a claim to rhetorical authority. In contrast, Cavendish is a guest in Henry Lawes's home. Whether she ever contributed an "Old Ballad" to the musical proceedings at Rutland House is unknown. More likely, as with her visit to the Royal Society in 1667, she was "all admiration" (Pepys 781) at the vocal pyrotechnics of Mary Knight, Lawes's prize pupil. Yet, like her musical evenings with the Duartes, her repeated visits to a royalist space known to feature the poetry and performance of women and devoted to the preservation of courtly poetry and music testify to her political sympathies as well as to her longing for the rhetorical power associated with "Nature's Musicians" that evaded her at Goldsmiths' Hall and that she strove so consistently to secure in her published works. In these accounts, Cavendish, a writer fascinated with the acoustic potency of the speaking and singing voice, taps into the close affinities between music and rhetoric circulating in humanist texts. Within the royalist space of the salon and the textual spaces of her published works, song – the ballad in particular – becomes for Cavendish not simply a pastime or the superficial ornament of a gentlewoman, but a politicized, civilizing, and ultimately self-authorizing rhetorical tool that makes possible her intellectual performance.

For Said, "the intellectual does not represent a statue-like icon, but an individual vocation, an energy, a stubborn force engaging as a committed and recognizable voice in language and in society with a whole slew of issues, all of them having to do in the end with a combination of enlightenment and emancipation or freedom" (*Representations* 55). It is difficult to imagine a more persistently public intellectual force in the mid-seventeenth century than Margaret Cavendish, Duchess of Newcastle. Writing at a time when both royalist and parliamentarian women were forced to assume greater political responsibilities and when the loosening of censorship created new openings for women to contribute to public debates, Cavendish positions herself in her texts as a radical spokesperson for her society, a speaker – and a singer – gifted with natural wit and reason who holds the capacity to mitigate strife prompted by rhetorical misuse. Her exploration of song's affective force sheds new insight on the politics of musical performance in the early modern context and demonstrates the extent to which vocal genres and the spaces within which songs were circulated and performed could facilitate public intellectual action for women. If Cavendish's civilizing songs help to situate her as a potent truth teller in mid-seventeenth-century England, however, they testify equally strongly to music's ongoing significance in our contemporary society as a vital rhetorical practice and a mode of intellectual performance that holds the potential to edify, to unify, and to effect lasting sociocultural and political change.

NOTES

Earlier versions of this essay were presented at the 2009 Renaissance Society of America conference and the 2011 International Margaret Cavendish Society conference. I am grateful to the audiences at both of these meetings for their feedback. I would also like to thank Joel Faflak, James Fitzmaurice, Jason Haslam, Linda Hutcheon, Alysia Kolentsis, Rebecca Laroche, Mary Trull, and Sarah Williams for contributing valuable insights as the chapter developed.

1 See Boose and Dolan.

2 For recent studies of women's rhetorical and intellectual practices in early modern England, see, for example, Bennett; Clarke and Clarke; Daybell; Donawerth; Harris and Scott-Baumann; Larson; Luckyj; Richards and Thorne.

3 Civility has a complex history, particularly in relation to women. Etymologically, the word carries political connotations (*cives, civitas*), whether relating to civil government or the humanist education that prepared men for public state roles. By the seventeenth century, civility was primarily associated with politeness, gentility, and proper modes of social interaction within and among social classes. The word could also denote modesty or sexual propriety. See Elias and, more recently, Bryson; Burke; Ingram; Mendelson, "Civility"; Richards; and Shapin.

4 See, for example, Clucas, ed.; Cottegnies and Weitz; Romack and Fitzmaurice.

5 Cavendish went to France in 1643 as a maid of honour to Queen Henrietta Maria. She lived out the Civil Wars and the short-lived English Republic in Paris and in Antwerp with her husband, William Cavendish, later First Duke of Newcastle. A general of the royalist forces, he fled to the continent after his defeat at the 1644 Battle of Marston Moor; his estates were subsequently sequestered by Parliament. Cavendish and her husband returned to England following the restoration of the monarchy and the accession of Charles II in 1660. Their return did not entirely alleviate their sense of exile, however, since they did not receive the favour that they expected from the new monarch.

6 Cavendish's experience exemplifies Said's notion of the "condition of exile" as "the state of never being fully adjusted, always feeling outside the chatty, familiar world inhabited by natives, so to speak, tending to avoid and even dislike the trappings of accommodation and national well-being. Exile for the intellectual in this metaphysical sense is restlessness, movement, constantly being unsettled, and unsettling others" (*Representations* 39).

7 See Chalmers 78–82.

8 The amusing comment reverses later cultural assumptions connecting operatic success with the requisite appearance of the "fat lady."

9 Her attention to the oral interpretation of her texts provides good evidence for communal reading practices in the period. It also betrays profound authorial anxiety, testifying to Cavendish's obsession with controlling her readers' reactions (see Fitzmaurice, "Reading").

10 See Bloom; Smith, *Acoustic*.

11 See Clark; Fitzmaurice, "'When'"; Smith, "Female." Patricia Fumerton reads the "nomadic journey of provisional subjectivities" (504) afforded by the ballad as a way of articulating homelessness and displacement. Although she focusses on early modern vagrancy and the space of the alehouse, her argument serves as an important reminder that Cavendish's account of herself as a ballad singer in *Sociable Letters* dates from her years living in exile.

12 Ballads that publicized the confessions of condemned prisoners or documented the details of sensational crimes and social downfalls constitute an important subgenre in this regard. Such ballads often warned of the consequences of transgressive social behaviour while also inviting sympathy from audience members (see, for example, Trull; Wiltenburg). Cavendish's self-representation as a ballad singer arguably works strategically to confront anxieties about her gendered singing/writing body, reinforcing her commitment to virtue by positioning herself as an implicitly moralizing didactic musical force.

13 See McElligott; Knoppers; and Würzbach 149–50.

14 On the ballad's association both with nostalgia and with topicality, see Smith, "Afterword."

15 The association between ballads and truth telling was well established by the mid-seventeenth century. Shakespeare's Autolycus, for instance, capitalizes on this notion in *The Winter's Tale* (1609–11), claiming that the broadsides he sells are "[v]ery true" and "very pitiful, and as true" (4.4.257, 270). Similarly, the clown Lavatch in *All's Well That Ends Well* (1602–6) professes himself a "prophet" who "speak[s] the truth" by quoting a ballad (1.3.51–3).

16 Cavendish develops a similar contrast in *The Comical Hash*: "For my part," declares Lady Solitary, "I had rather hear a plain old Song, than any *Italian* or *French* Love Songs stuff'd with Trilloes" (574).

17 Stephen Clucas defends Cavendish's rejection of authority in her philosophical and scientific writings as characteristic of the "essayistic and probablistic discourses of mid-century philosophers" ("Variation" 200).

18 Cavendish is in this regard very much a product of her time, aligning with writers like Montaigne, Bacon, and Lipsius who advocated a simpler approach to oratory and, ironically, with the Royal Society's defense of individual experience and reason as the basis for knowledge.

19 Steven Shapin has persuasively elucidated the strong association between civility and truth in seventeenth-century England, though without extending his argument to women. On the importance of civil truth-telling for Cavendish, see Larson 154–65.

20 As Ian Spink notes, the declamatory style "increasingly depended on rhetorical qualities – the rhythm of the text and the rise and fall of the speaking voice – to govern the vocal line" (6).

21 See Sanders; and Tomlinson, "She that Plays."

22 See Chalmers 17–22.

23 As a member of the King's Music, Lawes accompanied Charles on progress in 1633 and again in 1634, and was at the Cavendish estates, Welbeck Abbey and Bolsover Castle, when Ben Jonson's *Loves Welcome* and *Loves Welcome at Bolsover* were performed. Lawes's close connection to the Egerton family also brought him into contact with Newcastle's daughter Elizabeth; one of Lawes's London concerts was devoted to a celebration of the tenth wedding anniversary of the Earl and Countess of Bridgewater (Spink 97; Whitaker 136). Margaret Cavendish and her stepdaughter Elizabeth may well have crossed paths at Lawes's home. Lawes also included a setting of a poem by Cavendish's late brother Charles Lucas in his first book of *Ayres and Dialogues* (1653).

24 Milton had firsthand knowledge of Lawes's work as a composer; the pair collaborated on *A Masque Presented at Ludlow Castle* in 1634. Despite their political differences, they maintained their connection during the Civil Wars. Milton's nephew, Edward Phillips, did not share his uncle's fierce parliamentarian beliefs; he was a guest at Lawes's Interregnum royalist musical gatherings in London and contributed a dedicatory poem to his first book of *Ayres and Dialogues*.

25 See Whitaker 136; Tomlinson, *Women* 154, 162; and Chalmers 19–20, 80–2.

26 See also Chalmers 20–1.

27 See Larson 138–65.

WORKS CITED

Austern, Linda. "The Siren, the Muse, and the God of Love: Music and Gender in Seventeenth Century English Emblem Books." *Journal of Musicological Research* 18.2 (1999): 95–138. Print. http://dx.doi.org/10.1080/01411899908574754.

Bennett, Lyn. *Women Writing of Divinest Things: Rhetoric and the Poetry of Pembroke, Wroth and Lanyer*. Pittsburgh: Duquesne UP, 2004. Print.

Bloom, Gina. *Voice in Motion: Staging Gender, Shaping Sound in Early Modern England*. Philadelphia: U of Pennsylvania P, 2007. Print.

Boose, Lynda E. "Scolding Brides and Bridling Scolds: Taming the Woman's Unruly Member." *Shakespeare Quarterly* 42.2 (1991): 179–213. Print. http://dx.doi.org/10.2307/2870547.

Bourdieu, Pierre. ""The Economics of Linguistic Exchanges." Trans. Richard Nice. *Social Sciences Information/Information sur les sciences sociales* 16.6 (1977): 645–68. Print. http://dx.doi.org/10.1177/053901847701600601.

Bryson, Anna. *From Courtesy to Civility: Changing Codes of Conduct in Early Modern England*. Oxford: Clarendon P, 1998. Print.

Burke, Peter. "A Civil Tongue: Language and Politeness in Early Modern Europe." *Civil Histories: Essays Presented to Sir Keith Thomas*. Ed. Peter Burke, Brian Harrison, and Paul Slack. Oxford: Oxford UP, 2000. 31–48. Print. http://dx.doi.org/10.1093/acprof:oso/9780198207108.003.0002.

Calvin, John. "*Geneva Psalter:* The Epistle to the Reader." *Source Readings in Music History*. Vol. 2. Ed. Oliver Strunk. New York: Norton, 1965. 155–8. Print.

Castiglione, Baldesar. *The Book of the Courtier*. Trans. Charles S. Singleton. Ed. Daniel Javitch. New York: Norton, 2002. Print.

Cavendish, Margaret, Duchess of Newcastle. *Bell in Campo. Bell in Campo and the Sociable Companions*. Ed. Alexandra G. Bennett. Peterborough, Ont.: Broadview P, 2002. 23–120. Print.

Cavendish, Margaret. *The Comical Hash*. *Playes*. London, 1662. 557–77. Print.

Cavendish, Margaret. *The Convent of Pleasure*. *The Convent of Pleasure and Other Plays*. Ed. Anne Shaver. Baltimore: Johns Hopkins UP, 1999. 217–48. Print.

Cavendish, Margaret. *The Description of a New World, Called the Blazing-World*. London, 1668. Print.

Cavendish, Margaret. *The Female Academy*. *Playes*. London, 1662. 652–79. Print.

Cavendish, Margaret. *Grounds of Natural Philosophy*. London, 1668. Print.

Cavendish, Margaret. *The Life of the Thrice Noble, High and Puissant Prince William Cavendish*. London, 1667. Print.

Cavendish, Margaret. *Loves Adventures*. *The Convent of Pleasure and Other Plays*. Ed. Anne Shaver. Baltimore: Johns Hopkins UP, 1999. 21–106. Print.

Cavendish, Margaret. *Natures Pictures Drawn by Fancies Pencil to the Life*. 2nd ed. London, 1671. Print.

Cavendish, Margaret. *Observations Upon Experimental Philosophy*. 2nd ed. London, 1668. Print.

Cavendish, Margaret. *Orations of Divers Sorts, Accommodated to Divers Places*. London, 1662. Print.

Cavendish, Margaret. *Philosophical and Physical Opinions*. 1st ed. London, 1655. Print.

Cavendish, Margaret. *Philosophical Letters*. London, 1664. Print.

Cavendish, Margaret. *Playes*. London, 1662. Print.

Cavendish, Margaret. *The Publick Wooing*. *Playes*. London, 1662. 367–421. Print.

Cavendish, Margaret. *Sociable Letters*. Ed. James Fitzmaurice. Peterborough, Ont.: Broadview P, 2004. Print.

Cavendish, Margaret. *A True Relation of My Birth, Breeding, and Life*. *Paper Bodies: A Margaret Cavendish Reader*. Ed. Sylvia Bowerbank and Sara Mendelson. Peterborough, Ont.: Broadview P, 2000. 41–63. Print.

Cavendish, Margaret. *The Worlds Olio*. London, 1655. Print.

Chalmers, Hero. *Royalist Women Writers, 1650–1689*. Oxford: Clarendon P, 2004. Print. http://dx.doi.org/10.1093/acprof:oso/9780199273270.001.0001.

Clark, Sandra. "The Broadside Ballad and the Woman's Voice." *Debating Gender in Early Modern England, 1500–1700*. Ed. Cristina Malcolmson and Mihoko Suzuki. Basingstoke: Palgrave Macmillan, 2002. 103–20. Print.

Clarke, Danielle, and Elizabeth Clarke, eds. *"This Double Voice": Gendered Writing in Early Modern England*. Basingstoke: Palgrave Macmillan, 2000. Print.

Clucas, Stephen, ed. *A Princely Brave Woman: Essays on Margaret Cavendish, Duchess of Newcastle*. Aldershot: Ashgate, 2005. Print.

Clucas, Stephen. "Variation, Irregularity and Probabilism: Margaret Cavendish and Natural Philosophy as Rhetoric." *A Princely Brave Woman: Essays on Margaret Cavendish, Duchess of Newcastle*. Ed. Stephen Clucas. Aldershot: Ashgate, 2005. 199–209. Print.

Cottegnies, Line, and Nancy Weitz, eds. *Authorial Conquests: Essays on Genre in the Writings of Margaret Cavendish*. Madison and Teaneck: Fairleigh Dickinson UP, 2003. Print.

Daybell, James, ed. *Early Modern Women's Letter Writing, 1450–1700*. Basingstoke: Palgrave Macmillan, 2001. Print. http://dx.doi.org/10.1057/9780230598669.

Dolan, Frances E. "'Gentlemen, I have one thing more to say': Women on Scaffolds in England, 1563–1680." *Modern Philology* 92.2 (1994): 157–78. http://dx.doi.org/10.1086/392230.

Donawerth, Jane. "'As Becomes a Rational Woman to Speak': Madeleine de Scudéry's Rhetoric of Conversation." *Listening to Their Voices: The Rhetorical Activities of Historical Women*. Ed. Molly Meijer Wertheimer. Columbia: U of South Carolina P, 1997. 305–19. Print.

Donawerth, Jane. "Conversation and the Boundaries of Public Discourse in Rhetorical Theory by Renaissance Women." *Rhetorica* 16.2 (1998): 181–99. Print. http://dx.doi.org/10.1525/rh.1998.16.2.181.

Donawerth, Jane. "The Politics of Renaissance Rhetorical Theory by Women." *Political Rhetoric, Power, and Renaissance Women*. Ed. Carole Levin and Patricia A. Sullivan. Albany: SUNY P, 1995. 257–74. Print.

Elias, Norbert. *The Civilizing Process*. Oxford: Blackwell, 1939. Print.

Fitzmaurice, James. "Shakespeare, Cavendish, and Reading Aloud in Seventeenth-Century England." *Cavendish and Shakespeare, Interconnections*. Ed. Katherine Romack and James Fitzmaurice. Aldershot: Ashgate, 2006. 29–46. Print.

Fitzmaurice, James. "'When an Old Ballad Is Plainly Sung': Musical Lyrics in the Plays of Margaret and William Cavendish." *Oral Traditions and Gender in Early Modern Literary Texts*. Ed. Mary Ellen Lamb and Karen Bamford. Aldershot: Ashgate, 2008. 153–68. Print.

Fumerton, Patricia. "Not Home: Alehouses, Ballads, and the Vagrant Husband in Early Modern England." *Journal of Medieval and Early Modern Studies* 32.3 (2002): 493–518. Print. http://dx.doi.org/10.1215/10829636-32-3-493.

Harris, Johanna, and Elizabeth Scott-Baumann, eds. *The Intellectual Culture of Puritan Women, 1558–1680*. Basingstoke: Palgrave Macmillan, 2010. Print. http://dx.doi.org/10.1057/9780230289727.

Hooke, Robert. *Micrographia*. London, 1665. Print.

Hulse, Lynn. "'Amorous in Music.'" *Royalist Refugees: William and Margaret Cavendish in the Rubens House, 1648-1660*. Ed. Ben van Beneden and Nora de Poorter. Antwerp: Rubsenshuis & Rubenianum, 2006. 83–9.

Ingram, Martin. "Sexual Manners: The Other Face of Civility in Early Modern England." *Civil Histories: Essays Presented to Sir Keith Thomas*. Ed. Peter Burke, Brian Harrison, and Paul Slack. Oxford: Oxford UP, 2000. 87–109. Print. http://dx.doi.org/10.1093/acprof:oso/9780198207108.003.0005.

Jennings, Jeremy, and Anthony Kemp-Welsh. "The Century of the Intellectual: From the Dreyfus Affair to Salman Rushdie." *Intellectuals in Politics: From the Dreyfus Affair to Salman Rushdie*. Ed. Jeremy Jennings and Anthony Kemp-Welsh. New York: Routledge, 1997. 1–21. Print.

Knoppers, Laura Lunger. "'Sing old Noll the Brewer': Royalist Satire and Social Inversion, 1648–64." *The Seventeenth Century* 15.1 (2000): 32–51. Print.

Larson, Katherine R. *Early Modern Women in Conversation*. Basingstoke: Palgrave Macmillan, 2011. Print. http://dx.doi.org/10.1057/9780230319530.

Lawes, Henry. *Ayres and Dialogues, for One, Two, and Three Voyces*. London, 1653–1658. Print.

Lawes, Henry. *The Second Book of Ayres, and Dialogues, for One*. London: Two, and Three Voyces, 1655. Print.

Luckyj, Christina. *"A moving Rhetoricke": Gender and Silence in Early Modern England*. Manchester: Manchester UP, 2002. Print.

Marsh, Christopher. "The Sound of Print in Early Modern England: The Broadside Ballad as Song." *The Uses of Script and Print, 1300–1700*. Ed. Julia Crick and Alexandra Walsham. Cambridge: Cambridge UP, 2004. 171–90. Print.

McElligott, Jason. "The Politics of Sexual Libel: Royalist Propaganda in the 1640s." *Huntington Library Quarterly* 67.1 (2004): 75–99. Print. http://dx.doi.org/10.1525/hlq.2004.67.1.75.

McShane Jones, Angela. "*The Gazet in Metre; or the Rhiming Newsmonger*: The English Broadside Ballad as Intelligencer." *News and Politics in Early Modern Europe (1500–1800)*. Ed. Joop W. Koopmans. Leuven and Paris: Peeters, 2005. 131–52. Print.

Mendelson, Sara. "The Civility of Women in Seventeenth-Century England." *Civil Histories: Essays Presented to Sir Keith Thomas*. Ed. Peter Burke, Brian Harrison, and Paul Slack. Oxford: Oxford UP, 2000. 111–25. Print. http://dx.doi.org/10.1093/acprof:oso/9780198207108.003.0006

Mendelson, Sara. "Playing Games with Gender and Genre: The Dramatic Self-Fashioning of Margaret Cavendish." *Authorial Conquests: Essays on Genre in the Writings of Margaret Cavendish*. Ed. Line Cottegnies and Nancy Weitz. Madison and Teaneck: Fairleigh Dickinson UP, 2003. 195–212. Print.

Milton, John. *A Masque Presented at Ludlow Castle. John Milton: The Complete Shorter Poems*. 2nd ed. Ed. John Carey. Harlow: Pearson Longman, 2007. 173–234. Print.

Milton, John. "To Mr H. Lawes, on his Airs." *John Milton: The Complete Shorter Poems*. 2nd ed. Ed. John Carey. Harlow: Pearson Longman, 2007. 294–5. Print.

Peacham, Henry. *The Compleat Gentleman*. London, 1622. Print.

Pepys, Samuel. *The Shorter Pepys*. Ed. Robert Latham. London, New York: Penguin Books, 1985. Print.

Rees, Emma L. E. *Margaret Cavendish: Gender, Genre, Exile*. Manchester: Manchester UP, 2003. Print.

Richards, Jennifer, ed. *Early Modern Civil Discourses*. Basingstoke: Palgrave Macmillan, 2003. Print. http://dx.doi.org/10.1057/9780230505063.

Richards, Jennifer, and Alison Thorne, eds. *Rhetoric, Women and Politics in Early Modern England*. New York: Routledge, 2007. Print.

Rollins, Hyder E. "The Black-Letter Broadside Ballad." *PMLA* 34.2 (1919): 258–339. Print. http://dx.doi.org/10.2307/457063.

Romack, Katherine and James Fitzmaurice, eds. *Cavendish and Shakespeare, Interconnections*. Aldershot: Ashgate, 2006. Print.

Said, Edward W. "The Public Role of Writers and Intellectuals." *The Public Intellectual*. Ed. Helen Small. Oxford: Blackwell, 2002. 19–39. Print. http://dx.doi.org/10.1002/9780470775967.ch1.

Said, Edward W. *Representations of the Intellectual: The 1993 Reith Lectures*. London: Vintage, 1994. Print.

Sanders, Julie. "Caroline Salon Culture and Female Agency: The Countess of Carlisle, Henrietta Maria, and Public Theatre." *Theatre Journal* 52.4 (December 2000): 449–64. Print. http://dx.doi.org/10.1353/tj.2000.0122.

Shakespeare, William. *All's Well That Ends Well. The Norton Shakespeare*. Ed. Stephen Greenblatt et al. New York, London: Norton, 1997. 2175–244. Print.

Shakespeare, William. *The Winter's Tale. The Norton Shakespeare*. Ed. Stephen Greenblatt et al. New York, London: Norton, 1997. 2873–953. Print.

Shapin, Steven. *A Social History of Truth: Civility and Science in Seventeenth-Century England*. Chicago: U of Chicago P, 1994. 1–18. Print.

Small, Helen. "Introduction." *The Public Intellectual*. Ed. Helen Small. Oxford: Blackwell, 2002. 1–18. Print. http://dx.doi.org/10.1002/9780470775967.ch

Smith, Bruce R. *The Acoustic World of Early Modern England: Attending to the O-Factor*. Chicago: U of Chicago P, 1999. Print.

Smith, Bruce R. "Afterword: Ballad Futures." *Ballads and Broadsides in Britain, 1500–1800*. Ed. Patricia Fumerton and Anita Guerrini. Farnham: Ashgate, 2010. 317–23. Print.

Smith, Bruce R. "Female Impersonation in Early Modern Ballads." *Women Players in England, 1500–1660: Beyond the All-Male Stage*. Ed. Pamela Allen Brown and Peter Parolin. Aldershot: Ashgate, 2005. 281–304. Print.

Spink, Ian. *Henry Lawes: Cavalier Songwriter*. Oxford: Oxford UP, 2000. Print.

Tomlinson, Sophie. "'She that Plays the King': Henrietta Maria and the Threat of the Actress in Caroline Culture." *The Politics of Tragicomedy: Shakespeare and After*. Ed. Gordon McMullan and Jonathan Hope. New York: Routledge, 1992. 189–207. Print.

Tomlinson, Sophie. *Women on Stage in Stuart Drama*. Cambridge: Cambridge UP, 2005. Print.

Trull, Mary. "'Odious Ballads': Fallen Women's Laments and *All's Well That Ends Well*." *Translating Desire in Medieval and Early Modern Literature*. Ed. Craig A. Berry and Heather Richardson Hayton. Tempe: Arizona Center for Medieval and Renaissance Studies, 2005. 133–54. Print.

Whitaker, Katie. *Mad Madge: The Extraordinary Life of Margaret Cavendish, Duchess of Newcastle, the First Woman to Live by Her Pen*. New York: Basic Books, 2002. Print.

Wiltenburg, Joy. "Ballads and the Emotional Life of Crime." *Ballads and Broadsides in Britain, 1500–1800*. Ed. Patricia Fumerton and Anita Guerrini. Farnham: Ashgate, 2010. 173–86. Print.

Woolf, Virginia. *A Room of One's Own*. New York: Harcourt Brace & Company, 1929. Print.

Würzbach, Natascha. *The Rise of the English Street Ballad, 1550–1650*. Trans. Gayna Walls. Cambridge: Cambridge UP, 1990. Print.

6 Get Happy! American Film Musicals and the Psychopathology of Hope

JOEL FAFLAK

Overture

In *Summer Stock* (1950), Jane Falbery (Judy Garland), who runs the family farm, offers her barn to her sister's boyfriend/director Joe Ross (Gene Kelly) to rehearse his new show. For Falbery, theatre is a frivolous diversion from real life. But when her sister bails to pursue fame on Broadway, Jane trains like hell to replace her and falls in love with Ross. Planting cultural production between Broadway and Hollywood in the American Midwest, the film treats entertainment as serious business. Family, community, and a strong work ethic ensure decent folk with untrained talent can perform their way to happiness. At the end of the film, barn stage becomes soundstage, and a chorus of men in black, dancing against white clouds on an orange sky, help Jane sing the film's signature musical number:

Forget your troubles, c'mon get happy!
 You better chase all your cares away.
 Shout hallejulah, c'mon get happy!
 Get ready for the judgement day.

The sun is shinin', c'mon get happy!
 The lord is waitin' to take your hand.
 Shout hallejulah, c'mon get happy!
 We're goin' to the promised land.

"Get Happy!" shifts the film's message, that hard work brings just rewards, to a higher register. Moving from the labours of theatrical illusion to the seamless imaginary of cinema, the number sublimates happiness as a natural and transcendent right. Rather than work begetting happiness, happiness begets itself; the ultimate capitalist call is to get – to consume, to appropriate – happiness. Of course, the invitation cuts two ways: "judgement day" and "promised land" should make one giddy; yet because apocalypse and deliverance are still pending, better make bliss an evangelical imperative, just in case.

Garland filmed the number after a two-month hiatus to forget her own troubles (she looks better here than in the rest of the film) and then started a vacation, from which MGM called her back to film *Royal Wedding*.[1] Still overworked and exhausted, she couldn't go on and parted with MGM after a fifteen-year career in which her films (almost all musicals) made more money for the studio than those of nearly any other of Louis B. Mayer's stars. Returning to shoot "Get Happy!" is perhaps Garland's first "comeback," as if to answer the habituation to happiness the number demands. Asking myself, as always, "What would Judy do?," I started with this quip (and clip) recently when I addressed my university's Senior Alumni Association on psychiatry and the American film musical. Afterward, an audience member gave my talk an unexpected spin: "During the Depression we lived in poverty. Going to the movies kept us going, especially musicals." Musicals didn't pay the bills (indeed, even 1930s admission prices were an indulgence); but they showed others in the business of making others happy. Silvery illusions of how life might or should be were a lie that kept mass audiences going; they staged the luxury of survival when many couldn't afford it. I used to criticize my mother for being duped by the same lies. I now know better.

The above scenes stage what I call the psychopathology of hope as a psychic glitch that is constitutive of our desires.[2] Like faith, hope differs from belief, in which one seems certain that something exists. Belief doesn't need hope: the believer imagines he already has what he's wished for. (From this point of view, because belief makes little distinction between it and its object, it can seem even more psychopathological than faith, indeed even psychotic.) A believer is convinced, has no doubts, whereas one who has faith risks conviction; he commits to something knowing full well it might not be true or even exist. To have faith is to hope even when all hope is lost; it can thus seem foolhardy, reckless, even pointless. Such persistence makes it resilient but also, paradoxically, fragile, vulnerable to attack. Hope leaves itself open to ideological seduction or political manipulation. To hope is to risk our illusions, to suspend disbelief. But, again, if hope tarries with disappointment, disillusion, despair, even death, it also suggests at once a desire to go on and to commit, as well as a distance from the object of one's desire. Hazarding hope risks what Julia Kristeva, speaking as psychoanalyst, novelist, and social activist appealing to the dark intelligence of the public intellectual, calls "*energeia* in the Aristotelian sense of thought as act, the actuality of intelligence" (14). Hope mobilizes an informed scepticism yet a *commitment to* scepticism – against what Kristeva calls the "malady of ideality" (18) afflicting our culture – at the risk of breeding new myths by which to live.

This chapter reads film musicals as cultural phenomena exemplifying this "actuality of intelligence," for worse and better. Their political unconscious contains the rise of psychiatry as a science of happiness, the historical and cultural relevance of which I shall address in the next section. Like psychiatry, musicals take their cue from a social commitment to disclose, orchestrate, and thus instruct both private and public desires, as I argue in my second section. This commitment indicates the implicit value of both the field of psychiatry and the form of musicals as modes of intellectual pursuit within a broader cultural arena, as ways of exploring and explaining human drives and aspirations. It also makes them organs of social regulation. Between desire and discipline, happiness and its instrumentalization, psychiatry and musicals powerfully index hope's cultural capital in the public sphere. The psychiatric imperative of film musicals, that is to say, cuts both ways. On one hand, it reflects back to an entire population the pitfalls and potentialities of its social project. On the other hand, it suspends intellectual and political urgency within the spectacle of mass representation: in the case of psychiatry, first as the institutional archipelago that mapped an entire psychiatric industry in the nineteenth century and eventually in the twentieth century as the more effective therapeutic conditioning of the body politic via an obsession with self-help and well-being and the triumph of pharmacology; in the case of musicals, via the advent of cinema and its powerfully seductive hold on public imaginations, to which Jason Haslam's chapter in this volume speaks. At stake in this struggle, as I shall explore in my final section, are the risks of what Deborah Britzman, speaking of the complexities of transference informing the learning process, calls "difficult education." Film musicals use cinema to conduct a particular kind of communal experience, a national classroom that at once transports, inspires, instructs, challenges, and indoctrinates its audience, a mobile and shifting pedagogical capital that is their most profitable and exploitative asset.

Act One

Psychiatry emerged from advances in medical science via its curiosity about the brain and its nervous circuitry. But this medical desire had a far-reaching sociopolitical object. Fuelled by late eighteenth- to early nineteenth-century ideals of revolution and reform, early psychiatry was a utopian project dedicated to curing madness. Inventing the term *Psychiaterie* in 1808, German physician and physiologist Johann Christian Reil wrote: "A bold race of men dares to take on this gigantic idea, an idea that dizzies the normal burgher, of wiping from the face of the earth one of the most devastating pestilences" (cited in Shorter 8). In 1794, Philippe Pinel, overseer of the Bicêtre asylum in Paris, unchained its inmates, and in 1801 published one of psychiatry's ur-texts, *Traité médico-philosophique sur l'aliénation mentale*. Pinel advocated *traitement moral* ("moral" meaning "psychological" or "emotional" as well as "moral"), which stressed the physical, behavioural, and spiritual rehabilitation of the insane in isolated confinement over physical restraint and social ostracization. William Battie's 1758 *Treatise on Madness* had earlier argued that "*management did much more than medicine*" (68), and by the early nineteenth century, moral treatment or management characterized psychiatry in England, France, Germany, Italy, and the United States.

At first, psychiatry seemed headed towards psychoanalysis. In Germany, for instance, *Psychiker* ("the psychically oriented") "had little interest in heredity or brain pathology and preferred to spend long hours talking to their patients about their subjective experiences" (Shorter 30). Early psychiatric speculation and sympathy, dedicated to putting psycho-medical advances into the best socio-therapeutic practice, however, were quickly overshadowed by a "biological psychiatry [that] dominated the discipline throughout the nineteenth century" (32). This more scientific turn helped to legitimate psychiatric theory and practice and to facilitate the field's disciplinary and institutional expansion, and by the later 1800s in Europe and the United States the number of asylums, and their numbers, exploded. As custodianship shifted from family and community to institution, psychiatry shifted from therapy to bureaucracy, from rehabilitation to maintenance. This Foucauldian Great Confinement turned a pan-social enterprise into an oddly dissociative isolationism.[3] In 1817, French psychiatrist Jean-Etienne-Dominique Esquirol, in the spirit of the Tuke family, who founded the York Quaker retreat in 1792, advocated the "removal from family and friends," which "would contribute greatly to diverting the patient from the previously unhealthy passions that had ruled his or her life" (Shorter 13).[4] It seems unclear, however, if this therapeutic community marks a prophylactic repair *of* or *from* a psychopathologically wounded body politic. An increasingly sentimental view of family and friendship grew intolerant of threats to its "picture of bliss" (50), the pressures of which normative sociality produced their own discontents.

Numbers also mushroomed because social awareness of madness, facilitated by disciplinary expansion and an exploding print culture, made psychopathology viral in the public sphere. In an odd way, psychiatry survived culturally because of its therapeutic failure. The inchoate eighteenth-century taxonomy of "insanity" looked crystalline against the proliferation of definitions and diagnoses of psychopathology in the nineteenth century. In *An Essay on the Prevention and Cure of Insanity* (1814), George Nesse Hill fears that "even physicians daily habituated to view madness find it occasionally difficult to be clear and satisfactory in their decision" (393). Making the psyche behaviourally accessible, moral management exposed a remote and protean psychic motility that defied rehabilitation and speculation. Science's attempt to chart the increasingly florid terrain of psychopathology started to seem like madness itself. One can recall that in 1805, Samuel Taylor Coleridge coined the term "psycho-analytical" (2:2670) three years before Reil's *Psychiaterie*. It would take nearly a century for Coleridge's hunch to pay off in Freud's theory of the unconscious. Nonetheless, by registering the time's more than latent awareness of and thus deference to the mind's darkness, Coleridge's term haunts psychiatry's desire to make this darkness visible, yet also suggests how psychiatry flourishes by thriving upon the psyche's fundamental inaccessibility.

From early on, then, psychiatry signifies a broader obsession to diagnose the nervous body politic of a post-Napoleonic culture of unprecedented technological and scientific advancement, unbridled population and market growth, and threatening political and religious enthusiasms. Andrew Scull notes that by the Victorian period the psychiatric profession had "failed most abjectly," but its "insidious and worrying capacity to suppress non-conformity in the name of mental health [...] proved highly efficacious as a repressive instrument for controlling large numbers of people" (155–6). We can trace this tendency in the previous century's attempt to deal with the psychological complexities of social, political, and economic exchange.

Early psychiatry is also sustained by the spirit of moral philosophy and political economy, which based the cohesion of progressive and profitable civil society in sympathy, the focus of recent critical reassessments. Discussing Adam Smith's dictum that we can only imagine, not share, the other's suffering, David Marshall argues that Smith, unable to see "fellow-feeling [as] automatic or even natural," explores "what it is like to want to believe in the fiction of sympathy, and what it's like to live in a world where sympathy is perhaps impossible" (180, 181). Sympathy's theatre or spectacle of witnessing, that is, stresses self-mastery over empathy. As Vivavsan Soni puts it, Smith's *Theory of Moral Sentiments* (1759)

> becomes a conduct manual, teaching those who suffer how to manage their behaviour so that the spectator can sustain the fiction of sentimental communion; it is less interested in sentimental concern for suffering than the regulation of sentiments. In this perverse shift, *The Theory of Moral Sentiments* turns into very nearly its opposite: it places responsibility not with the spectators, but with those who are afflicted, enjoining them to regulate their conduct in such a way as to occasion as little disturbance as possible in the equanimity of spectators. (310)

Aestheticizing sympathy as participation in others' tragedy, Smith makes us vicarious witnesses who experience self-satisfaction rather than pathos, a sentimental veneer of ethical concern that masks a sadistic narcissism: "all men for others" is really "every man for himself."

Soni's account suggests a different spin on psychiatry's implicit assumption of benevolence and a natural right to happiness.[5] In his classic text of future political economy, *The Wealth of Nations* (1776), Smith's feeling subject is also a yeoman, whose self-commanding moral sentiment licences his taking charge within the body politic. Smith's view reflects the Scottish Enlightenment ethos of Common Sense, defined by Thomas Reid as "that degree of judgment which is common to men with whom we can converse and transact business" (421). Edinburgh also being the epicenter of modern medicine in the eighteenth century, one sees an implicit connection between market leader and psychiatrist, both at once self-developed, empathic, and self-interested individuals disciplined in the efficient deployment of healthy feelings. In short, good psychiatry is good business: keeping bad feelings at bay ensures a healthy citizen, who ensures a healthy marketplace and the wealth of nations.

The equation seems pat, yet emerging between capitalist expansion and social regulation, psychiatry, failing to cure madness, succeeds in mobilizing the *desire* for moral management. Texts like Thomas Trotter's 1807 *A View of the Nervous Temperament* (Trotter also wrote one of the first tracts against drunkenness) sounded the call for sobriety: "the temperate man is observed to bear sickness with more patience and resignation, than those accustomed to indulgence" (137). Moderation restores vitality to the body politic by managing its habits, which, Trotter claims, "if not restrained soon, must inevitably sap our physical strength of constitution; make us an easy conquest to our invaders; and ultimately convert us into a nation of slaves and ideots [sic]" (xi). The anxiety is ironic given the Empire's profitable trade in habituates, but in light of this uncanny traffic between intemperance and sobriety, one can rephrase early psychiatry's aborted excursions into psychopathology as success by another route. The failure itself instilled the *idea* of its success – what one might call the psychiatric consciousness of a desire to domesticate the perils of looking inward for the collective payoff of getting people oriented towards the habit of wanting to be better people. To rephrase my earlier equation: the ethical exercise staged by Smith's theatre of sympathy becomes the desire for the desire *for* happiness. *Whose* happiness remains to be seen.

The spirit of Pinel's revolution at the Bicêtre asylum found its way across the Atlantic[6] to the Philadelphia Hospital, where Benjamin Rush, pioneer of prison reform and founder of American psychiatry, designed a chair for spinning mentally ill patients in order to dispose them towards the blandishments of psychotherapy.[7] Spinning caught the patient's attention, a different version of Pinel's or English psychiatrist John Haslam's method of holding his patient's eye in order to "obtain the confidence, and conciliate the esteem of insane persons," thus "procuring from them respect and obedience" (Haslam 295). With these "constraints" in mind (one recalls that Pinel removed shackles, but replaced them with straightjackets), it is not such a leap of faith from spinning away madness in the City of Brotherly Love to a different kind of spin: singing and dancing on a soundstage in Culver City, where film musicals write the socio-therapeutic example of psychiatry large as visual spectacle. For as Soni's argument suggests (see note 5), the eighteenth century's misplaced politics of happiness produced in its place a rather more enduring and compulsively repetitive culture of happiness, though not without its own ideological and political implications.

Roughly paralleling the rise and fall of the Broadway musical, film musicals are hybrids of opera, operetta, music halls, vaudeville, minstrel shows, as well as Broadway and the birth of cinema itself. After *The Jazz Singer* (1927), the first talkie, and *Broadway Melody* (1929), the first musical to win Best Picture Oscar, musicals seemed to flag (although, as Andrea Most's chapter for this volume reminds us, Ernst Lubitsch's early 1930s films for Paramount prove otherwise). The form revived at Warner Brothers in three 1933 films: *42nd Street* and *Footlight Parade*, both directed by Lloyd Bacon, and *Gold Diggers of 1933*, by Mervyn Leroy (Busby Berkeley choreographed and staged musical numbers for all three). These films innovate the "show within a show" or "let's put on a show" narrative of the "backstage musical," which laid bare the economics, aesthetics, and collaborative labour of film diegesis, thus advertising and applauding the technology and culture of studio production. This self-referentiality epitomizes the genre's endless capacity to retool, refashion, and rebrand itself (musicals are among the most incestuously intertextual cultural products). The genius of this reproductive drive was to grasp the essence of film semiosis for both its celebration and encryption of cinematic experience and mirror this experience back to a yearning public.[8] Using film to replicate the logistics of how to put America back to work, musical "can-do" ideology, as my senior alumnus testified, helped to materialize the end of the Depression.

As the country got happier, film musicals followed suit. Their capital rose with the sunnier Astaire/Rogers films at RKO in the later 1930s, and their heyday was at MGM roughly from *The Wizard of Oz* (1939) to *Gigi* (1958). The demise of the studio system also witnessed some of the most aesthetically challenging musicals, such as *The Pirate* (1948), *Singin' in the Rain* (1952), *The Bandwagon* (1953), and *West Side Story* (1961). As if working overtime to cure the time's dissociated ideological sensibilities, this creative fever coincided with post-WWII American optimism as it met its paranoiac doubles abroad in the Cold War and at home in McCarthy's witch hunts. The times were not so unlike post-Revolutionary Britain, whose psychiatric development parallels that of the United States. For in the traumatic aftermath of 1790s politics – Treason Trials, Gagging Acts, war and the threat of foreign invasion, economic vagaries at home and the burden of colonizing and managing the marketplace abroad – Britain marshalled its resources towards building a second Empire better than the first (whose demise was signalled by George III losing the Colonies), which required perfecting and exporting a civilizing mission that would put a benign cultural face on an otherwise ideologically suspect political anatomy. The times required getting people in the habit of believing in hope by repeatedly staging a society making a spectacle of its desire for happiness. But the aesthetic results of this spectacle aren't as benign as they seem.

Act Two

Richard Dyer argues that film musicals are collaboratively produced entertainments whose mode of

> "escape" or "wish fulfillment" point[s] to [their] central thrust, namely, utopianism. Entertainment offers the image of [...] something we want deeply that our day-to-day lives don't provide. Alternatives, hopes, wishes – [...] the sense that things could be better, that something other than what is can be imagined and maybe realized. Entertainment does not, however, present models of utopian worlds [...] Rather the utopianism is contained in the feelings it embodies. (18)

Dyer distinguishes a film's representational elements, such as stars, characters, or setting, from its nonrepresentational elements such as "colour, texture, movement, rhythm, melody, camerawork," which intensify cinematic experience and are thus key to how numbers materialize utopian feelings. For Dyer this manufactured happiness turns the otherwise improbable break between narrative and musical number into a constitutive negotiation between social reality and utopian longing. By revitalizing the entropies of everyday life, musical numbers stage the utopian correction of quotidian deficiencies. For instance, that Busby Berkeley numbers from the 1930s shift abruptly from reality to fantasy suggests overwhelming social problems, whereas *On the Town* (1949), one of the first musicals shot on location, by moving more seamlessly between narrative and number, as when sailors start to dance on the streets of New York, marks a smaller rift between real and ideal in optimistic post-WWII America.

One can push Dyer's argument further. If the narrative demands a transformational relationship with numbers, the numbers also insist upon their estranging distance, as if to fetishize an impossible metamorphosis. This freakish compensation signifies what Kristin Thompson might call the excess of cinematic experience in general. This excess is generated when a film's "unifying structures" (e.g., the heterosexual romance or backstage musical plots) clash with the images and sounds of film's "*materiality*," which defamiliarizes these normalizing strategies in order to "intrigue us by [film's] strangeness" (498). This filmic lure materializes the "astonishing phenomenon *where the illusion of reality is inseparable from the awareness that it is really an illusion*, without, however, this awareness killing the feeling of reality" (Morin 225). Hence, "the real emerges into reality only when it is woven with the imaginary, which solidifies it, gives it consistency and thickness – in other words, *reifies* it" (227). Reading illusion's reifying nature in terms of the Lacanian Real, Slavoj Žižek speaks of the "*Real of the illusion itself*" (81). Žižek describes the Real as "a certain GRIMACE of reality, a certain imperceptible, unfathomable, ultimately illusory feature" (80) that marks our irrevocable distance from reality. Utopia would be this perfect apprehension if reality functioned seamlessly, except that both utopia and the desire for it would then be void. Illusion exists *as* illusion to hide "the remainder of [our] *authenticity*" (45), the place where we *are* but can never *be* or *know* in its fullness, but "whose traces we can discern in an imperfect mechanical reproduction" (45). The Real both necessitates and guarantees illusion by not calling attention to it *as* illusion, which in turn gives our existence's imaginary nature its "consistency and thickness" precisely by ignoring the lack of this integrity.

Perhaps this is why musical numbers make us uncomfortable: by so palpably staging our illusions *as* illusions they threaten to expose our frail grasp on reality, in turn making reality itself *all too real*, the site of an impossible transformation. Something about utopia makes us uneasy, despite its yearning for a better world. The inadequate bridge between narrative and numbers, then, is symptomatic of how musicals *necessarily* fail to negotiate between real and ideal, a failure constitutive of film musicals' desiring economy. Mapping both the social space of their collaborative labour and the cultural matrix of their hybrid development onto the "no-place" of utopia, film musicals are at once self-fulfilling, self-referential, and self-cannibalizing. By so zealously insisting upon happiness, numbers encrypt the concentrated but volatile potentiality of all experience, which threatens to turn against itself, as in the number "Cool" from *West Side Story*. "Cool" choreographs this redundant energy as a raw sexuality that has to be sloughed off, not *before* it explodes, but as the anticipatory choreographing of an impending and inevitable violence. Driving this economy is a technology of utopianism that at once orchestrates and then feeds upon its audience's very desire *for* hope. Promising hope by endlessly frustrating or deferring its satisfaction, musicals are instead in the business of manufacturing good feelings. The glitch in their mechanical reproduction of happiness ensures the payoff is never so high as to preempt the game's repetition, though part of the high that comes with being swept up in a number's Dionysiac frenzy is the implicit lure that *this* will be the number to beat all numbers, a telos one both desires and wants to have frustrated so that the number can go on forever.

In this sense musicals at once transform and repeat capitalist ideology and its effects. Two early examples of the backstage musical exemplify this tension between ideology and utopia, repression and wish fulfillment, within the same social mechanism.[9] At the same time, they suggest a critique of this delicate balance as the insidious equilibrium of hope's mythmaking ideology. The backstage musical stages the business of stage business in order to sell America on entertainment as a way to forget one's troubles in the name of building social cohesion. To do so, however, it has to work through the troublesome politics of democracy itself: for the collective to work, some individuals will shine and some must subsume their individuality, nonetheless allowing the group to thrive on the latter's spent energy. To paraphrase Chantal Mouffe's notion of liberal democracy, the backstage musical identifies democracy with "the defence of human rights" rather than "popular sovereignty" (4). To cite Daniela Garofalo citing Mouffe, liberalism compromises democracy by "forfeiting equality for individual self-development" and "is more consistent with a meritocracy in which everyone in theory is free to develop according to his or her talents, unhampered by traditional privilege" (130). Feeding off this meritocratic (and meretricious) ideal, the backstage musical shows just how cannibalistic liberalism can get.

In the ur-backstage musical, *42nd Street*, Julian Marsh (Warner Baxter) is a director both recovering from and verging on a nervous breakdown because he's given everything to "that gulch" Broadway, a harsh mistress from whom he's made a lot of money, but who has extorted a high cost for his talent. Having lost everything in the crash of 1929, Marsh signs on to direct *Pretty Lady*, against his doctor's warning that continued hard work might precipitate a relapse. Repeated troubles with *Pretty Lady* demand that Marsh marshal his energy to keep the company on its toes and morale high. A final crisis comes when his fading star, Dorothy Brock (Bebe Daniels), breaks her ankle in a drunken fight with her boyfriend, whom she thinks Peggy Sawyer (Ruby Keeler), a wide-eyed newcomer, is trying to steal. In desperation Marsh plucks Sawyer from the chorus, works her to the limits of her (clearly limited) talent, and overnight transforms her into a star (also ensuring Sawyer gets the young male lead, Billy Lawler, played by Dick Powell).[10] Their key number is "Young and Healthy," in which, to woo Sawyer, "a bundle of humanity" who is "oh so hard to kiss," Lawler sings: "I'm young and healthy, / And you've got charms; / It would really be a sin / Not to have you in my arms." Sawyer can't resist: "That ain't my nature, / I'm full of vitamin 'A,' say!" To visualize the song's flimsy prophylactic between chaste repose and reproductive urgency, the camera pans through a long tunnel of parted women's legs, a running crotch shot that comes to rest on Keeler's and Powell's impossibly sunny faces.

"Young and Healthy" extols the virtues of monogamy against the earlier number, "You're Getting to be a Habit with Me," in which the older Brock is hand(l)ed from man to man. But the later number also encrypts the guilty and costly pleasure of serial encounters in its otherwise sublime spectacle of faceless female bodies. Notice that Lawler doesn't sing, "I would love to have you in my arms," instead posing the spectre of turpitude ("It would *really* be a sin *not* to have you in my arms") that the number both fights against and entertains. Its terminus might be heterosexual bonding, but its sexual economy works by a more cyclical desire, thus staging the uneasy tension between production values and reproductive value. A rather inhuman and dispassionate repetition of female "innocence" supports the healthy sentiments of communal identity, both a mask and justification for Broadway compromise. That Keeler goes in a youngster but comes back a star means she's already poised to become seasoned, and between youth and age there is a moment of desperate consummation that can't be sustained forever. As Sawyer also sings to Lawler, "So let's be bold. / In a year or two or three / Maybe we will be too old." Ironically, the film closes outside the theatre with an exhausted Marsh, who overhears departing audience members accuse him of trying to take all the credit for the show's success when he should be thankful to have a star like Sawyer.

Key here is Marsh's ambivalent signification. On one hand, he is either patient or victim: Broadway's machinery of hope will either cure or consume him. On the other hand, he is either doctor or conqueror: he'll either get better in order to help others, or he'll tap their energy to become his species' fittest survivor, suggesting both the ethical and narcissistic drives of sympathy explored earlier (he's Smith's yeoman as passive/aggressive leader). Both artist and manager, he is the film's polestar for a number of dirty but necessary collaborations: art and commerce, talent and luck, sincere creativity and callous economics, genuine feeling and faceless drive, Broadway and Wall Street. For the *film's* audience the messy social education represented on the screen by Broadway economics (on the East coast) renders invisible the equally complex politics of the industrial apparatus (in the West) that makes the representation possible. Broadway hope comes at a price; cinematic hope wraps its audience in the silvery illusion of a seamless ideological enterprise. But the film's conscience isn't entirely clean. Whether patient or doctor, Marsh ends up exhausted, defeated again by his faith in any social project. Moreover, the film also sells off its most valuable commodity: the youthful energy and innocence of its new star. The suggestion that youth is the price it pays to sustain itself follows a social Darwinism not uncharacteristic of Depression-era film, but nonetheless startling for a musical.

Which makes Berkeley's staging of "Lullaby of Broadway" in *Gold Diggers of 1935* not only a commentary on the film's own time but a powerful apotheosis of the musical form itself early in its history. The story is set in a luxury resort for rich people trying to survive the Depression. The plot pairs the medical student Dick Curtis (Dick Powell) with Ann (Gloria Stuart), daughter of the wealthy but tight-fisted Mrs Prentiss (Alice Brady), who fall in love against the mother's wishes. The mother wants Anne married to millionaire T. Mosely Thorpe (Hugh Herbert), who is being blackmailed by the hotel stenographer (Glenda Farrell). When not bailing her son Humboldt (Frank McHugh) out of bad marriages, the elder Prentiss funds the resort's annual charity show by hiring broke stage director Nicoleff (Adolphe Menjou), who goes overboard with the show's production in order to skim money off the top, thus nearly bankrupting his patroness. Eventually the show goes on, and Humboldt comes clean by marrying Curtis's fiancé Aline (Dorothy Dare), an inverse of Curtis's union with Ann, proving that a soberly industrious (read: upwardly mobile) working class, rather than succeed by extortion, can check upper-class intemperance (Mrs Prentiss relents that it'll be good to have a doctor in the family) and thus revitalize the economy.

But Berkeley's direction of the film, reflecting the more cynical social vision of Ernst Lubitsch's musicals for Paramount and MGM (1929–34), and as if dissatisfied with any hopefully convenient match between reality and idealism, pushes cynicism further.[11] The film closes with "Lullaby of Broadway," the show that secures Prentiss's investment in "charity." Curtains part on the resort stage, and the camera pans towards the distant face of entertainer Wini Shaw against a black background. As she finishes, her head fills the screen, then turns upside down and transmogrifies into a map of Manhattan in which Broadway bifurcates her face (she's at once "the gulch" and its victim). This abstract disfiguration further disembodies the woman's face as the eyes into the soul of the cautionary tale she is to become, re-anatomized as the unfolding topography of her moral crimes, what Žižek might call the "Real of the illusion itself" that marks the "GRIMACE of reality." The number then stages this grimace's para-reality as an extended film within a film, which pits hardworking daylight reality against the gaily abandoned nightlife of the Broadway Baby, Shaw herself. The final scene of this show within a show within a show is another show: a musical number set in a nightclub, witnessed from a table above seating Dick Curtis and the Baby (the kind of woman he *shouldn't* marry). The number builds from a languid tango to the mechanical precision of a whole rally of dancers who then mutate into an anarchic Dionysian frenzy, which sweeps a willing Baby into its irresistible momentum only then to drive her off the nightclub balcony to her death. The denouement is a return to daylight as the Big Apple morphs back to Shaw reprising the song's final refrain.

That the number restores the anthropomorphic humanity of Shaw's face comforts us that this is morality play, not real life. But the preceding trauma scars irrevocably the film's glistening veneer. *Someone* has to pay for the economic and moral excesses that precipitated the Great Crash; someone also has to pay to keep the working class working and the rich spending. If the number's inhuman spectacle – its lockstep choreography, the abstraction of the human body into mechanized set pieces that subsume individuals into a larger machinic whole – leads us to question Berkeley's politics, it also stages a rather worrisome political ambivalence. Well in advance of the genre's later self-critiques such as *Singin' in the Rain*, *Cabaret* (1972), *All that Jazz* (1979), or *Dancer in the Dark* (2002), Berkeley's film-within-a-film stages how far film musicals – and the society for which they speak – will go to do the dirty work of utopianism of *any* stripe, what sacrifices a society has to make to sustain its own vitality. If musicals work to perfect a "natural" shift from narrative to number, Berkeley's number exposes the naturalistic determinism of utopianism itself. The tragic payoff for its overabundance of pleasure isn't so much Aristotelian – cathartic and socially ameliorative – as Nietzschean, aware of the Dionysian cost of maintaining Apollonian sobriety and equipoise.

Berkeley's vision is at once *mise-en-scène* and primal scene of capitalism's fanatical desire to satisfy the same want it endlessly produces. Musicals don't just produce the feeling of utopia; they show

how the feeling is produced in order to show how it can then be consumed, an excess that at once excites transformation and demands containment. Returning from narrative to number contains the excess, but leaves the transformation wanting, in turn leaving the audience wanting more. In the final nightclub scene of "Lullaby of Broadway," Powell and Shaw mirror an eager participation in spectacle. The girl succumbs as the boy remains unscathed, an inevitable gendering of the psychic survival of the socially fittest that in turn mirrors the audience's vicarious moral satisfaction while offering the pleasures of witnessing, at once implicating, justifying, and getting us off the hook. Evoking the work of Mouffe among others, Karyn Ball, discussing truth and reconciliation hearings in South Africa or Canada, argues that public repentance for past crimes stages a spectacle of social catharsis that allows democracy to feel better about itself in order to get on with the addictively dirtier business of capitalism ("Democracy"). The genius of Berkeley's staging is to glimpse at once film's utopic mechanism and its entropic drive: the film musical as a collaborative manufacture of hope that exposes the political technology of utopianism as something at once habitual, compulsively repetitive, and thus habit forming in its audience. The mindlessly cyclical nature of this determinism points to the spirit of sacrifice necessary to ensure the survival of democratic capitalism, a disease within its utopian longings necessary to insure the endurance of social *cum* psychic health. Hope and happiness mask the trauma of collaboration: the fact that everyone can be equal, though some more equal than others. By insisting upon and then exceeding its own social order, Berkeley's number conveys something darker about democracy. Our love for our neighbours makes us cohere as social entities, but it also allows us to take from others as a way of disavowing what we lack in ourselves – and to feel good about this in the process. Which takes us back to Adam Smith: the fact that we can only *imagine* the suffering of others is a fortunate fall, a *failure* of sympathy that also accrues to the benefit of one person's fantasy over the other's. The myth of hopeful collaboration masks the less savoury fact of human nature: we get along by thriving on the misfortunes of others, psychic survival of the socially fittest.

Closing Credits

Berkeley's lesson proved to be the exception rather than the rule, at least with mass audiences. If his vision seems to evoke the dangers of political commitment and its faith in the illusion of communal betterment, such a critique wasn't bound to survive the headier optimism and patriotism that got America out of the Depression, into WWII, and on top of the world after that, an idealism epitomized by MGM's hegemony in Hollywood during that time. It is no small irony that film musicals passed out of favour towards the end of the 1950s, not just because the studio system was in decline or because society had grown too savvy for their clunky idealism, but perhaps because they had effectively indoctrinated the masses with their obsession for and with happiness, a habituation partly taken up by the medium that challenged the studios' demise: television. It would be difficult to prove an immediate link, but the eventual outcome is hard to dispute. The cover story of a recent issue of *Harper's* (September 2010) is titled "The War on Unhappiness: Goodbye Freud, Hello Positive Thinking," by Gary Greenberg, practicing psychotherapist, depression patient, and author of *Manufacturing Depression: The Secret History of a Disease* (2010). The article was written after Greenberg attended the Evolution of Psychotherapy Conference at the Anaheim Convention Centre. Taking the conference's temperature, Greenberg delivers his diagnosis: psychoanalysis has been a colossal failure, Freud is dead, and psychotherapy needs to mourn the loss and move on.[12] At the turn to the twentieth century, the story goes, Freud foisted upon civilization the analysis of its discontents: the inscrutable and intractable nature of the human mind and the individual's unavoidable psychosexual evolution. Sailing with Jung into New York Harbour in 1909 en route to Clark University, where both had been invited to speak, Freud refers to their visit as bringing the plague to America. Not surprisingly, his idea that humanity needed to settle for ordinary unhappiness met with a kind of implacable resistance in a country that had enshrined within its constitution the right to pursue happiness.

As Greenberg notes, in 1926 the New York Psychoanalytic Society "decree[d] that only physicians could practice psychoanalysis." The decision infuriated Freud because it "abandoned study of 'the history of civilization and sociology' for anatomy and biology, culture for science" (29). Medicine was the wrong training for the subtleties of dealing with "psychic suffering." For a man steeped in nineteenth-century scientific materialism, anxious about his own scientific respectability, and defensive about rifts within the discipline he claims to have founded, Freud's anger is ironic. In spite of his warning, psychoanalysis became especially popular in the United States in the mid-twentieth century, when various spectres haunted an otherwise triumphant post-WWII American psyche. Yet American psychoanalysis, by largely championing the ego's ability to surmount threats from both within and beyond its defences (an ego psychology that French psychoanalyst Jacques Lacan railed against), could not for long entertain living with the more inscrutable and indeterminate aspects of unconscious life. As Greenberg's article suggests, American culture avoids the leap of faith required to live with ambiguity. Patriotic optimism and faith in its Manifest Destiny help to explain this avoidance, as does a post-9/11 world of increasingly global entanglements, political uncertainty, and economic volatility. Time for decisive action rather than sustained self-reflection, one might say.

"Still," Greenberg powerfully notes, "[Freud's] notion of an unseen other – the mysterious unconscious self who bedevils our every decision, who eludes us yet must be sought – [...] courses through the white noise of our lives" (29). While the times often require social engagement and activism, one wonders if our sometimes ceaseless call to action isn't a way of avoiding a restlessness of thought that asks us to tarry with our decisions. As Freud knew all too well, the painful and often resistant introspection over past traumas produced delays, detours, and evasions, embedded in the transference between analyst and analysand, which were, precisely because they indicated a resistance to remembering, essential to clinical practice. In the later twentieth century the model has shifted towards something like cognitive behavioural therapy (CBT), which circumvents what Philip Reiff calls the "deliberate anti-efficiency" of psychoanalysis (334): "Identify and repair the glitches in our operating system – *dysfunctional thoughts* that arise automatically from our unduly negative *core beliefs* – and we will find no adversity we cannot meet with resilience. We will be programmed for success" (Greenberg 31). Put another way, whereas CBT takes the illusions of sympathy for real, and thus avoids the costly, protracted time of psychoanalysis, Freud understands the sympathy of theatre as a performance playing out the unavoidable complexities of human nature and human relations. To use one's illusions about others without imagining one should master either of them was especially key to a Jew forced to flee Vienna in 1938. If illusions were an unavoidable fact of culture, one needed to question how to proceed with them.[13]

Greenberg goes on to note that the political and ideological significance of CBT has not been wasted on its heirs, like Martin Seligman, inventor of positive psychology, who writes the individual desire for happiness large as a capacity for "human flourishing" (cited in

Greenberg 32): cultures flourish because they fit their individuals for success. In the 1960s Seligman conducted experiments that subjected dogs to electric shocks, many of whom "simply whined and curled up in a ball" after "the first jolt." Applied to humans, this "learned helplessness" was a key cause of depression: learn to identify and avoid the sources of trauma and one could be a happier person. Most recently, the American military (to the tune of $10–$15 billion annually) has deployed positive psychology "'to create an Army that is just as psychologically fit as it is physically fit,'" in the words of an American defence official. Or more to the point, Greenberg adds, "soldiers who learn optimism will heal faster when they are wounded on the battlefield" (34). In a rather ironic twist on the orientalist stereotype of the threat posed to Christian civilization by insensate Muslim hordes steeled by opium, Seligman offers this: a happy army is an invincible army. If biographer Ernest Jones noted that Freud's grudge was against America itself, Greenberg wonders otherwise: "[Jones] might have deduced that a country dedicated in its infancy to the pursuit of happiness would grow up to make it a compulsion" (35). One is reminded of the mutually beneficial relationship Hollywood formed with the war machine during WWII, which played no small part in sustaining morale, at the very least. Marking the uncanny connection between happiness and torture, Slavoj Žižek goes further: happiness has become our "supreme duty," our new "biomorality" (44, 45).[14] Žižek hastens to add, "This is *not true* of psychoanalysis" (45), which is bent on demystifying such illusions. However, we refuse to get on board with happiness at our and the state's peril. The earlier reference to opium proves equally prescient. If eighteenth-century moral philosophy and political economy produced Jeremy Bentham's "felicific calculus" (McMahon 213), which found solutions in John Stuart Mill's utilitarianism or in psychiatry as institution, if not as cure, a further eventuality has been the spectacular growth of pharmacology and the pharmaceutical industry, which bypasses thought altogether by putting good feelings directly into the population's veins.

Early on I alluded to the sceptical struggle of faith that comes with hope. Perhaps in the face of an exploding global population confronted by increasingly complex social, political, environmental, and economic issues, scepticism has become our least sustainable intellectual resource. Time to stop wasting time tarrying with the chimeras of speculative thought, and get on with the real business of solving problems. But I'm reminded one last time of Greenberg's article: "the single factor that makes a difference in outcome [in psychotherapeutic practice] is faith: the patient must believe in the therapist, and the therapist must believe in his orientation. For therapy to work, both parties must have faith, sometimes against all reason, that their expedition will succeed" (29). This isn't blind faith but a commitment that one must work through the psychic and social complexities that entail any process of improvement. Belief in the goal of improvement (which *would* suggest blind faith in the outcome) is rather beside the point. As moral management sought to diagnose and cure psychopathology, it came up against something else: what Christopher Bollas calls the "epistemophilic demand" of a "noumenal transference" (*Mystery* 9–10) in which, by calling upon others to answer to our unhappiness, "the illusion of understanding breaks down" (*Being* 8), and we confront the "ultimate realization that communication recognize[s] the impossibility of itself" (13). Shouldering the burden of this mystery evokes another scene of sympathy that Deborah Britzman calls "difficult education." Britzman argues that "education makes us nervous, and psychoanalysis touches upon raw nerves," for both remind us that learning is never about the mere acquisition of knowledge (3). The human inability and unwillingness to take things in creates an anxious lack of comprehension that assaults the ego's fragility. Paraphrasing André Green, Britzman writes:

> our history of learning [is] a condensation of many fragments of events, even as shards of experience that return when least expected. This leads [Green] to describe history for the psyche through its absences and gaps and as drawing into its narrative what has happened, what we wish had happened, what happened to others but not to us, what happened but cannot be imagined, and what did not happen at all. Such is the creative expression of what we do with the meeting of phantasy and reality. Here and there, history is the return of affect: pining, disappointment, envy, and wish. It is also the narration of and resistance to these shadowy experiences. And it is precisely with this strange and estranging mixture that the otherness of our education archive returns, now as psychoanalytic inquiry. (3)

There is always a lag between knowledge and perception, learning and its labours. This is perhaps what Greenberg means by the "white noise" that nags at our certain beliefs. Continually attending to this "white noise" is rather arduous. Britzman continues: "After the experience of education, there is still the problem of education," which rehearses a "drama that stages the play between reality and phantasy and a question that leaves its trace in something interminable about our desire to know and to be known" (16, 9).

Film musicals, expressing psychiatry's spirit of well-being, would stage "the play between reality and phantasy" as a spectacle that harmonizes the white noise into melody as a celebration of the capacity for things to get better. The cultural phenomena addressed in this chapter suggest both the aspirations and perils of this utopian project. Film musical entertainment offers the imagination a far more complex experience than mere diversion, a different form of public intellectualism.[15] Yet precisely by staging this education *as* entertainment, film musicals beg the question of the extent to which all education risks its own illusions. One final irony is the most chilling of all: the right to happiness we have manufactured for ourselves might be our acceptance of a failure to deal with the complexities of real problems under the guise *of* dealing with them – the inevitable outcome of Ayn Rand's call to an utterly narcissistic capacity for self-development, or more recently Sarah Palin's blind subscription to the myth of improvement. If hope is film musicals' most protean and volatile resource, perhaps the most portable commodity this hope has produced is not the capacity for human flourishing but failure itself as insurance against the threat of deep thought. Success at any cost: the right to fail – spectacularly.

NOTES

I thank the Social Sciences and Humanities Research Council of Canada and the Faculty of Arts at the University of Western Ontario for their financial support of research and travel associated with the writing of this essay. I would like to thank audiences at Memorial University, Concordia University, the Department of English Language and Literature and MA Program in Popular Culture at Brock University, and the Centre for the Study of Theory and Criticism at Western University, all of whom heard versions or parts of this chapter and offered generous and constructive feedback. Finally, I thank my coeditor Jason Haslam for his generous response and encouragement.

1 Garland was signed to MGM in 1935 at the age of thirteen, though her first stage appearance was in Vaudeville at the age of two. By the time Garland started working on *Summer Stock* she was only twenty-eight years old, but fifteen years of nonstop work in MGM's studio system had produced a

number of emotional and professional problems that left her addicted to drugs prescribed by studio doctors to keep her productive and saw her institutionalized at least twice in her remaining few years on the MGM lot. The two-month hiatus from shooting *Summer Stock* was another attempt to get her back into shape for work, with Louis B. Mayer's promise of a long vacation once the film wrapped. The vacation she was given was rather more terminal.

2 In a similar vein, Vivavsan Soni argues that "the eighteenth century's very obsession with happiness culminates in the political obsolescence of the idea," so that happiness is "better understood as the pathological symptom of an insoluble problem than as evidence of a viable political concern" (3, 4).

3 Here I invoke in psychiatric historiography the profound influence of Foucault's *Madness and Civilization* (1965), an abridged form of the original French publication, *Folie et Deraison: Histoire de la Folie a L'Age Classique* (1964), the whole of which has since been translated as *History of Madness* (2006). "The Great Confinement" is, of course, Foucault's term for the epistemological and sociopolitical imperative, beginning in the seventeenth century and the rise of the Enlightenment, to diagnose, classify, and thus contain insanity as a (perceived) threat to social order. For my present purposes I set aside the anti-psychiatry debates that ensued in the wake of Foucault's text, but do intend the phrase "the Great Confinement" to evoke his critique of biopolitics.

4 The idea of confinement goes back to Battie, who in Section X of his *Treatise*, "The Regimen and Cure of Madness," advocates that madness "requires the patient's being removed from all objects that act forcibly upon the nerves, and excite too lively a perception of things, more especially from such objects as are the known causes of his disorder" (68).

5 Indeed, one of Soni's key points is that the Declaration of Independence "muffles its own call for a politics of happiness" (460), which is in turn "deliberately omitted from the Constitution" (20), and that eighteenth-century moral and political philosophy, recognizing the impossibility of such a politics, instead "finds a home only in the realm of the family and marriage," which comes to define a "sentimentalized conception of happiness" in the nineteenth century and beyond (20–1). Soni's essential point is that the politics of happiness, emerging with such utopian urgency in eighteenth-century thought, immediately turns into a melancholic endeavour.

6 For the discursive and cultural roles of sympathy and sentiment in driving Manifest Destiny and building American national identity, see Barnes, Burgett, Burstein, or Hendler. Each is informed by the tutelary spirit of

Sacvan Bercovitch's notion of an American Jeremiad rooted in the astringent spirituality of early American Puritan culture as it translates into a later evangelical political fervour.

7 I thank Jason Haslam for pointing out the rather ironic connection between Rush's innovations. Recall as well that Jeremy Bentham, mathematician of the "felicific calculus" of utilitarianism (which I mention later) and co-pioneer in prison and other institutional reforms, was also social architect of the panopticon, a sort of penitentiary theatre in the round choreographing the observation of criminal behaviour, but an invention, as Haslam reminded me recently via e-mail, that Bentham conceived as a mobile social form adaptable to a variety of institutional settings from madhouses, to prisons, to schools. The panopticon might be one of the objects of Fosse's social satire in "Cell Block Tango," a number from his 1975 *Chicago*, filmed in 2002 by Rob Marshall.

8 For a fascinating account of this (re)producibility of the Deleuzian economy of film musical experience, its tension between difference and repetition, see Herzog.

9 This is Frederic Jameson's point about utopia (xi–xvi).

10 As Brock says to Sawyer, "Now go out there and be so swell you'll make me hate you." As Marsh says just before Sawyer goes on, explaining to her that the lives of 200 people depend on her not screwing up, "You're going out there a youngster, but you've *got* to come back a star!"

11 In my reading of Lubitsch's Paramount films I veer significantly from that of Andrea Most's essay in this volume.

12 The hilarious caricature on the cover of *Harper's* depicts a beefy security guard wearing a tight t-shirt evicting Freud, whose nametag reads "Hello, my name is Sigmund," from the conference.

13 I pause here to mention Simcha Jacobivici's 1997 documentary, *Hollywoodism: Jews, Movies, and the American Dream*. Jacobivici's point, based on Neal Gabler's 1989 book, *An Empire of Their Own: How the Jews Invented Hollywood*, is that, moving away from persecution (or worse) in Europe and elsewhere, those Jewish emigrants to America who migrated to California (specifically the five main studio heads) invented the utopian no-space of Hollywood as a way of reinventing for themselves a sense of home they never possessed. They did so by setting aside their ethnic and cultural inheritance in order to assimilate themselves to their adopted home – yet precisely by creating the very myths that made this home seem "homegrown." The ur-expression of this longing is, of course, "Over the Rainbow." Nonetheless, one can read in these films' subtexts the profound dislocation and yearning of the immigrant experience. One of

the more telling symptoms of this act of cultural (re)invention is the fact that, despite its considerable (some might say unprecedented) cultural clout, mainstream Hollywood was slow in tackling the Holocaust.

14 Speaking of the new discipline of "happiness studies," specifically its psychological as opposed to sociological branch, which combines cognitive science research and New Age wisdom, Žižek writes: "[This] combination of cognitive science and Buddhism [...] is here given an ethical twist: what is offered in the guise of scientific research is a new morality that one is tempted to call *biomorality* – the true counterpart to today's biopolitics. And indeed, was it not the Dalai Lama himself who wrote: 'The purpose of life is to be happy'" (45).

15 I set aside here Lauren Berlant's related notion of "cruel optimism," the "condition of maintaining an attachment to a problematic object *in advance* of its loss" (94). This is different from melancholia, "which is enacted in the subject's desire to temporize an experience of the loss of an object or scene with which she has identified her ego continuity." In melancholia, the subject doesn't know that loss has occurred and so encrypts loss itself as, well, the lost object that she imagines she *hasn't* lost. "Cruel optimism" is a condition past mourning, as it were, in which the subject persists by consciously, but also paradoxically and ironically, embracing loss as a stay against getting on with dealing with loss. This isn't so much denial as living *with* loss that indicates a survival in which people "choose to ride the wave of the system of attachment they are used to, to syncopate with it, or to be held in a relation of reciprocity, reconciliation, or resignation that does not mean defeat by it" (97). "Cruel optimism" is perhaps most aptly and devastatingly staged in a Lars von Trier's 2000 indictment of the film musical utopianism, *Dancer in the Dark*, beyond my present discussion.

WORKS CITED

Ball, Karyn. "A Democracy Is Being Beaten." *English Studies in Canada* 32.1 (2007): 45–76. Print. http://dx.doi.org/10.1353/esc.2007.0063.

Barnes, Elizabeth. *State of Sympathy: Seduction and Democracy in the American Novel*. New York: Columbia UP, 1997. Print. http://dx.doi.org/10.2307/3201339.

Battie, William. *A Treatise on Madness*. London: [printed for J. Whiston and B. White], 1758. Print.

Bercovitch, Sacvan. *The American Jeremiad*. Madison: U of Wisconsin P, 1978. Print.

Berlant, Lauren. "Cruel Optimism." *The Affect Theory Reader*. Ed. Melissa Gregg and Gregory J. Seigworth. Durham, NC: Duke UP, 2010. 93–117. Print.

Bollas, Christopher. *Being a Character: Psychoanalysis and Self Experience*. New York: Hill and Wang, 1992. Print.

Bollas, Christopher. *The Mystery of Things*. London: Routledge, 1999. Print. http://dx.doi.org/10.4324/9780203361009.

Burgett, Bruce. *Sentimental Bodies: Sex, Gender, and Citizenship in the Early Republic*. Princeton: Princeton UP, 1998. Print.

Burstein, Andrew. *Sentimental Democracy: The Evolution of America's Romantic Self-Image*. New York: Hill & Wang, 1999. Print. http://dx.doi.org/10.2307/366810.

Britzman, Deborah. *After-Education: Anna Freud, Melanie Klein, and Psychoanalytic Histories of Learning*. Albany: SUNY P, 2003. Print.

Chicago. By Bob Fosse. Dir. Bob Fosse. 46th Street Theatre, New York. 3 June 1975. Performance.

Chicago. Dir. Rob Marshall. Miramax, 2002. Film.

Coleridge, Samuel Taylor. *The Collected Notebooks of Samuel Taylor Coleridge*. Ed. Kathleen Coburn and Merton Christensen. 4 vols. New York: Bollingen Series: Pantheon Books, 1957–1990. Print.

Dancer in the Dark. Dir. Lars von Trier. Zentropa Entertainment et al., 2000. Film.

Dyer, Richard. *Only Entertainment*. 2nd ed. New York: Routledge, 2002. 19–34. Print.

Forty-Second Street. Dir. Lloyd Bacon. Warner Brothers, 1933. Film.

Gabler, Neal. *An Empire of Their Own: How the Jews Invented Hollywood*. New York: Anchor, 1989. Print.

Garofalo, Daniela. *Manly Leaders in Nineteenth-Century British Literature*. Albany: SUNY P, 2007. Print.

Gold Diggers of 1935. Dir. Busby Berkeley. Warner Brothers, 1935. Film.

Greenberg, Gary. "The War on Unhappiness: Goodbye Freud, Hello Positive Thinking." *Harper's Magazine* 321.1924 (September 2010): 27–35. Print.

Haslam, John. *Observations on Madness and Melancholy*. 2nd ed. London, 1809. Print.

Hendler, Glenn. *Public Sentiments: Structures of Feeling in Nineteenth-Century American Literature*. Chapel Hill: U of North Carolina P, 2002. Print.

Herzog, Amy. *Dreams of Difference, Songs of the Same: The Musical Moment in Film*. Minneapolis: U of Minnesota P, 2010. Print.

Hill, George Nesse. *An Essay on the Prevention and Cure of Insanity; with observations on the rules for the detection of pretenders to madness*. London: Longman, Hurst, Rees, Orme & Brown, 1814. Print.

Hollywoodism: Jews, Movies, and the American Dream. Dir. Simcha Jacobovici. Paradox, 1998. DVD.

Jameson, Frederic. *Archaeologies of the Future: The Desire Called Utopia and Other Science Fictions*. New York: Verso, 2005. Print.

Marshall, David. *The Surprising Effects of Sympathy: Marivau, Diderot, Rousseau, and Mary Shelley*. Chicago: U of Chicago P, 1988. Print.

McMahon, Darrin M. *Happiness: A History*. 1st ed. New York: Atlantic Monthly P, 2006. Print.

Morin, Edgar. *The Cinema; or, The Imaginary Man*. Trans. Lorraine Mortimer. Minneapolis: U of Minnesota P, 2005. Print.

Mouffe, Chantal. *Radical Democracy*. London: Verso, 2000. Print.

Reid, Thomas. *Essays on the Intellectual Powers of Man. The Works of Thomas Reid*. 8th ed. Vol. 1. Ed. William Hamilton. Edinburgh: James Thin, 1895. Print.

Reiff, Phillip. *Freud: The Mind of the Moralist*. Chicago: U of Chicago P, 1979. Print.

Scull, Andrew. "Psychiatry and Social Control in the Nineteenth and Twentieth Centuries." *History of Psychiatry* 2.6 (1991): 149–69. Print. http://dx.doi.org/10.1177/0957154X9100200603.

Shorter, Edward. *A History of Psychiatry: From the Era of the Asylum to the Age of Prozac*. New York: Wiley, 1997. Print.

Soni, Vivavsan. *Mourning Happiness: Narrative and the Politics of Modernity*. Ithaca: Cornell UP, 2010. Print.

Summer Stock. Dir. Charles Walters. Metro-Goldwyn-Mayer, 1950. Film.

Thompson, Kristin. "The Concept of Cinematic Excess." *Film Theory and Criticism: Introductory Readings*. 5th ed. Ed. Leo Braudy and Marshall Cohen. New York: Oxford UP, 1999. 487–98. Print.

Trotter, Thomas. *A View of the Nervous Temperament*. London: Longman, 1807. Rpt.: New York: Arno, 1976. Print.

Žižek, Slavoj. *In Defense of Lost Causes*. New York: Verso, 2008. Print.

7 To Be (Or Not To Be): Ernst Lubitsch's Irrepressible Theatrical Liberalism

ANDREA MOST

You've gotta have hope!
Mustn't sit around and mope.
Nothin's half as bad as it may appear;
Wait'll next year and hope.

When your luck is battin' zero,
Get your chin up off the floor.
Mister you can be a hero;
You can open any door,
There's nothin' to it but to do it.

Jerry Ross, "Heart"[1]

I

American culture, since its inception, has been deeply committed to a politics of hope, dreams, and aspirations. Nowhere was this hope more passionately and consistently expressed than in the Broadway musicals and Hollywood film comedies of the early and mid-twentieth century (the complicated hopes of the former being the subject of this volume's previous chapter, by Joel Faflak). Jerry Ross's paean to hope, above, and his connection of hope with action ("there's nothin' to it but to do it") is typical of the sentiments of countless songs and scripts of the time. American liberalism is, at its foundations, an expression of the hope that individual freedom and democratic government will lead to happiness and justice for all. This culture of hope is renowned for its inspirational pull – the hope of greater freedom, justice, and prosperity inspired millions of immigrants to leave their homes around the world and to make a new start in America. In the early twentieth century, this ethos of hope became the basis for a new form of popular culture, one which combined the utopian aspects of romantic comedy with a passionate embrace of the theatre, theatricality, and above all, *acting*, as the most moral path to creating a self and imagining a community. This kind of popular culture, which I call theatrical liberalism, was largely created by first- and second-generation Jewish immigrants, who combined Judaic values and practices with aspects of Protestant Enlightenment liberalism in a remarkably successful set of movies and plays which quickly achieved a central role in American culture, reinventing definitions of American identity for the twentieth century.[2]

Americans have long wrestled with questions about where the "truth" of a self lies. For most Protestants, while action in the world has often been seen as a sign of good internal character, *internal*, private faith is the driving force that animates action (rather than the other way around); faith, and the kinds of character traits that allow for and support Christian faith, determine one's chances of salvation and move one to act morally in the world. This Protestant separation of action in the world from private faith deeply influenced early liberal thinkers and helped to shape American attitudes about the separation of church and state. For John Locke, for example, religion was largely a matter of faith, and faith is a private, not a state, matter. Separating church from civil government in this way allowed Locke to argue for civil rights not only for Catholics and Protestants, but also for Jews, because a Jew's faith was not – in his liberal philosophy – the concern of the civil sphere (Locke 240). When Jewish thinkers began to engage with liberal ideas, they revealed the ways in which Protestant Enlightenment notions of religious toleration imperfectly fit the lives Jews actually lived. Eighteenth-century Jewish philosopher Moses Mendelssohn responded to Locke by exploring the tension in Judaism between action and faith. In *Jerusalem* (1783), he wrote: "Among all the prescriptions and ordinances of the Mosaic law, there is not a single one which says: *You shall believe or not believe*. They all say: *You shall do or not do* [...] Nowhere does it say: *Believe, O Israel, and you will be blessed; do not doubt, O Israel, or this or that punishment will befall you*" (100). Mendelssohn acknowledges that faith is required for one to accept the obligations of a Jewish life, but points out that professions of faith are not required in and of themselves. He points to one of the key defining moments for Judaism when Moses, after receiving the Ten Commandments on

Mt. Sinai, recited them aloud to the assembled Israelites at the foot of the mountain. The people then agreed to the terms of the covenant with God, saying, "na'aseh v'nishma," the exact Hebrew translation of which is "we will do and we will hear" (Exodus 24:7). This phrase has been the source of centuries of discussion amongst Jews because of the apparently reversed order of the verbs. Shouldn't we hear first and do afterwards? On the contrary, argue Jewish thinkers across the ages. *Na'aseh v'nishma,* we will do and we will hear, argues for the importance of following laws, of acting, of living a life according to Jewish law, *in order to* learn or "hear" why, in order to develop greater understanding of the divine, and in order to bring the world closer to redemption.[3]

Freedom of religion as inscribed in the American Constitution is generally interpreted in Protestant terms as *freedom of conscience,* the freedom to believe whatever you'd like.[4] For those whose religion focusses on deeds and actions in the world, this definition of religious freedom has led to some challenging quandaries. Up until the modern period, to be a Jew was not primarily to profess a particular set of beliefs, but to act Jewishly in everything one did: from the foods one ate; to the clothes one wore; to the ways in which one interacted with other members of the community; to the role one took in caring for one's house, crops, livestock, or the earth itself. Thousands of Jewish immigrants arrived on America's shores with this kind of direct, lived experience of a traditional society deeply concerned with the ethical and spiritual implications of everyday behaviour. Accustomed to a culture that asserted the primacy of ritual and deed over declarations of faith, these immigrants confronted in early twentieth-century America the oppositional force (and seductive energy) of a liberal political and social model that granted them freedom of belief and freedom of speech, but not necessarily the cultural freedom to *act* in accordance with those beliefs. For the most part, no civil law in America circumscribed the practice of Jewish rituals like *kashrut,* Sabbath observance, or the covering of heads. But an apparently secular but deeply Protestant cultural and social worldview shaped all of the contours of modern American life, from the calendar, to the proper place and time for religious practice, to the forms and content of public education, to attitudes towards social life, eating, fashion, relations between the sexes and between parents and children. This transparent overlay of Christian social practice in America made it almost impossible for Jews to become fully accepted Americans without giving up outward signs of religious difference. Yet while most American Jewish writers and thinkers of this generation departed from traditional Jewish practice, even the most assimilated of them resisted a worldview that privileged intention over action. Rather, Jewish writers and performers shaped a new kind of American public sphere, one which relocated the Jewish spiritual obligation to *act* in the world from an Old World religious context to a legitimately *American* arena, the world of popular entertainment.

In new entertainment genres of the early twentieth century – vaudeville routines, Tin Pan Alley songs, backstage musicals, and fast-talking Hollywood comedies – Jewish writers, directors, producers, and performers responded to their encounter with Protestant liberalism by developing a secular form of Judaism – theatrical liberalism. This secular Judaism was expressed in the most popular forms of entertainment of the early twentieth century and appealed broadly to the American public. It rarely overtly expressed its debts to Judaism and Jewish culture, but was nonetheless distinctive in its values and worldview. Four key features distinguish works of theatrical liberalism from other works of American popular culture. First, these works resist traditional Protestant suspicion of the theatre, instead reconstructing the theatre as a sacred space, a venue for religious expression and the performance of acts of devotion, thereby turning theatricality into a respectable American cultural mode. The works of theatrical liberalism are almost all about the theatre or about the performance of identity. Most contain meta-theatrical elements, and many are part of a new genre invented to express the worldview of theatrical liberalism – the backstage musical (or backstage play) which combines the conventions of romantic comedy with the drama of putting on a show and offers the ideal structure in which to consider basic liberal and Judaic questions about individual choice, self-fashioning, and communal obligation. Second, in celebrating theatricality, these plays and films privilege a particularly Jewish attitude towards action and acting in the world, stressing the external over the internal, public over private. Third, these works strenuously resist essentialized identity categories, promoting a particular kind of individual freedom based on self-fashioning. Theatrical liberalism guaranteed secular Jews the freedom to perform the self, a freedom particularly cherished by a people so often denied the right to self-definition, whether by Christian dogma or racial science. And fourth, these works circumscribe individual freedom according to a set of incontrovertible obligations to the theatrical community. In these plays and movies, there is a palpable tension between the liberal rhetoric of rights and the Judaic rhetoric of obligation (*mitzvot*) and the moral weight of these stories turns on the fulfilling of theatrical obligations, even at the expense of individual rights. And while these shows embrace the commercial demands of the free market – indeed their success is most often judged on the basis of their popularity – when theatrical obligations come into conflict with the logic of the marketplace, the obligations take priority. "The show must go on" became the new dogma of the theatrical liberal.

II

Among the most influential practitioners of theatrical liberalism in the first half of the twentieth century was German-Jewish director Ernst Lubitsch, an inventor and master of the Hollywood "screwball" comedy. Lubitsch believed deeply in external action – acting – as the only reliable source of truth in judging individuals. His early comedies offer a primer on an ethics of action that Lubitsch celebrated throughout his long career. As we shall see, his later comedy *To Be or Not to Be* (1942), produced on the eve of America's entry into World War II, pushes this ethics even further, combining his characteristic theatrical flair with an unshakeable optimism in the powers of theatricality to resist evil and to guarantee freedom. Born the son of a Jewish tailor, Lubitsch began a career on the stage in his teens, receiving his early theatrical training in Max Reinhardt's Deutsches Theater. He worked as an actor in early silent films, often playing Jewish comic stereotypes. The silent films he directed were enormously successful in Germany, and silent screen star Mary Pickford convinced him to emigrate to America in the 1920s, where he achieved even more remarkable success in Hollywood, directing a steady stream of hits for nearly twenty years.[5] Lubitsch found his niche in the emerging Hollywood musical, and became famous for his sophisticated and stylish films. Lubitsch worked with a string of talented writers, nearly all of them Jewish, and together they created an alternate universe in which a particular mode of skilful and self-conscious performance grounds the characters in a moral system that turns a blind eye to sexual impropriety and "minor" breaches of law like stealing or drinking in public, but insists on absolute fidelity to the laws of the stage.[6] Lubitsch was deeply invested in theatre and artifice, but his films tended to explore not actors per se, but the impact which acting, and the particular theatrical skills actors practice, can have in the social world of the street, the drawing room, and the bedroom. Even in the one film that takes a company of actors as its central characters – *To*

Be or Not to Be – the bulk of the story focusses on what happens when those actors make use of their talents in a "real world" situation, when acting is taken as not just an artistic pursuit, but a way of life. Thriving in the new genre of the screwball comedy, Lubitsch produced comedies almost exclusively, and the comedy of manners became his greatest success, both critically and at the box office. Made for adults, characterized by skilful implication and elegant sexual wit, these films embodied the cynical and urbane style that became known as the "Lubitsch touch." Lubitsch's style was distinctive, and was considered "European" or "cosmopolitan" because of his disregard for American sexual mores. But the "Lubitsch touch" is better understood in terms of theatrical liberalism – as a passionate embrace of acting as the most interesting, most effective, and most ethical way to construct a self.

This embrace of action as an ethical position has deep Jewish roots and became particularly important to American Jewish thinkers of the early and mid-twentieth century. Mordecai Kaplan, the founder of the Reconstructionist Movement in Judaism, famously preached that Judaism is "what Jews do," and developed an entire theory of Judaism as a civilization on this basis. Abraham Joshua Heschel, one of the most important American Jewish theologians of the twentieth century, saw practice and action as the key to Jewish theology: "A good person is not he who does the right thing," Heschel wrote in his magnum opus, *God in Search of Man,* "but he who is in the habit of doing the right thing" (345). Heschel argued for the importance of *acting* Jewishly, even if one doesn't understand exactly why or doesn't feel spiritually moved to do so: "Judaism insists upon the deed and hopes for the intention" (403). Action is the first step to spiritual illumination, not the last. Inverting a famous line of Proverbs, Heschel insists "The way to pure intention is paved with good deeds." From doing will eventually come understanding: "It is the act that teaches us the meaning of the act" (404). Acting on the stage and acting Jewishly clearly have many affinities, and this common ground provided a space for secularizing Jews to maintain a familiar stance towards everyday behaviour while simultaneously dispensing with the overtly religious rituals that formed obstacles to acculturation to the American way of life.

In the self-consciously theatrical world of many early twentieth-century plays and films, a good performance was the measure of a good actor. What an actor did on the stage is what mattered; what an actor believed – who an actor *really was* – was of little interest. In Jewish-authored plays, films, and novels of the early twentieth century, *acting* becomes a central moral and dramatic subject. But not any kind of acting – this is self-conscious and theatrical acting. There is a strong Jewish tradition of acting with deep self-consciousness: centuries of debates on the how, what, where, when, and why of doing particular actions have kept Jews always aware that the actions they perform are not spontaneous expressions of personal faith (although these actions may inspire this sort of passion) but rather carefully rehearsed rituals laden with historic and symbolic significance. Just as Heschel insists that "we do not have faith because of deeds; we may attain faith through sacred deeds" (282), the plays and films of theatrical liberalism argue for the power of acting to shape belief and feeling.

Ernst Lubitsch is unapologetic in his celebration of all types of acting in *The Love Parade* (1929), his first Paramount musical. The film adeptly ignores American moral concerns about artifice and theatricality, asserting instead, simply and directly, the effectiveness of acting both as the only moral way to be in the world and as the means of inspiring emotional or spiritual transformation. The film features Maurice Chevalier, a well-known French entertainer, as Count Renard, recently returned to his native Sylvania from Paris under a cloud of scandal. As he waits for an interview with the queen (played by Jeannette MacDonald) to determine his fate, he asks the queen's guardsman how he should act: "Should I be humble, proud, apologetic?" The guard replies that he should say as little as possible because the guard "do[es]n't think [Renard's] French accent will please her majesty." Making a joke of the fact that Chevalier is playing a "Sylvanian" with a thick French accent, the dialogue both draws attention to the fact that Chevalier is acting and dismisses this lack of realism as a serious concern. He asks the guard (in barely understandable English), "Is it still very notice-able?" "No," the guard replies (in clear American English). "It's very noticeable [...] How did you acquire it?" Chevalier/Renard explains that once in Paris he had a bad cold and when he went to the doctor to cure it, he encountered a beautiful woman. He ended up losing the cold but gaining a "terrific French accent."

The queen of Sylvania (MacDonald) is looking for a husband, but no man of position will accept the limited role of prince/consort. Count Renard decides to marry the queen to avoid being thrown in jail. He doesn't quite realize what he is getting into, and quickly becomes bored and angry with his subordinate position. The couple fights, and Renard refuses to appear at the opera with the queen. Interestingly, his refusal to appear is based not on the expected reason – that he recoils from the falsity of pretending to be happy when he isn't – but rather because he is angry and wants to assert his agency in the only way available to him. The queen goes to the opera alone, but Renard ultimately shows up to support her ("because he once loved her"). It turns out that he is a better actor than she is, and the crowds are delighted by the appearance of this loving husband. The film fully supports the performance, believing, along with the queen, Renard, and the courtiers, that putting on a good performance for the crowd is a necessary part of public life. Of course, Renard's triumphant performance leads to a reconciliation between the two, the queen acknowledges his acting skills, and they end up in love again by the end.

Acting also leads to love in another early Lubitsch musical, *The Smiling Lieutenant* (1931). In a complex series of plot twists, the lieutenant Niki (Chevalier) is forced to marry an innocent and prudish princess whom he doesn't love (Miriam Hopkins), thereby giving up the sexy musician Franzi (Claudette Colbert) whom he does. Ultimately, Franzi realizes she will never get Niki back, and she selflessly decides to ensure Niki's and the princess's happiness by teaching the princess how to seduce Niki. Franzi's tutorial in proper dress, behaviour, voice, and gesture is enormously successful. Convinced by the princess's seductive acting, Niki falls for his wife and they live happily ever after.

Lubitsch's most brilliant collaborative effort – with Samson Raphaelson, who also wrote the immensely popular Jewish immigrant melodrama *The Jazz Singer* (1927) – was *Trouble in Paradise* (1932), a film that offers an elegant and passionate argument for acting as a higher truth within a most unlikely setting – the shady world of con games and bank robberies. Focussing on the love and career of two con artists, the film demonstrates the seductive power of brilliant acting, and critiques those who extol sincerity but ultimately behave hypocritically. The film opens in Venice, with a "Baron" (Herbert Marshall) and a "Countess" (Miriam Hopkins) at dinner. She convincingly performs the role of an aristocratic lady, but as the scene progresses, it becomes clear that neither the baron nor the countess are what they seem to be. The countess receives a phone call from a friend whom she pretends is another aristocrat, but when the film cuts to the person at the other end of the phone line, we see the "Countess's" down and out roommate. A robbery is discovered in the hotel and the countess informs the baron she knows about his illegal activities, that he has stolen the missing wallet from the room down the hall. "Baron," she says, "you are a crook. You robbed the gentleman in 253-5-7-and-9. [Pause.] May

I have the salt?" The baron tells her in return that she is a thief, that she has snatched the stolen money from him. The accusations escalate, becoming increasingly incredible. In the course of their brief encounter, it turns out he has taken her brooch ("one very good stone"), she has taken his watch ("it was five minutes slow but I regulated it for you"), and when he finally reveals that he has stolen her garter without her suspecting it, she leaps on him, shouting "Darling! Tell me all about yourself. Who are you?"

Thus begins a passionate and resilient love affair. They love one another not for their honesty or sincerity, but for their ability to trick, deceive, and con. And yet this love is, within the ethical parameters of the world of the film, true love. At the end, after a madcap adventure in which they attempt to con a fabulously wealthy and beautiful heiress, neither is punished for their illegal activities. On the contrary, they are rewarded with a happy ending. The only person ultimately punished is the heiress's banker, who is revealed to have been stealing from her for years. The difference between them? The banker insists on his sincerity and constancy ("I have enjoyed the confidence of this family for more than forty years"). His protestations of virtue make him a hypocrite. Gaston and Lily live in another moral universe, one in which acting, becoming someone else, is a celebrated life skill. Their crimes are inconsequential as they only steal from very rich people who don't suffer from their losses. The film therefore is not promoting stealing and deception, but rather arguing for acting as a higher truth. The self-conscious performance of the crooks leads not only to true love, but to a kind of honest passion that sincerity and confidence (which the banker professes) could never achieve. For Lubitsch, and for many other writers of popular theatre and film of the time, the truth of a person cannot reside inside the self – how can one ever know what lies inside? The truth resides in *action*; the only way to judge character is to observe what people *do*. The only way to *be* someone is to *act*.

III

Theatrical liberalism represented for Jewish writers not only a celebration of action, but also a means by which to integrate into American society, to gain the freedoms inherent in social and economic mobility, and to ensure the widest possible application of these freedoms for all Americans. In exchange for the long-sought-after rights promised by liberalism, Jews transformed Judaism from a complete way of life to a more limited kind of private religious faith that closely resembled American and Protestant ideas about religious practice. By making this shift, modernizing Jews transformed themselves into viable American citizens. But in doing so, a new quandary arose. For centuries, European Jews had married within their own communities and led lives largely separate from their Christian neighbours. Traditional Jews defined themselves as a displaced nation and God's chosen people, carrying out a sacred task until the arrival of the messiah and the long-awaited return to Jerusalem. But as Jews began to leave traditional communities, enter the public sphere of European and American culture, and adopt the dress, habits, and citizenship of mainstream Christian society, this national and religious identity was destabilized, and the question of "who is a Jew" became a pressing one both for modernizing Jews and for the Christian societies into which they were integrating. Multiple possibilities for communal self-definition arose – Zionist, socialist, Yiddish secularist, cultural humanist, assimilationist (i.e., French, German, American), and many others.[7]

Anxious about the integration of Jews and Christians in modern metropolises, and the increasing difficulty of distinguishing between assimilated Jews and non-Jews, liberal Christian societies and governments looked for ways to assimilate Jews and, at the same time, to articulate markers of Jewish difference. By the late nineteenth century, European and American Jews were popularly regarded not as a nation (since national identity conflicted with the project to incorporate Jews as citizens of the United States and other liberal democracies) but as a race. The rise of racial science in America and Europe in the mid-to-late nineteenth century reinforced a hierarchy of peoples (with, following the demarcations of the time, "white" Anglo-Saxons at the top and "black" Negroes at the bottom), and offered security to those at the "top" of the race-defined ladder made anxious by the instability of identity in liberal cosmopolitan society. The rhetoric of race played a major role in the response to Jewish immigrants in America around the turn of the century. In the heavily racialized American society of the early twentieth century, Jews were labelled Hebrews (or Semites, or sometimes Orientals), a distinct race which was situated somewhere in the middle of the racial hierarchy, not "white," but also not quite "black," and whose physical, psychological, and intellectual features were assumed to be transmitted genetically. Individual American Jews, whether or not they participated in Jewish religious or communal activities, and whether or not they self-identified as Jews, were considered to be racially marked. In a nation divided by race, racial status played a major role in the distribution of rights and privileges, and race was a central feature of discussions over immigration and citizenship policy.[8] While many Jews at first embraced racial self-definition as a mode of self-identification that asserted belonging while demanding little in the way of communal or religious obligation, with the rise of nativist immigration policies and American anti-Semitism in the 1920s and 1930s it quickly became clear that "off-white" racial designations (or indeed any labels imposed by outsiders) were dangerous for Jews and could prevent them from achieving full civil rights in America.[9] With the rise of Nazism in the early 1930s, the trap of a race-based identity became horribly apparent.

In response, American Jewish writers and artists used nonracial and anti-essentialist models of identity in order to argue forcefully against the snare of racial self-definition. In doing so, they unwittingly drew upon an eighteenth- and nineteenth-century ideal of self-formation initially embraced by German Jews eager to gain political rights. The German Enlightenment produced a new ideal for the rising middle class, a secular and aesthetic mode of self-creation through education known as *Bildung*, in which success in social and political life was awarded on the basis of merit and achievement, as opposed to noble birth. As David Sorkin has shown, Jewish emancipation in nineteenth-century Germany was deeply intertwined with this notion of *Bildung*, and Jews implicitly accepted a situation in which they would "regenerate" themselves via *Bildung* – in other words, educate themselves in Enlightenment values and discard "backward" Jewish practices in exchange for citizenship or at least a measure of civil rights. Understandably eager for emancipation, a generation of German Jews passionately embraced the principles of *Bildung*, in effect re-creating themselves as secular, highly educated, cultured members of the German middle class.[10] This embrace of *Bildung* became a defining feature of middle- and upper-class Jewish life not only in Germany, but also in other liberal republics (especially France and England) and eventually made its way to the United States, where Jews quickly became among the most avid consumers and purveyors of higher education and all forms of high culture. With the wholesale adoption of racial science and the rejection of the notion of personal self-formation, the rewards promised by *Bildung* turned out to be specious in Germany, but they remained real in the United States, where the Jewish embrace of self-formation was reinforced and encouraged by the ideals of perfection inherent in certain strains of liberal

Protestantism (especially those most famously articulated by Ralph Waldo Emerson).[11] By the mid-twentieth century, this notion of self-formation was a defining feature of Jewish success in America. In theatrical liberalism, as in Enlightenment thought, *Bildung* is a ticket to freedom: in guaranteeing the agency to *create* the self anew, theatrical liberalism gives actors the ability to escape oppression, to embrace multiplicity, and to determine one's own identity definitions in response to the challenges, threats, and seductions of modern American life

A remarkable number of American comedies created by Jews feature characters who are running for their lives. These characters escape their enemies and achieve freedom not by outrunning or outshooting their oppressors, but by transforming themselves into someone else. The ability to create and re-create a self is fundamental to the freedom of theatrical liberalism, and the late 1920s and 1930s witnessed an explosion of Jewish-created popular performance styles that celebrated changeability itself. The ethnic comedians of vaudeville, who could adopt a character with the change of a hat, a nose, a feather, or coloured face paint, were a central feature of such high-class Broadway revues of the 1920s and '30s as the *Ziegfeld Follies* and the *George White Scandals*. In a flash, Eddie Cantor transformed himself from Jewish neurasthenic to Greek cook, to black errand boy, to Indian chief and back again in the play and film *Whoopee* (1928). Fannie Brice was well known for her ability to do "imitations." Willie Howard, in the smash hit Gershwin stage musical *Girl Crazy* (1930), miraculously transformed himself from Jewish taxi driver, to a woman, to a variety of famous performers (including, among others, Maurice Chevalier) to a Western sheriff, to an Indian chief.[12] In *Betty Boop* (created by the Fleischer Brothers) and *Looney Tunes* cartoons (created by a team of Warner Brothers artists and voiced by Mel Blanc), characters regularly changed shape, size, character, gender, costume, and performance style in order to outwit pursuers or seduce lovers. In "A Hare Grows in Manhattan," one of a number of stories of Bugs Bunny's early years, Bugs spends the entire cartoon escaping a pack of enormous dogs on the Lower East Side by putting on various costumes, voices, accents, and characters. Likewise, in explaining the origin of his iconic line, "What's Up Doc?," in yet another animated bio-pic, Bugs Bunny shows how he turned the trope of transformation and escape (from Elmer Fudd) into theatrical gold.[13] Superheroes Superman and Batman, invented by Jewish comic book artists in the 1930s, similarly based their success on their ability to change identity, thereby eluding and ultimately triumphing over their enemies.

A brilliant argument for the liberating possibilities of theatricality, Ernst Lubitsch's 1942 film *To Be or Not to Be* tells of the escape of a Polish theatre company from the Nazis immediately following the Nazi invasion. The mixed company of Jewish and non-Jewish actors uses every theatrical technique at their disposal to escape the worst threat to Jewish freedom in the modern age while also skewering the intensely anti-theatrical philosophy of the Nazis themselves. The film opens with the startling image of Adolf Hitler walking the streets of Warsaw, only to be revealed, a few minutes later, as a member of the Polish theatre company dressed in costume for a production about Nazis that is about to open on the stage. Before the actor has a chance to play Hitler, the Nazis invade Warsaw, the production is cancelled, and the theatre is closed. The actors become involved with a member of the Polish Underground, and use all of their talents to save the resistance from destruction. In the process, the lead actor (of both the theatre company and the film), Joseph Tura, played by Jack Benny (born Benjamin Kubelsky), impersonates a Nazi SS officer and then a Nazi spy. In the first scene, Tura, dressed in the costume for the cancelled play, momentarily fools the Nazi spy Siletski by playing the role of Colonel Ehrhardt. Tura's broad impersonation ("So they call me Concentration Camp Ehrhardt!") seems dangerously unconvincing until we meet the real Colonel Ehrhardt, who turns out to be as vulgar and oafish as Tura imagined him to be. Tura's ability to "play" a Nazi so successfully clearly undermines Nazi power and raises questions about the purity of Nazi ideology. In the second scene, Tura, now dressed as the recently murdered spy Siletski, enters Nazi headquarters for a meeting with Ehrhardt, only to discover in the waiting room the *real* body of Siletski. In a tight spot, Tura thinks fast and, pulling a fake beard from his pocket, replaces the dead Siletski's real beard with the fake one. When Ehrhardt enters, Tura insists that he is the *real* Siletski, and demonstrates his point by revealing that the dead Siletski is wearing a fake beard. The Nazis are, at this point, totally confused, and Tura goes free. The Nazis' inability to distinguish between reality and performance once again undermines their power, turning them into the straight men for yet another Jewish joke. It also raises questions about Nazi racial ideology – if they can't distinguish the real Siletski from the fake one, how can they possibly distinguish a Jew from an Aryan?

By insisting on *actor* as the most liberating of all identities, directors and writers of theatrical liberalism such as Lubitsch and Raphaelson created a secular, universal rhetoric that protected Jews' newly acquired and deeply treasured civil rights. At the same time, this kind of rights-based freedom – the individual right to self-fashion – is deeply rooted in Enlightenment liberalism and liberal Protestantism and differs in important ways from Jewish jurisprudence. In works of theatrical liberalism, the rhetoric of rights – the right to be oneself, to self-fashion, to take advantage of opportunities and advance to fame and fortune free of interference – is in constant tension with another legal rhetoric, emerging from a different legal culture, the system of *obligation* or what in Hebrew is called a *mitzvah*. The theatrical community has a complicated relationship to a system of individual rights. Theatre is fundamentally a collective practice, and the ultimate source of authority in the theatre is the collective itself. In other words, without a number of participants each fulfilling a set of prescribed obligations – producer, director, actors, designers, technicians, house staff, and of course audience – the show cannot proceed and the entire theatrical system would cease to function. In the unwritten, but universally acknowledged, laws of the theatre, all members of the company are obligated to do what they can to make sure that the show goes on.

Although the self-fashioning at the centre of theatrical liberalism draws its authority from the American liberal ideology of individual rights, the freedom to shape the self in Lubitsch's movies is embedded within and circumscribed by a set of communitarian obligations that more closely resemble Jewish *mitzvot* (commandments). In twentieth-century America, while the individual freedom to perform (and, if one is very talented and lucky, to become a star) was central to the ethos of theatrical liberalism, this freedom was only possible within a system of obligations imposed by the covenant of The Theatre, and shared by each member of the theatrical community. In works espousing theatrical liberalism, when a character in a play or movie insists to his or her co-star that "the show must go on," the conversation is over. There is no alternative. Members of a theatrical community are responsible to each other, to the audience, to the producers, but even more importantly to the higher calling of the theatre, to ensure that the show goes on night after night and that it is the best show it can be.

The final climactic escape scene in *To Be or Not to Be* offers an extraordinary illustration of theatrical liberalism and comments especially strongly on the role of obligation in Lubitsch's work. In this scene, every actor is literally playing for his or her life. They depend absolutely on one another; the show *must* go on or the company, and the members of the Polish resistance, and, by implication, the cause of freedom itself, will all be lost. The performance begins when a Jewish member of the company, Greenberg, agrees to serve as a decoy by reciting Shylock's speech ("Hath not a Jew eyes?") before an audience of real and fake Nazis (his fellow actors), thereby protecting the members of the resistance in Warsaw and enabling the escape of the entire theatre company. It ends with the company safely on a plane to England, where we are assured in the final scene that the show does indeed go on. Filmed in 1941, this successful high-stakes performance is both poignant and powerful. On one hand, the scene is clearly a fantasy – by 1941 Lubitsch must have known that the dangers of such a performance would have been unlikely to be rewarded with freedom. On the other hand, the scene expresses Lubitsch's optimistic hope that – in America at least – theatricality can protect performers (and by extension, anybody) from the entrapment of essential identity and ensure freedom from oppression. In the liberal utopia of *To Be or Not to Be,* even a Jew playing a Jew *in front of Adolf Hitler himself* can escape if he gives a good enough performance (and has a loyal company of actors to back him up). Hitler insisted that biology was destiny; Lubitsch protested that freedom means the right to play whatever role you choose. For Lubitsch, as for all the creators of theatrical liberalism, this freedom to perform, to *act,* to fashion a self, opened the door to a more hopeful and more just world.

NOTES

1 "Heart," by Richard Adler (music) and Jerry Ross (lyrics), from the musical *Damn Yankees* (book by George Abbott and Douglass Wallop), which opened on Broadway in 1955 at the 46th Street Theatre.

2 An earlier version of the portion of this chapter on action was published as "The Birth of Theatrical Liberalism" in *After Pluralism: Reimagining Religious Engagement.*

3 See Heschel 281. Other relevant commentaries on this text include a compilation of well-known *midrashim* on Exodus 24:7, detailed in Ginzberg 593. Also see Talmud Bavli, Tractate Shabbat, 88a; Talmud Bavli, Tractate Kiddushin, 40b; and on the meaning of "*sh'ma*" (hearing), see also Sefer Abudarham (1340), Dinay Kriat Sh'ma.

4 The notion of "free exercise of religion" was clarified in Reynolds v. The United States (1878), which ruled that "Laws are made for the government of actions, and while they cannot interfere with mere religious beliefs and opinions, they may with practices." The ruling was based on Thomas

Jefferson's "Danbury Letter" on the separation of church and state, which states: "Believing with you that religion is a matter which lies solely between Man & his God, that he owes account to none other for his faith or his worship, that the legitimate powers of government reach actions only, & not opinions, I contemplate with sovereign reverence that act of the whole American people which declared that their legislature should 'make no law respecting an establishment of religion, or prohibiting the free exercise thereof,' thus building a wall of separation between Church & State" (Jefferson). For the full description of the case and the resulting opinions, see Reynolds.

5 Having seen his German comedies, Pickford was impressed and asked Lubitsch to come to Hollywood to work for her studio, United Artists, as a director. Lubitsch agreed, and in 1922 he directed Pickford in *Rosita.* The relationship was not successful, however, and Lubitsch was quickly signed to a directing contract by Warner Brothers. See Eyman for more biographical details.

6 Lubitsch certainly was not the first to celebrate artifice in this way. Oscar Wilde is his clear forebear, and Lubitsch was a huge fan of Wilde's (he made a particularly celebrated silent film of *Lady Windermere's Fan* in 1925). Lubitsch is distinctive in his ability to bring this sensibility to a place – America – Wilde considered notably incapable of the kind of ironic stance necessary to appreciate it.

7 A great deal has been written on the pathways to Jewish modernity. For a particularly provocative and interesting narrative, see Slezkine.

8 On the racialization of Jews and other immigrants, see Brodkin, Goldstein, and Jacobson.

9 See Goldstein, especially chapter 1, for an excellent discussion of how Jews adopted a racialized identity in the late nineteenth century.

10 Stephen Greenblatt locates a similar idea of "self-fashioning" (a term he coined) in Early Modern England, in the theatre of Shakespeare.

11 See, for example, the ambivalence about this form of theatrical self-fashioning in the *Autobiography of Benjamin Franklin* in which Franklin, on the one hand, worked hard to build character but, on the other hand, considered "going to plays and other places of amusement" one of the "great errata of my life, which I should wish to correct if I were to live it over again" (39).

12 See extended discussions on *Whoopee* and *Girl Crazy* in Most, *Making Americans,* chapter 2.

13 Jews were not the only writers and performers to celebrate transformation as a pathway to freedom. But it is interesting to note that the groups

that made use of this theatrical device in American popular entertainment shared a common heritage of being a minority culture within an often hostile majority. The trickster figure is ubiquitous in African American culture, and also in Irish American comedy. Indeed, Bugs Bunny has a subtly Irish identity in the cartoons I discuss here. What distinguishes the Jewish version of this celebration of transformation is that Jewish-created narratives of transformation managed to become "universal," applying not only to a single identity group, but to American-ness as a whole.

WORKS CITED

Adler, Richard, and Jerry Ross. "(You've Gotta Have) Heart." *Damn Yankees.* Dir. George Abbot. 46th Street Theatre. 1955. Print.

Brodkin, Karen. *How Jews Became White Folks and What That Says About Race in America.* Newark: Rutgers UP, 1998. Print. http://dx.doi.org/10.1353/ajh.2000.0005.

Eyman, Scott. *Ernst Lubitsch: Laughter in Paradise.* New York: Simon, 1993. Print.

Franklin, Benjamin. *The Autobiography of Benjamin Franklin.* New York: Penguin, 2003. Print.

Ginzberg, Louis. *Legends of the Jews.* 7 vols. 1909–1938. 2d ed. Trans. Henrietta Szold. Philadelphia: Jewish Publication Society, 2003. Print.

Goldstein, Eric L. *The Price of Whiteness: Jews, Race and American Identity.* Princeton: Princeton UP, 2007. Print.

Greenblatt, Stephen. *Renaissance Self-Fashioning: From More to Shakespeare.* Chicago: U of Chicago P, 1981. Print.

Heschel, Abraham Joshua. *God in Search of Man: A Philosophy of Judaism.* 1955. New York: Farrar, 1976. Print.

Kaplan, Mordecai. *Judaism as a Civilization.* New York: Macmillan, 1934. Print.

Jacobson, Matthew. *Whiteness of a Different Color: European Immigrants and the Alchemy of Race.* Cambridge, MA: Harvard UP, 1998. Print.

Jefferson, Thomas. "To messers. Nehemiah Dodge, Ephraim Robbins, & Stephen S. Nelson, a committee of the Danbury Baptist association in the state of Connecticut." 1 Jan 1802. *Library of Congress Information Bulletin* 57.6 (1998): n. pag. Web. 14 April 2013.

Locke, John. *Two Treatises of Government and A Letter Concerning Toleration.* Ed. Ian Shapiro. New Haven, Conn.: Yale UP, 2003. Print.

Lubitsch, Ernst, dir. *The Love Parade.* Paramount Pictures, 1929. Film.

Lubitsch, Ernst, dir. *To Be or Not To Be.* United Artists. Film, 1942.

Lubitsch, Ernst, dir. *Trouble in Paradise.* Paramount Pictures. Film, 1932.
Lubitsch, Ernst, dir. *The Smiling Lieutenant.* Paramount Pictures. Film, 1931.
Mendelssohn, Moses. *Jerusalem, or, On Religious Power and Judaism.* 1783. Trans. Allan Arkush. Hanover, NH: University Press of New England, 1983. Print.
Most, Andrea. "The Birth of Theatrical Liberalism." *After Pluralism: Reimagining Religious Engagement.* Ed. Courtney Bender and Pamela Klassen. New York: Columbia UP, 2010. 127–55. Print.
Most, Andrea. *Making Americans: Jews and the Broadway Musical.* Cambridge, MA: Harvard UP, 2004. Print.
Reynolds v. U.S. 98 U.S. 145. Supreme Court of the US. 1878. *FindLaw.* Web. 1 Feb. 2011.
Slezkine, Yuri. *The Jewish Century.* Princeton: Princeton UP, 2004. Print.
Sorkin, David. *The Transformation of German Jewry.* New York: Oxford UP, 1987. Print.

8 Inglourious Criticism, Basterd Fantasies: Rancière, Tarantino, and the Intellectual Spectacle of Hope

JASON HASLAM

My chapter begins with two indictments of the role that culture plays in creating a democratic civic nation: one, the seeming denial of (popular) culture's aesthetic value in the face of its social context; the other, the seeming denial of its social and political efficacy in the face of its aesthetic structure. The first was proclaimed by Theodor Adorno, when he famously stated that "To write poetry after Auschwitz is barbaric" (34). Adorno's oft-quoted statement, easily read solely as a commentary on the impossibility of beauty in an age of mechanized genocide, is, however, made in the context of a nostalgic malaise concerning what he saw as the barbarism of culture itself in the modern era, and the impossibility of critiquing that culture from within: "Traditional culture," he writes, "has become worthless today [...], its heritage [...] expendable to the highest degree, superfluous, trash. And the hucksters of mass culture can point to it with a grin, for they treat it as such" (34). Culture, for Adorno, becomes a problem the moment it becomes its own subject, attempting to separate itself disciplinarily from the world around it, even as, for Adorno, such separation is impossible because of the dialectical structure of society. This false vision of culture thus, for Adorno, furthers a false vision of the liberal intellectual within such a culture: "the liberal, who sees no way out, makes himself the spokesman of a dictatorial arrangement of society even while he imagines he is opposing it," for "the very intelligentsia that pretends to float freely is fundamentally rooted in the very being that must be changed and which it merely pretends to criticize" (47). Whereas another, more "authentic" kind of culture – synecdochically represented in the poetry that can no longer be written in these barbarous and brutal times – could, as he supposes Spengler feared, "expose contradictions which a regimented economic system had allegedly eliminated" (63), culture in the contemporary world instead becomes constituted of a flattened landscape of undifferentiated surfaces without depth. The second denial of culture comes from Laura Mulvey, who argues that, in order to disrupt the psychologically formative (and invasive) patriarchal functions of film, the first step must be to "destroy[ ] the satisfaction, pleasure and privilege" of feeling like the "invisible guest" who voyeuristically identifies with film's scopophilic gaze, which reduces women – and in fact the passively viewing audience as a whole – to undifferentiated surfaces without depth (18). My parallel language is purposeful, of course: both critics present, from different angles, a dire if not hopeless view of mass culture and the social efficacy of cultural production in the creation of an intellectual public.

It is worth noting that both authors moved away – to varying degrees – from these, arguably their best known, statements, but the foundational conceit of these original positions – that popular or mass culture functions first and foremost in the realm of ideological (re)production, by which an audience can either be passively enthralled, or against which it can agentially resist – remains. This conceit leaves the public role of culture and, indeed, of the cultural critic in a tense position: cultural criticism is, at best, left in the resistant space, either sneering at contemporary cultural products as merely vehicles for an ethically and aesthetically bankrupt society (a position Adorno himself critiqued as pointless), or gesturing to moments of ideological resistance within a culture that nonetheless can never truly move beyond its own ideological landscape. To use Foucault's terms, within these visions there can be no "great Refusal" of one's surrounding ideological condition (96). Both Adorno and Mulvey thus lament the impossibility of, but at the same time nostalgically re-create the need for, a socially efficacious art, which leads in a direct line from artist to medium to spectator, where the last of those is transformed not into a passive victim of commodification culture, but into an active agent of social change. Not so, they say, in the contemporary world, where there is such a direct line, but it is a line that culminates in a spectator who is only a passive vessel, filled with the emptiness of ideology, at best only ephemerally able to challenge epistemological systems from within small fractures or discordances within those systems.[1]

These resistant spaces have been configured in many ways.[2] The British tradition of Cultural Studies, arising from the Birmingham School and its various offshoots, has tended to focus on the ways in which consumers "write back" against the ideological formations contained within mass culture. One of the better-known examples comes from Dick Hebdige's study of punks and their seemingly unsafe use of safety pins, as part of a resistance (un)contained in a cultural practice of *bricolage*. As in Mulvey's argument, here the consumer's agency is expressed only at a moment of and through an act of defamiliarization: an active rejection of the traditional frames and uses of culture. Likewise, one can compare Mulvey's call for a defamiliarization of filmic pleasure to Brecht's or Artaud's radical attack on passive spectatorship. The consumer or audience member as such, the person who not only participates in culturally prescribed ways but also *enjoys* doing so, is generally read as the passive victim of ideological critique: the un-defamiliarized familiar of popular culture's magical control.

In these revisions, which have been used both to erase and reinstate a line between "high" and mass or popular culture, the cultural object itself (be it a safety pin, a film, a television show, or *The Tempest*) is important only insofar as it functions in relation to a material moment; it is both ideologically and historically contingent. As with the audience, it can be resistant (think of Mulvey's unpleasurable cinema), or it can engage in a hegemonic reproduction of the status quo, and sometimes it can do both, but what it cannot do is escape its own materiality. The materialist turn is, after all, a profoundly anti-Kantian move, one that denies the transcendence of art because such transcendence serves as a mask to hide often grotesque ideologies of dominance. Art cannot be transcendent – that is, it cannot free us or "itself" from our own ideologically conditioned position(s) in the world – because any declaration of transcendence is itself a sign of ideological interpellation. And certainly this argument holds true: one has only to juxtapose Kant's arguments for the possibility of universal aesthetic or other judgments with his profoundly racist arguments against the rationality of non-white peoples to see the problem with his own claims of universal, because disinterested, sources of judgment.[3]

I do not wish to contest these conclusions: notions of artistic transcendence have been used to justify many forms of bias, from the mundane to the horrific.[4] As Jacques Rancière has recently argued, however – taking up the passive/active spectator dyad of Brecht's and Artaud's different theatrical practices – the materialist renunciation of the emancipatory project of art relies on a logic that denies, or at best undermines, its own methodologies. If, for Adorno, Mulvey, and any range of their critical descendants, the scene of interpellation consists of a palimpsest of a (minimally complex) popular culture placed onto a (minimally complex) audience, and this scene can only be socially or politically meaningful in its disruption, then the critic must somehow position himself or herself beyond both, in a rarefied atmosphere of intellectual and therefore ideological distance that can both reflect on and denounce that interpellation. In other words, whatever complex theoretical dance is performed, the dancer must be offstage, in a space of transcendence from which to critique the impossibility of transcendence. Of course, to say that as dismissively as I just have is to engage in its mirror image, the position that Adorno explicitly critiques and which Mulvey, to a point, engages: that other *de rigueur* critical stance which denounces the elitism of the former criticism, only to replace it instead with a cynical vision of the impossibility of such critical and ideological distance, and a recognition that any resistance is effectively reappropriated by the very machinery of ideology one is attempting to resist. As Rancière writes, this position "makes any protest a spectacle and any spectacle a commodity. It makes it an expression of futility, but also a demonstration of culpability" (*Emancipated* 33). In both of these critical positions, however, an unreconstructed popular or mass culture and the audience that actually *enjoys* said culture are looked upon with varying levels of disdain or scientific objectification; the only difference between the two critical perspectives is that in the latter the cultural critic – perhaps sneeringly – sees him- or herself as an object of (almost) equal disdain.

Building on Rancière's discussion of these and related critical trends, I turn to Quentin Tarantino's film, *Inglourious Basterds* (2009) in order to argue that, rather than denounce the mundane nature of mass culture, as Adorno so often does, and rather than try to escape the pleasure of identification, as Mulvey does, Tarantino instead undertakes the task of rebuilding a distance between culture and history that allows simultaneously for the reintegration of pleasure and for the creation of a critical – because subjective and unpredictable – intellectual engagement. Going back to the nadir of modern mass consumption in WWII and the Holocaust, Tarantino attempts to rebuild the spectator's engagement with popular culture from the ground up, explicitly burning the assumptions lying behind theories of commodity fetishism – and burning materiality itself, as it turns out – and taking his audience on journeys through the destruction and reconstitution of an intellectual and hopeful engagement with popular culture.

I Rancière and the Inglorious Critic

I want to start with a discussion of Rancière not only because he frames my approach, but because, in its own way, Tarantino's film makes a parallel argument to that of the French philosopher. Updating his 1987 study, *The Ignorant Schoolmaster*, Rancière's *The Emancipated Spectator* (2008), for example, attempts to analyse spectacle – and the image as such – as what he calls the "third thing" that exists between and beyond both the artist and the audience (15), thus offering an intervention into the understanding of the relationship between text (widely defined), its audience, and social and political life. Using live theatre (as opposed to cinema), Rancière offers a history of recent critical thought regarding the position of the spectator vis-à-vis the performance. Rancière argues that the fact that "there is no theatre without a spectator" has been rendered as a problem for creators and critics, because,

> at least according to the accusers, being a spectator is a bad thing for at least two reasons. First, viewing is the opposite of knowing: the spectator is held before an appearance in a state of ignorance about the process of production of this appearance and about the reality it conceals. Second, it is the opposite of acting: the spectator remains immobile in her seat, passive. To be a spectator is to be separated from both the capacity to know and the power to act. (*Emancipated* 2)

While he does not directly analyse them here, one can see echoes of my use of Adorno and Mulvey as the exemplary poles of a bifurcated criticism of popular culture. But, for both, the relationship between culture and its spectators is a vicious circle that, as Rancière describes, swirls around a spectator who is devoid of subjectivity outside of its parasitic relationship with the image, a spectator without a self: in other words, a consumer. One is left, then, with the figure of the citizens of Huxley's *Brave New World* (1932): whether Alpha or Epsilon, whether finding escapist satisfaction in the feelies (Huxley's vision of cinema) or in their labour, the inhabitants of this brave new cultural landscape are locked in place by a conditioning of which they are unaware and from which they cannot escape.

Implicit in Adorno's argument and explicit in Mulvey's, however, is the desire to fill in that selfhood of the spectator, somehow to allow for an engagement with culture that is both critical and, therefore, politically active. No longer passive nor ignorant, this spectator is an agent for social change against the ruling forces that would otherwise keep it subjected in its Blob-like state. Where Adorno calls for "[c]ritical intelligence" to break free of its "self-satisfied contemplation" (162), Mulvey calls for a cinema that will deny the very pleasure its spectators seek; both, in other words, await Steve McQueen to fight against the cultural Blob coming to pacify him. Neither, however, seems too sure of his arrival.[5]

All well and good, but this positing of a need for action rather than passivity, doing rather than watching, does not answer Adorno's question: from what position can we decide which is which? If we are entranced with the reification of the corrupted and corrupting culture that consumes us even as we supposedly consume it, who is it who can decide which actions are truly and unambiguously "good"? If there is no poetry after Auschwitz, with the concomitant assertion that cultural criticism only serves to further that lack, then how is the critic or revolutionary to stand outside in order to convince the audience to stand up and participate – or, more to the point, how is one to assure that such audience participation isn't simply a sing-a-long to the musical of the State? Rancière points to this as the self-defeating paradox at the heart of both critical and theatrical schools in the post-Marxist era, of whatever theoretical flavour. In an earlier book, he does address this issue with reference to Adorno, whose "modernist rigour," Rancière argues, which aims "to expurgate the emancipatory potential of art of any form of compromise with cultural commerce and aestheticized life," instead "becomes the reduction of art to the ethical witnessing of unrepresentable catastrophe" (*Aesthetics* 131). The avant-garde may resist such "cultural commerce," but its only reply is "to put up a 'resistance' that is nothing but the endless work of mourning" (130). Thus, he continues in *Emancipated Spectator*, "The current disconnection between critical procedures and any prospect of emancipation simply reveals the disjunction at the heart of the critical paradigm. It can mock its illusions, but it reproduces its logic" (45). This argument may sound eerily similar to Adorno's proclamation, but note the phrase "prospect of emancipation": it is not culture or even the critical reliance on it that reproduces the alienation of the masses; instead, it is the constative assumption that the masses are alienated to begin with that leads to the paradoxical situation in which critical inquiry finds itself. After all, Rancière writes,

> What makes it possible to pronounce the spectator seated in her place inactive, if not the previously posited radical opposition between the active and the passive? Why identify gaze and passivity, unless on the presupposition that to view means to take pleasure in images and appearances

> while ignoring the truth behind the image and the reality outside the theatre? Why assimilate listening to passivity, unless through the prejudice that speech is the opposite of action? These oppositions – viewing/knowing, appearance/reality, activity/passivity – are quite different from logical oppositions between clearly defined terms. (*Emancipated* 12)

The critical dismissal of (popular) culture and its effect on its audience, in other words, *must* presuppose passivity (and, frankly, stupidity) on behalf of the spectating audience.

To argue against this passivity, however, is not necessarily to reproduce Hebdige's argument concerning the agential redeployment of culture against itself. Rancière is not arguing for a defamiliarizing or alienating experience that removes the spectator from the enjoyment of the text or the replacement of the text into a new material relation that in turn reconditions its meaning. Instead, Rancière could be said to deny the notion that aesthetic enjoyment as transcendent activity is necessarily a disguise for ideological engagement. Whether reproductive or resistant, the spectator in such an Althusserian analysis is not individually active so much as an embodiment of a push-and-pull of varying ideological forces. It is this presupposition, central to so much film and cultural theory of the post-Marxist period,[6] that Rancière says we must, and that I argue Tarantino does, abandon in favour of a vision that instates as its presupposition the notion of the spectator's intellectual engagement with culture, predicated on culture's formal separation from its material surroundings. Later critiques of Althusserian and other film analyses, particularly those of the Birmingham School, with which Rancière's work shares some similarities, would emphasize those discords in the music of ideology which would allow for multiple identifications and interventions between spectator and film, but in practice these critical approaches would still posit a primarily ideological relation (with some possibility for resistance).[7] Rancière and Tarantino, conversely, posit a (return to) a radical split between aesthetic object and its viewer, in which freedom is possible. "Emancipation begins," Rancière writes, "when we challenge the opposition between viewing and acting […]. The spectator also acts, like the pupil or scholar. She observes, selects, compares, interprets. […] This is the crucial point," he continues, "spectators see, feel and understand something in as much as they compose their own poem, as, in their way, do actors or playwrights, directors, dancers or performers" (*Emancipated* 13).

Of course, this argument sounds Kantian – all too Kantian. After all, Kant similarly derides the need to call attention to the artifice of an artistic creation, writing that "In [dealing with] a product of fine art we must become conscious that it is art rather than nature, and yet the purposiveness in its form must seem as free from all constraint of chosen rules as if it were a product of mere nature. It is this feeling of freedom in the play of our cognitive powers, a play that yet must also be purposive, which underlies that pleasure which alone is universally communicable" (173–4). Like Kant, Rancière is interested in the "freedom [of] play" in one's engagement with culture, and in the ways in which that play is created by the inherent separation between the aesthetic image and the social world. But, for Kant, this freedom is paradoxically constrained by what he deems the "universal," which *is*, as we know from such writers as Althusser and Barthes, simply a cover for particular ideologies. It is in the seemingly subordinate, yet actually constative, clause, "yet must also be purposive," that we can see the distinction between Kant and Rancière, allowing Rancière (and Tarantino) to avoid altogether the biased baggage of humanism while simultaneously allowing for a free-flowing and unpredictable engagement with cultural texts, an engagement that may run parallel to ideological formations and material history but is not limited to those. As Rancière writes, "Whatever might be the specific type of economic circuits they lie within, artistic practices are not 'exceptions' to other practices. They represent and reconfigure the distribution of these activities" (*Politics* 45). For Rancière, the answer lies in understanding spectatorship itself as an *active* and *freeing* engagement in that redistribution, and in seeing aesthetic separation as a function of intertextual and multimedia conversations occurring on the same surface.

This active viewing, connecting an aesthetic object to the lived experience of a subject's own positionality, is best seen, Rancière argues, as an act of translation, in which the social power of an audience as a collectivity derives from "the power each of them has to translate what she perceives in her own way, to link it to the unique intellectual adventure that makes her similar to all the rest in as much as this adventure is not like any other" (*Emancipated* 16–17). In other words, rather than the Kantian view, in which it could be said that art is a vehicle through which "a man with a *broadened way of thinking*" can "override[] the private subjective conditions of his judgment [...] and reflect[ ] on his own judgment from a *universal standpoint*" (Kant 161; emphasis in original), culture for Rancière is the space precisely for the subjective engagement of an enculturated subject who, by virtue of what Eve Kosofsky Sedgwick calls the "nonce taxonomy" of our lived experience (23), always has an individual intellectual engagement with that culture.[8] If Kant's ideal judgment is always a disinterested one, Rancière's active spectator is active only insofar as she is necessarily *interested.*[9] Avoiding a Habermasian neoliberal vision of an active public sphere based on a universal rationality even as he avoids the circularity of his former colleague Althusser's interpellative cycle, Rancière here reimagines Foucault's agency within subjection, his "plurality of resistances, each of them a special case" (96). But, Rancière performs agency as a function of interpretation, with the aesthetic images of culture itself, rather than power differentials, being his ground against which the figure of community is created. Individuality originates in, but is precisely not identical with, its historical moment, and so spectatorship exists within, but cannot be contained by, one's multifaceted ideological development.

II Exploding Film

Tarantino points to the critical space between material history and mass culture that Adorno, Mulvey, and the Birmingham School (and all of their critical descendants), in different ways, collapse, while denying the "universality" of "common sense" and beauty that Kant says inhabits that space. Tarantino echoes Rancière's vision, in *The Politics of Aesthetics*, of a (mechanical) culture that is socially efficacious precisely because it is set at a remove from social relevance as an aesthetic object (31–4): culture here constitutes Rancière's aforementioned "third thing," which "is not the transmission of the artist's knowledge or inspiration to the spectator [...] whose meaning is owned by no one, but which subsists between them, excluding any uniform transmission, any identity of cause and effect" (*Emancipated* 15). Rather than deny either the political possibilities or the aesthetic values of mass culture, *Inglourious Basterds* forces us to recognize that popular culture constitutes its own public intellectual space insofar as, as a set of aesthetic objects that migrate between varying media and audiences, it is irreducible to any given parallel set of material surroundings.

Inglourious Basterds is Tarantino's most reflexive commentary on film to date, as many critics, including Tarantino himself, have pointed out. As Tarantino has, rather directly, said, "In this story, cinema changes the world, and I fucking love that idea!" (Cox; also qtd. in "Revenge of the Giant Face"). But, as Charles Taylor writes, "It's not simply cinephilia that has led Tarantino to create a world where the war is fought by movie stars, film critics, [and] theatre owners" (104). Taylor argues – picking up on the film analysed by Andrea Most at the conclusion of the previous chapter of this volume – that "These characters use what the movies have taught them to win the war in the same way that the theatrical troupe members in Ernst Lubitsch's 1942 anti-Nazi comedy *To Be or Not to Be* used the illusions of their profession" (104). More than just cinema itself, or its characters, however, *Inglourious Basterds'* representation of cinema is one that highlights the role of the viewer, and specifically emphasizes the acts of intellectual and other translations in which viewers must engage when watching any film. The film follows two central plots, which come together at the end: the first, the story of Shosanna Dreyfus (Mélanie Laurent), a Jewish theatre owner in Paris, who at the beginning of the film is spared by the so-called Jew Hunter, Colonel Hans Landa (Christoph Waltz), even as he murders her entire family. The second plot follows the titular Basterds, a group of Jewish American soldiers, and one former German soldier, whose sole purpose in France, as their commander, Lieutenant Aldo Raine (Brad Pitt), puts it, is "killin' Nazis." The plots come together when Shosanna is asked to host the premiere of Joseph Goebbels's (Sylvester Groth) latest propaganda film, *A Nation's Pride,* which will be attended by the entire Nazi elite, including Hitler (Martin Wuttke). Shosanna agrees to host the film, but only so that she can lock the Nazis in and burn the theatre down using her cache of highly explosive silver nitrate film. Unbeknownst to her, the Basterds are also in the theatre, planning to blow up themselves and the Nazis using their own explosives. In the end, Shosanna's plan works, as does that of the Basterds, with two of them exploding along with the theatre just after one of them kills Hitler, reducing the fascist's head to pulp with machine-gun fire.

Some have viewed Tarantino's film as the most simplistic kind of cinematic wish fulfilment, through which the audience loses its own critical engagement with material history and its horrors in exchange for an apolitical, counter-historical fantasy of revenge; others have read that revenge fantasy as a positive statement of the necessity to continue a fight against the evils of anti-Semitism and fascism; while yet others have viewed it as a purely anti-Semitic film that presents the Nazis sympathetically and Jews as sadistic controllers of media, while reading the plot as tantamount to Holocaust denial.[10] While I would argue against these last assertions, it's not my purpose to enter into that debate – although I necessarily do – but rather to explore the film's self-referential representation of culture as a primary site for such public intellectual debate. Tarantino's film, like Rancière's critical explorations, thematizes the figure of (popular) culture as the space for precisely this kind of active viewing, in which, it should be pointed out, the responses are ultimately uncontrollable by any but the spectator herself. *Inglourious Basterds* thus doesn't necessarily lend itself to or resist specific readings, as much as it thematizes, through the film's intradiegetic refraction of both audience and screen, the activity of a spectator's translation and interpretation through that person's individual journey, to use Rancière's terms.

Ultimately, then, it is the passive viewer/interpellative film dyad that Tarantino wants to explode in this movie. In the climactic theatre scene, a film of pure fascist propaganda is literally burned away, along with its perfectly interpellated Nazi audience: "the only people who should be allowed in the room," the film's star explains to Goebbels earlier, "are people who will be moved by exploits on the screen"; "this a German night, a German event, a German celebration," he says, and only those who are willing to "fight" for the limited seats will be able to enter. In other words, it is a perfectly sympathetic audience, willing and ready to be told again what it already knows, desirous of the suppression of its own intellectual engagement to the superficial ideological message of the film. This is, in other words, a representation of popular culture and the consumer-spectator as defined by critical theory. That passive spectator here becomes the Nazi, the fascist who is by definition also a passive figure of group-think even while being simultaneously the figure of violent suppression of non-conformity. A simplistically ideological film and a simplistically uniform audience exist here in a purely tautological relationship; it is this image that *Inglourious Basterds* wipes from the screen.

The fire that will eventually kill the Nazis in the audience starts behind the screen, when Marcel (Jacky Ido), Shosanna's romantic and business partner (whose race, as a black man, is clearly significant), sets the silver nitrate film on fire. Just before the flames build under the screen, Shosanna and Marcel's own reel of film replaces the final reel of the Nazi propaganda film, revealing Shosanna's face as she says, in English "I have a message for Germany," responding to the main character in the Nazi film shouting to the American enemy sarcastically, "Do you have a message for Germany?" Shosanna, as the active viewer, responds "I have a message for Germany: that you are all going to die. And I want you to look deep into the face of the Jew who is going to do it," all while Goebbels yells impotently for someone to "shut off the projector" since, as he perhaps obviously shouts, "I don't know what's going on! That doesn't belong in my movie!"

It may be tempting here to read this disruption as Mulvey's disruption of pleasure, that the Nazi audience is awakened to the fourth wall, and thus shaken from their passive voyeuristic reverie. And, indeed, this scene could be read as a metacinematic representation of Tarantino's own much discussed techniques derived from the French avant-garde. Tarantino is well known for adopting the methods of Jean-Luc Godard, famous for attempting to import Brecht's theatrical distancing into film, in order to create that alienating effect, and to wake the audience from its passive dreaming.[11] For Tarantino, these techniques include sudden and inexplicable narration, jump cuts, the use of text overlays, the insertion of excerpts from other films (in one telling case in *Inglourious Basterds*, a scene from Hitchcock's *Sabotage* – in which a bus is blown up using silver nitrate film – is shown while Samuel L. Jackson narrates the flammability of such film), and other general reminders of the constructed nature of cinema. And if that's what's happening here, my argument falls flat on its giant face: Tarantino's film – and Shosanna's – would not, then, reimagine spectatorship itself, but would in fact engage in the dismissive opinion of the passive nature of spectatorship I have been aiming to critique. In this particular instance, however, the alienation of the Nazi audience is explicitly *not* alienating for Tarantino's audience. We are aware of why there has been a break in the Nazi's film, and it serves simply to further our film's primary narrative. It seems as if Tarantino is highlighting the very lack of distinction between avant-garde alienating effects and the pleasures of spectatorship.

Furthermore, one needs to recall that Shosanna is not just on the screen, but is also watching the screen, and the film constantly focusses on her eyes. She is the hybrid viewer-actor that Rancière says we all are (not only does she disrupt the Nazi's film, but she kills its star and biographical subject, Fredrick Zoller (Daniel Brühl) – it would be difficult to imagine a more active critical response to a film). Even within the film, the recorded Shosanna has two audiences: after her speech to the Germans, she then says "Marcel, burn it down," speaking literally to the other side of the screen. Her film thus simultaneously addresses two sides of the screen, the front and back, the Germans on one side, Marcel on the other: the fascist and racist audience and, quite literally, that audience's vision of a *bête noir*. As the smoke builds, we see her face become a ghostly and intangible projection onto the smoke, as she laughs, and Marcel, after lighting the fire with his discarded cigarette, disappears into the background as all of the Nazis die. Shosanna's is a film that simultaneously addresses two ideologically, diametrically opposed audiences at the same time, creating both pleasure and alienation for the two audiences who respond with completely opposed actions, even as this film is running in one theatre, for one show only. These may be read as two ideologically opposed groups; but I would argue, given the as yet unacknowledged position of the audience of Tarantino's film itself, that they figure the audience member as the historically located individual, yes, but also as someone who creates either pleasure or pain from his or her reading of the screen based on her or his intellectual relationship with the history and aesthetic images that surround him or her. At the very least, Tarantino highlights the necessary ambiguity of the "message" of film by representing the most diametrically opposed audiences possible present at the same film.

III Revenge of the Giant Face: Spectacle's Return

This haunting, beautiful, terrifying scene refracts film in several directions, but what I want to focus on as I conclude is the fact that this scene – and Tarantino's filmic, textual, generic, and other interruptions, allusions, and overlays – renders in film the effect that Rancière says culture is always already in the midst of creating: what he calls "dissensus." "What 'dissensus' means," Rancière writes, "is an organization of the sensible where there is neither a reality concealed behind appearances nor a single regime of presentation and interpretation of the given imposing its obviousness on all. It means that every situation can be cracked open from the inside, reconfigured in a different regime of perception and signification" (*Emancipated* 48–9). In other words, the very images of culture, those superficial appearances so detested, vilified, or viewed as simplistic by the critical regimes with which I opened this chapter, are rendered as being that which is important to social and political life. In this scene in the film, Shosanna is rendered into pure image, after all: the fire starts when Marcel burns the material reality of film history, a pile of silver nitrate film that, in being destroyed, gives life to an image that moves beyond its connection to that material. The fire even consumes the screen, leaving the image hanging in the air as it literally goes up in smoke. The scene clearly plays on a dual meaning of consumption: film is consumed in fire and consumed as image, the burning of its material existence being the precondition to the ability of the spectator to view its spectral image. The image is portrayed simultaneously as the destruction of any rigid meaning and as the creation of its symbolic power. Shosanna's laughter echoes over the dead and dying fascist regime that would dictate its "single regime of presentation and interpretation," imposing if not its obviousness, then its will on all, and does so even as the reality behind that image, Shosanna herself, lies dead in the projection booth. This spectral Shosanna is not a historical figure, nor is she necessarily a metaphor for history, nor is she even a representation of a character presented as a person under the guise of realism: she is the viewed image "itself."

And yet this image, and the film, is precisely not "itself." The film is ostensibly a remake of the 1978 film of the same title (although Tarantino's version is gloriously misspelled with an extra "u" in the first and an "e" in the second word). The 1978 film, a so-called macaroni war film (in the tradition of the "spaghetti western") was shot by Italian director Enzo G. Castellari (who has cameos in both his own and Tarantino's versions: in the original as an American commander yelling "Fire!" to signal the beginning of a battle; in the latter as a Nazi yelling "Fire!" when the screen bursts into flame). The original is a more-or-less straight-up action film, what Tarantino has called a "bunch of guys on a mission movie" (Hohenadel), focussing on a group of American deserters near the end of WWII who escape from their prison transport and attempt to fight their way through France to Switzerland, killing Germans and Americans on the way, refusing openly to show allegiance to either side even though they eventually, of course, fulfil an important mission for the Americans, in which most of them die. Ultimately, this film has little to do with Tarantino's remake, with Tarantino taking the general setting and title but little else. But, it's important to recognize the connection for several reasons. First, Tarantino – ever the generous director attempting to salvage lost careers – was insistent in helping to remarket this, one of his favourite films, placing his own film in a position of spectator to the earlier film. In fact, the relationship between the earlier film as both source text and object of the second film's gaze is emphasized by the fact that Castellari appears in Tarantino's film as a film viewer. Second, the original *Inglorious Bastards* is notable for its lengthy history of retitling, repackaging, and remarketing. Released theatrically in Italy under the title *Quel maledetto treno blindato* (1978), or, *That Damned Armored Train*, it was released – not widely – in the United States as *Inglorious Bastards*, and then at various points released to home video as, among other titles, *Hell's Heroes, Deadly Mission*, and *Counterfeit Commandoes*, and was then (possibly) recut by the Blaxploitation studio, Xenon Pictures, with a focus on the character played by Fred Williamson, and released to home video as *G. I. Bro*. And all of this builds on the foundation of a film that is basically a retelling of the narrative of *The Dirty Dozen* (1967), which Tarantino references in the climactic scene of his remake (in *The Dirty Dozen*, a group of Nazis are similarly locked in a small room and firebombed). Third, both the original film and Tarantino's dialogue with it also introduce a multinational, multilinguistic space, as Castellari's original, like Sergio Leone's westerns, were international productions, with many languages being spoken on set. The Nazi film-within-a-film discussed above, meanwhile, can also be read as homage to, and political inversion of, *To Hell and Back* (1955), which tells the story of – and stars – American war hero Audie Murphy. To these various inter-filmic references made by Tarantino, Ben Walters adds even more, beyond those that arise from the relation to Castellari's original: "The score is filched from other films, characters are named for obscure actors and filmmakers, and there are innumerable references to UFA, G. W. Pabst, and Leni Riefenstahl; there's even a riff on King Kong as representative of 'the story of the negro in America'" (20).

I mention these details precisely because they point to the ways in which watching and retelling – in the form of revision and adaptation – are at the centre of the film industry, and thus point to the ways in which the notion of a passive viewing audience is belied by the blurring of culture consumer and culture producer that enables the creation of film itself. And, of course, Tarantino is more than aware of this: all of his major films are meditations on specific film genres, retellings not of individual films but of entire methods of cinematic storytelling. The spectral image of film thus becomes a discursive site of intertextuality, in which the dialogues between films exponentially expand into dialogues between dialogues of films, and so on. More a fractal explosion of signs than a mise en abyme, this endless swirl of refracted images is another way of viewing Rancière's dissensus. His discussion of a scene in Pedro Costa's film, *In Vonda's Room* (2000), could be translated onto Tarantino's climactic image of film consuming itself: "the film cannot be the presentation of this sensible world," he writes. "Cinema cannot be the equivalent of the love letter or music of the poor" or, one may add, of Jewish resistance against Nazi genocide. Instead,

> It must split itself off; it must agree to be the surface on which an artist tries to cipher in new figures the experience of people relegated to the

> margins of economic circulation and social trajectories. [...] And if its political effect stems from its very exteriority to the formatted distribution of thoughts and sensations to formatted audiences, this means that there can be no anticipating that effect. [...] [A]ll forms of art can rework the frame of our perceptions and the dynamism of our affects. As such, they can open up new passages towards new forms of political subjectivation. But none of them can avoid the aesthetic cut that separates outcomes from intentions and precludes any direct path towards an "other side" of words and images. (*Emancipated* 82)

The distance between image and audience is here necessarily insurmountable, and thus leaves subsequent interpretations, translations, and transubstantiations of that image unpredictable. The aesthetic distance, and therefore spectacle itself (Tarantino's stock and trade), is thus the only space for hope: hope for transformation, newness, change.

I will end on what every discussion of *Inglourious Basterds'* climactic scene touches on: its dialogue with *The Wizard of Oz*. The climactic theatre scene takes place in the final chapter of the film, which is titled "The Revenge of the Giant Face." The image of a ghostly face projected onto smoke with a fire beneath it references, of course, the famous image of the green-faced "wizard" in the 1939 MGM masterpiece. Released in the year that would mark the beginning of the war that Tarantino rewrites, *Oz* performs its own dance through the minefield of spectatorship, the image, and the real. A film that technically highlights the transformation from the drab sepia of the mundane to the glorious Technicolor of fantasy, *Oz*, on its surface, warns us not to mistake the image for the real, telling us that, like Dorothy (and her little dog, too), we must always look behind the curtain, or we risk not getting back to Kansas after all, and we might mistake real courage, intelligence, and affect for the mere images thereof.

Not so Tarantino: *Inglourious Basterds* would have it that the image is significant, for it is on and from the surface of the image that the viewer can construct and find a space for intellectual engagement and hopeful social transformation.[12] That dynamic instant of transformation from sepia to Technicolor, from reality to fantasy, is the moment that we all live in as hybridizations of viewers and living subjects: this is the space that Tarantino asks the audience to recognize itself in when, at the very beginning of the film, he forces together fairy tale fantasy and historical horror, as the screen offers the tagline, "Once upon a time ... in Nazi-occupied France," and Lander, the figure for the material realities of the Holocaust and anti-Semitism in the film, inexplicably allows Shosanna to live, moving into a fantasy where she can escape down the yellow-brick road to the magical land of Paris, which allows her to take her phantasmagoric revenge through a manipulation of the silver screen image. Precisely because the Wizard is not and can never be the same as the man behind that screen, the image can never be a space of simple subjection or resistance, but can only ever be the ground and figure of an intellectual public who translates that image into a sensible object in its own variable ways "This is what a process of political subjectivation consists in," Rancière tells or reminds us: "in the action of uncounted capacities that crack open the unity of the given and the obviousness of the visible, in order to sketch a new topography of the possible" (49). Here, the image itself takes revenge on those who would deny it its image-ness, a power at once more ephemeral and more material than that of the woman or man behind the curtain, but only because the meaning of that image remains necessarily foggy: this is the point that McLuhan makes with regard to the unperfected technologies of early television, but he should have taken it to the level of image itself.[13] Whether sepia or Technicolor, silver nitrate or digital, low or high def, the image – culture itself – is never a perfect transmission.

And that's what makes the image perfect. Refusing to submit to the dichotomy of passive and active audience, a reading of culture as important because it is at a remove from the material world allows the critic or spectator to present, as Rancière writes, "a new scene of equality where heterogeneous performances are translated into one another" where "to know that words are merely words and spectacles merely spectacles can help us arrive at a better understanding of how words and images, stories and performances, can change something of the world we live in" (22–3). It is through the always distant surface of the spectacular image and the constant fascination with and interpretations of it that, perhaps, the audience – and the inglourious critic – can learn how to stop worrying about the culture industry and find intellectual engagement and hope in loving its basterd fantasies.

NOTES

I would like to thank audiences at the Canadian Association for American Studies and Dalhousie University for their comments on earlier versions of this chapter. I would also like to thank the Dalhousie's Theory Reading Group (notably in this case Anthony Enns, Geordie Miller, and Erin Wunker) as well as

Trevor Ross for their willingness to discuss Rancière's work with me; Ainsworth Clarke and Joel Faflak for doing the same with Kant (and Joel for all of his other incisive comments); and the anonymous readers of this volume for all of their comments. I should also express my sense of gratitude and uncanny wonder to whomever it was who sent me – over the course of a few months, completely out of the blue, and long before this paper was conceived – copies of recent translations of Rancière's works. And, as always, I thank Julia M. Wright for her willingness to discuss the whole and its constituent parts.

1 My musical metaphor is borrowed from Althusser, who writes: "This concert [of Ideological State Apparatuses] is dominated by a single score, occasionally disturbed by contradictions (those of the remnants of former ruling classes, those of the proletarians and their organizations): the score of the Ideology of the current ruling class which integrates into its music the great themes of the Humanism of the Great Forefathers, who produced the Greek Miracle even before Christianity, and afterwards the Glory of Rome, the Eternal City, and the themes of Interest, particular and general, etc. nationalism, moralism and economism" (154–5).

2 In addition to the critical schools discussed, one could mention Brecht's and Artaud's differing theatrical processes, which nonetheless both aim to create or reawaken the active subject within the passively constructed audience. I discuss these in brief, below, when turning to Tarantino's cinematic borrowings from Jean-Luc Godard, but the reader should also see R. Darren Gobert's contribution to this volume, which discusses these and similar theatrical practices. See note 7, below, as well, for a more detailed discussion of the Birmingham School.

3 The best known of Kant's racist statements comes from his *Observations on the Feeling of the Beautiful and the Sublime,* in which he states of a "Negro carpenter" that "this fellow was quite black, from head to foot, a clear proof that he was stupid" (qtd. in Eze 57).

4 One significant example is, of course, the canon formation engaged in by the New Critics, many of whom denied to popular forms the sublimity of "true art," and in so doing also shunt to the side a connection to the particularities of history, preferring instead the totalizing assertions of a "universal history" of aesthetics and affect. Cleanth Brooks, perhaps the most cogent of the New Critics in the recognition that a fully realized universalism of criticism or (literary) history cannot exist, still summarizes this position, tying a Kantian disinterest to an attempt at a universal (literary) history (see esp. 237–8). His definition of this universal history is, however, explicitly tied to value judgments that result in the gendered critical denial of popular culture: "Can we even stop short of the young

lady who confesses to raptures over her confessions magazine? [...] [O]n the premises of critical relativism, have we not deprived ourselves of the right to say that her taste is 'desperately bad'?" (233). H. Bruce Franklin, in a more historical bent, traces the connections of some of the New Critics to implicitly or explicitly racist ideologies.

5 My allusions here are to the famous 1958 B-movie, *The Blob*, which is itself a meditation on the ways in which popular cinema projects the passivity of its audience back onto that audience, rendering a subject ripe for exploitation. At one point, the hero, Steve Andrews (Steve McQueen), and his girlfriend, Jane Martin (Aneta Corsaut) (described as "cats [who don't] dig spooky shows") go into the movie theatre to recruit friends to help the town. As they walk in, the voiceover of a particular "spooky show" states "I am here, the demon who possesses your soul. Wait a bit: I am coming for you. I have so much to show you." In what follows, as an old man tells them to be quiet and watch the movie, Steve has a hard time convincing his friends to leave to help save the town, since they "want to get [their] money's worth" from the movie ("none of us will, unless someone keeps quiet"), ending with one teen saying, "I'm part of this chair and I can't move": the demon of the cinematic spectacle does indeed possess the soul of the passive audience, leaving them ripe for the blob of mass culture to ingest. At a later point, as an audience laughs at a film that is itself seemingly made up only of images of laughing faces, the titular monster – a gelatinous image of the undifferentiated masses – absorbs the projectionist and proceeds to squeeze through the projection window onto the audience itself, which, in an oft-cited scene, runs screaming from the theatre, the only way the mass audience can save itself from the demon of passivity. As Hanna Fenichel Pitkin writes, using *The Blob* and other B-horror films as a model for Hannah Arendt's vision of the social, such a view sees the social world (specifically, I would say, in the cultural image) as "an evil monster from outer space, entirely external to and separate from us," which has "fallen upon us intent on debilitating, absorbing, and ultimately destroying us, gobbling up our distinct individuality and turning us into robots that mechanically serve its purposes" (4).

6 In addition to Mulvey, one can point here to the Situationists, who Rancière discusses, and to any number of discourse analysis media theorists.

7 The Birmingham School in many ways sets the stage for Rancière's work, especially in arguing that there is no simple or direct line of meaning or interpellation between culture producers and culture consumers. In addition to Hebdige's work, I think here of E.P. Thompson's attempt to recover

the working class as being composed of thinking and reflexive individuals, and of Stuart Hall's notions of "encoding" and "decoding," through which, like Rancière, he critiques overly linear models of cultural interpellation, what he calls "mass-communications research [that] has conceptualized the process of communication in terms of a circulation circuit or loop" (107). In his model, the spectator can fully buy into the hegemonic transmission of a spectacle, can "negotiate" a more "local" response to such a transmission, or can stand in "opposition" to this hegemonic message (115–16). Hall's theory lays the groundwork for a notion of the active spectator, but this spectator and the spectacle are still tethered to their separate states of production. Likewise, John Fiske reads television as a "producerly" text, which he defines in contradistinction to Barthes's "readerly" and "writerly" texts. The "producerly text," falling between these poles, is popular, and so doesn't "foreground" its structure, but still remains an "open" text, through which the reader can write her own "script" (96). But, for Fiske, the *medium* of television generates the supposedly active viewer, a process which thus, in turn, is a product of capitalist market relations. While Fiske is interested in cultural form, in the image, and in the spectator's active engagement with it, this relation is still one fully contained, as it is for Hall, by the material position and subsequent production of both. To connect these conclusions back to the Frankfurt School, one could argue that they sound like nothing so much as Benjamin's assertion that, when it comes to film, "The public is an examiner, but an absent-minded one" (241).

To quote Thoreau, the "distinction" I am drawing here may seem to be "without a difference" (97), insofar as I see Rancière largely agreeing with these premises but, by focussing on the spectacle, coming to different conclusions. The Birmingham School and its later adherents are often guilty of reducing those "concrete individual[s]" and their "positions, practices and operations" to a minimalist set of pre-ordained sociological metonyms. This assumption is tied to one that cannot see the spectacle as an *aesthetic* space of freedom for that audience. Perhaps this distinction could best be made via Tony Bennett, who states that the Birmingham School's essentially Gramscian approach offers a "conjunctural analysis [...] in which all moments of the social totality interact, however disjointedly, in ways which ultimately make for a complexly structured whole" (170); allowing for the aesthetic separation of the spectacle, on the contrary, permits for the potential shattering of that whole.

8 Sedgwick argues for the simple existence of a pragmatic "nonce taxonomy" of human identity in our day-to-day lived experience, one that

should be mirrored in theoretical discussions of identity, going beyond the "coarse axes" of "gender, race, class, nationality, [and] sexual orientation" to recognize that "people are different from each other" in myriad ways (22). In her argument, interactions with culture become systematically unsystematic, categorizable to the point of categories becoming largely useless. In this system, seeing an interaction with the image as either one of interpellation or resistance along whatever lines of identification becomes its own kind of myth.

9 My reading of Kant, it should be noted, is a blunt one, used as a stable ground against which to present Rancière's and Tarantino's works in relief, as it were. But, it needs to be noted that Kant's own work is not necessarily stable on the subject of universal judgement, nor is the relationship between the transcendent (and universal) and phenomenal (and hence specific) necessarily untroubled. As David Farrell Krell writes (in a book coincidentally titled *The Purest of Bastards*), within Kant's writings "a certain amount of 'not entirely avoidable obscurity' remains attached to every solution attempted by a transcendental critique of the power of judgement" (35). For a counter-reading of Kant's inevitable, if undesired, connection of the material to the transcendental, see Deleuze, who writes of the Kantian faculties of knowledge and desire, on the one hand, and "imagination, understanding, [and] reason" on the other (see, esp. 3–7), that their "higher form never abstracts them from their human finitude any more than it suppresses their difference in kind. It is *in so far as they are specific and finite* that the faculties – in the first sense of the word – take on a higher form and that the faculties – in the second sense – take on the legislative role" (69; my emphasis). Finally, for a reading that ties Deleuze and Rancière together through Kant, see Wolfe.

10 One has only to google "'Inglourious Basterds' antisemitism" to see a range of responses, from film reviewers decrying the film as anti-Semitic, to Nazi-sympathizer hate sites offering their own confused, idiotic "analyses," to others, including the Anti-Defamation League, lauding it as a film about the destruction of evil. For some responses that deal with the complexities of the revenge fantasy and the violence it entails, see Goldberg, Uni (in an article published during filming), and O'Hehir (who provides a meta-discussion of criticism of the film, including the two previous responses).

11 See, for example, Pisters, who analyses Tarantino's homage to Godard in *Pulp Fiction*, and also discusses the way in which Tarantino "plays with the power of the false in a masterly fashion," though she reads Tarantino as "completely den[ying] the classic distance [...] between reality and fiction"

seeing this denial as reinforced, rather than troubled, by his similar blurring of the line between "fiction and metafiction" (101).

12 I am tempted here to add yet more layers of intertextuality, this time between Tarantino's film and Mel Brooks's *The Producers* (1968), and its play-within-a-film, *Springtime for Hitler*. The recursive structure of Brooks's film also posits an aesthetic image completely disconnected from its conditions of production, in this case figured as the author's or producers' intent: as the audience laughs uproariously at what they have interpreted as comedy, the producers see their monetary scheme (premised on a certain knowledge of an opposite audience reaction) go up in smoke, while the Nazi author jumps up and shouts furiously "You shut up! I am the author! You are the audience! I outrank you!" The audience, watching a very different play from the one he sees, keeps laughing.

13 I am indebted for this point to Christine Handley, who makes a similar argument in her thesis, "'Playthings in the Margins of Literature': Cultural Critique and Rewriting Ideologies in *Supernatural* and *Star Wars* Fanfiction."

WORKS CITED

Adorno, Theodor W. *Prisms*. Trans. Shierry Weber Nicholsen and Samuel Weber. Cambridge, MA: MIT P, 1981. Print.

Althusser, Louis. *Lenin and Philosophy and Other Essays*. Trans. Ben Brewster. New York: Monthly Review P, 1971. Print.

Benjamin, Walter. *Illuminations*. Ed. and intro. Hannah Arendt. Trans. Harry Zohn. New York: Schocken, 1969. Print.

Bennett, Tony. "The Intellectual Genealogies and Possible Futures of Cultural Studies: An Interview with Tony Bennett." Interview by Huimin Jin. *Cultural Politics* 4.2 (2008): 161–182. Print. http://dx.doi.org/10.2752/1751743 08X310884.

The Blob. Dir. Irvin Yeaworth. Written by Kay Linaker and Theodore Simonson, from an orig. idea by Irvine H. Millgate. Paramount, 1958. Film.

Brooks, Cleanth. *The Well Wrought Urn: Studies in the Structure of Poetry*. 1947. New York: Harvest/HBJ, 1974. Print.

Cox, David. "Inglourious Basterds is cinema's revenge on life." *The Guardian* 20 August 2009. Web. 9 October 2010.

Deleuze, Gilles. *Kant's Critical Philosophy: The Doctrine of the Faculties*. Trans. Hugh Tomlinson and Barbara Habberjam. Minneapolis: U of Minnesota P, 1985. Print.

Fiske, John. *Television Culture*. London: Methuen, 1987. Print.

Foucault, Michel. *The History of Sexuality*. Vol. 1. Trans. Robert Hurley. New York: Vintage, 1990. Print.

Franklin, H. Bruce. *Prison Literature in America: The Victim as Criminal and Artist*. Expanded ed. of *The Victim as Criminal and Artist: Literature from the American Prison*. Oxford: Oxford UP, 1989. Print.

Goldberg, Jeffrey. "Hollywood's Jewish Avenger." *The Atlantic*. Sept. 2009. *theatlantic.com*. Web. 18 January 2011.

Hall, Stuart. "Encoding/decoding." *Culture, Media, Language*. Ed. Stuart Hall, Dorothy Hobson, Andrew Lowe, and Paul Willis. 1980. London: Routledge, 1991. 107–16. Print.

Handley, Christine. "'Playthings in the Margins of Literature': Cultural Critique and Rewriting Ideologies in *Supernatural* and *Star Wars* Fanfiction." MA thesis. Dalhousie University, 2010. Print.

Hebdige, Dick. *Subculture: The Meaning of Style*. London: Routledge, 1981. Print.

Hohenadel, Kristin. "Bunch of Guys on a Mission Movie." *New York Times*. 6 May 2009. Web. 18 January 2011.

Huxley, Aldous. *Brave New World and Brave New World Revisited*. New York: Harper, 2005. Print.

Inglourious Basterds. Writ. and Dir. Quentin Tarantino. Universal, 2009. Blu-ray.

Jameson, Frederic. *Archaeologies of the Future: The Desire Called Utopia and Other Science Fictions*. London: Verso, 2005. Print.

Kant, Immanuel. *Critique of Judgment*. Trans. Werner S. Pluhar. Indianapolis: Hackett, 1987. Print.

Krell, David Farrell. *The Purest of Bastards: Works of Mourning, Art, and Affirmation in the Thought of Jacques Derrida*. University Park: Pennsylvania State UP, 2000. Print.

Morley, Dave. "Texts, readers, subjects." *Culture, Media, Language*. Ed. Stuart Hall, Dorothy Hobson, Andrew Lowe, and Paul Willis. 1980. London: Routledge, 1991. 154–65. Print.

Mulvey, Laura. "Visual Pleasure and Narrative Cinema." *Screen* 16 (1975): 6–18. Print.

O'Hehir, Andrew. "Is Tarantino good for the Jews?" *Salon.com*. 13 August 2009. Web. 18 January 2011.

Pisters, Patricia. *The Matrix of Visual Culture: Working with Deleuze in Film Theory*. Stanford: Stanford UP, 2003. Print.

Pitkin, Hanna Fenichel. *The Attack of the Blob: Hannah Arendt's Concept of the Social*. Chicago: The U of Chicago P, 1998. Print.

The Producers. Writ. And dir. Mel Brooks. 1968. MGM, 2002. DVD.
Rancière, Jacques. *Aesthetics and Its Discontents*. Trans. Steven Corcoran. Cambridge: Polity, 2009. Print.
Rancière, Jacques. *The Emancipated Spectator*. Trans. Gregory Elliott. London: Verso, 2009. Print.
Rancière, Jacques. *The Politics of Aesthetics: The Distribution of the Sensible*. Trans. and intro. Gabriel Rockhill. Afterword by Slavoj Žižek. New York: Continuum, 2004. Print.
"Revenge of the Giant Face: 14 Notes on Quentin Tarantino's *Inglourious Basterds*." *The Film Doctor* 22 August 2009. Web. 9 October 2010.
Sedgwick, Eve Kosofsky. *Epistemology of the Closet*. Updated with a New Preface. Berkeley: U of California P, 2008. Print.
Taylor, Charles. "Violence as the Best Revenge: Fantasies of Dead Nazis." *Dissent* 57.1 (2010): 103–6. Print. http://dx.doi.org/10.1353/dss.0.0115.
Thompson, E.P. *The Making of the English Working Class*. London: Gollancz, 1963. Print.
Thoreau, Henry David. "Slavery in Massachusetts." *Reform Papers*. Ed. Wendell Glick. Princeton: Princeton UP, 1973. 91–109. Print. Writings of Henry D. Thoreau.
Uni, Assaf. "The Holocaust, Tarantino-style: Jews scalping Nazis." *Haaretz.com*. 7 October 2008. Web. 18 January 2011.
Walters, Ben. "Debating *Inglourious Basterds*." *Film Quarterly* 63.2 (2009): 19–22. Print. http://dx.doi.org/10.1525/FQ.2009.63.2.19.
Wizard of Oz. Dir. Victor Fleming. Perf. Judy Garland. 1939. Warner, 2010. Blu-ray.
Wolfe, Katharine. "From Aesthetics to Politics: Rancière, Kant and Deleuze." *Contemporary Aesthetics* 4 (2006). Web. 18 January 2011.

PART THREE

Public Matters

9 Beyond the Book: Reading as Public Intellectual Activity

DANIEL COLEMAN

Most people think of the public intellectual as a person. The problem with this notion is that it pins too much hope for change on the image of the romantic hero: some extremely smart or specially gifted person will arise who can explain to us the conditions of our lives and show us how to make a better world. If we follow Antonio Gramsci's original description of the organic intellectual, this person will be defined by the ability to articulate the conditions of our lives in such a way as to galvanize society to action against oppressive conditions and generate revolutionary change.[1] I do not dispute that such people have emerged in human history, but it's pretty rare. It seems that you have to wait a long time for conditions to converge so that one of these galvanizing figures can appear. So I am interested here in where we might find hope in the meantime, in less romantic and less personality-driven possibilities. I would like to suggest, though it means a minor tussle with Gramsci, that if we think of public intellectualism as a set of activities rather than a person, activities that many people already participate in, then perhaps we might be able to concentrate on the potentials within these activities for invigorating public life and addressing immense and seemingly intractable problems.[2]

Very simply, I submit that reading, plain and simple, but understood in broader terms than we often do, is public intellectual activity – or to put it the other way around, reading is a fundamental activity of the public intellectual. This claim may seem strange, because reading seems decidedly un-public, since most of us do it in private. It is precisely in the paradox of its privacy, however, that we can find hope, for reading is an activity that causes us to retreat from others in order to connect with them. Think about what happens when we read: we isolate ourselves with the text, but we do so to attend to thoughts and images generated by someone else, so our isolation is not solipsistic. Indeed, the privacy of reading fosters a unique vulnerability: we can open ourselves to the experiences and views of others without fear of immediate evaluation by them. We can try on unfamiliar ideas or behaviours offstage, as it were, before we decide how they fit our public lives. Solitary reading is, then, despite appearances, the scene of our active engagement with others, with worlds beyond our own immediate surroundings. This paradox makes reading profoundly intimate and private on the one hand, and publicly, socially active on the other. For readers cannot passively consume a text, but must imagine a dialogue with the (usually absent) author to construct meaning, image, and understanding. Reading nurtures a posture of attentiveness: it exercises our skills as active interpreters and counteracts the temptation to remain private and passive consumers.

I have developed these ideas at greater length in my book *In Bed With the Word*,[3] so I want to move on to a second paradox, which is that reading is also a nonconsumptive kind of consumption. In the words of Robert Bringhurst, "Reading [...] enables us to reach across the fence between the world and ourselves without destroying what we find" (9). Reading is like listening in the sense that it takes in without touching, eats without killing, harvests without cutting. The thing we read – whether a newspaper, a human face, or the needles of a pine tree – nourishes us *and* survives us. To stay alive, we must consume, we must eat the lives of others – plants, minerals, animals – and eventually, we too become the food of others when our bodies return to the earth. Reading is a great relief because it is one step removed from this necessary economy. Like eating, reading reveals our interdependency on the world around us. We depend upon others for the words in our own mouths, for our mental nourishment, just as they depend upon us. But to read is to consume without consuming. The object being read lives on after our reading, has its own life, retains its distinctness even after we have ingested it.[4]

The activity of reading, then, is a beam of hope in times when it seems there is no escaping the pandemic of consumption that characterizes Western history and culture. In the early nineteenth century, one in four British people died of consumption. The disease was called *consumption* because those it claimed seemed to be consumed from within. The idea of being consumed from within still echoes in what we now call "consumer culture." Indeed, if anything breeds cynicism in our times, it's the despair that, whatever we humans do, we consume and destroy the world around us, and with it, ourselves. Whether the cost is war in Iraq between 1990 and 2011 or the ecological disaster of British Petroleum's malfunctioning Deepwater Horizon well in 2010, shortsighted consumption is willing to destroy manifold forms of life so we can drive to the store and pack our purchases in plastic bags. In a culture that gauges its economic health by measures such as the Consumer Confidence Index, the inevitability of our consumption can cause twenty-first-century humans to lose hope in ourselves. Even readers are not exempt, when we turn objects of mental or spiritual nourishment into possessions that line our shelves or when we colonize the thoughts or creativity of others as if they were branch plants of our own egos. There are those who try, at least, to resist. Whether they plant a vegetable garden, install solar panels, or take the bus, they refuse the cynicism of consumption. They can imagine a relation to the other that is not consumptive, that sees the other as having a life that is as rich and precious and complex as their own. These are people who have not lost hope, who wish to respect the world around them, to engage the world without destroying what they touch. But it seems the larger forces in our culture press unstintingly towards bigger box stores, faster microprocessors, larger television screens, and extra lanes on the highway.

In a culture of rampant consumption, one wonders if there is any hope for reading and the private, let alone public, intellectual life that it makes possible. There are those who have been driven by this despair to hunker down in defence of the traditional book. They see the culture of the screen as the enemy. Whether it's TV, with its laugh tracks and advertising, its surround-sound and high-definition knockout punch, or whether it's the high-speed, commerce-saturated Internet, with its chimes and click-me pop-ups, tweets and twitters, the culture of the screen seems opposed to the posture of sustained attention associated with the printed page. The hope I see in reading, however, lies not so much in the medium itself as in the paradoxes of privacy-in-order-to-connect and consuming-not-to-consume that I think is its essential value. Let me illustrate what I mean by reading beyond the book, by reading a text that is not a printed document but that has circulated widely in North America for about four centuries.

I

Around 1613, two peoples found themselves thrown together in the same territory and on the same river by the burgeoning forces of colonial consumption. Dutch traders had travelled up what was later called the Hudson River into Haudenosaunee territory. The Haudenosaunee were and are a confederacy of at first five and then six Iroquoian-language-speaking nations, the Mohawks, Oneidas, Onondagas, Cayugas, and Senecas, who were eventually joined in the eighteenth century by the Tuscaroras. When the Dutch arrived in the territory, they marvelled at the densely populated towns, the fertile fields tall with the corn that sheltered crops of beans and squash. They eyed the forests of oak, sugar maples, and the tall white pines that would make perfect ship masts. The *sachems* or lords of the Haudenosaunee Confederacy council, along with the clan mothers and warriors, greeted the newcomers, and rather than overwhelming their ship and confiscating their goods, or requiring them to abandon their language and enter schools where they could be civilized and taught the rudiments of consultative democracy outlined in the *kayaneren'tsherakowa* or Great Law of Peace, they formed a friendship with them. For the Haudenosaunee, too, saw advantages in the arrival of these newcomers who would take pelts and hides in exchange for iron-headed axes, guns, and metal cooking pots.

After the two groups had become acquainted with each other, the time came for the Haudenosaunee to formalize this friendship. They therefore showed the Dutch traders a ceremonial belt of purple and white quahog shell-beads called wampum. Wampum was part of a widespread system of graphical communication that extended across early Amerindian cultures "from the Tupi-Gurani's *Ayvu Rapyta* or Origin of Human Speech, to the Yucatac-Mayan paper screenfolds, to the Algonquian *Walam Olum* or Red Score, Medewiwin or Grand Medicine Scrolls, and Mi'kmaw hieroglyphics" (Battiste, "Print Culture" 111). With ideographical patterns woven into strings or belts, wampum was a common communication medium throughout the northeastern region of Turtle Island. Among the Iroquois, it was used as a ceremonial-mnemonic system for recording agreements between peoples.[5] The accounts I have heard of the meeting of the Dutch and the Haudenosaunee come from oral history and have found their way into written form. The version I know best comes from articles written by Tuscarora scholar Richard Hill, who recounts the story as he heard it from Jacob Thomas, an elder Cayuga chief, now deceased, who was

Figure 1. Cayuga Chief Jacob Thomas holding replicas of the Two Row Wampum and a related wampum known as the Friendship Belt in 1988. Courtesy of the American Philosophical Society.

an adjunct professor at Trent University and whose father had been a wampum keeper; and from Huron Miller, a respected Onondaga culture-bearer. The belt the Haudenosaunee brought in ceremony to the Dutch is called the *Aterihwihsón:sera Kaswentah*, in English the Two Row Wampum, because two rows of purple beads run horizontally across the belt, uniformly parallel so they never veer apart nor merge together into one.[6] The two purple rows divide the belt into three background rows of white beads, each three beads wide.

The Haudenosaunee pointed to the white beads and explained that they represented the river the Dutch had been sailing on. The river was the Creator's gift to all people, including two-legged ones such as the Haudenosaunee and the Dutch. It provided them with much of their livelihood, and it gave them ease of travel. They then pointed to the two purple rows and explained that one row represented the Dutch sailing vessel, while the other represented the Iroquoian canoe. They would share the Creator's river, neither interfering with the other's progress nor boarding the other's vessel. This is how to conduct a friendship, they said: the two parties would share the water and the life sustained by it, especially when they remembered that the three bands of white beads on which the two vessels floated represented the three principles of peace, friendship, and respect.

The Dutch traders did not understand what they were hearing. How could they? Everything they had been taught about the people they would encounter in America insisted they were illiterate savages with no civilization, no government, and no god. They were utterly unprepared for the *Aterihwihsón:sera Kaswentah* with its iconography of equity, autonomy, interrelationship, and ecological responsibility. They did not know how to read this kind of text. So, like most people would do, they translated it into their own notions of how to sweeten talks with people who sit upon resources you wish to extract. They expressed their respect for the Haudenosaunee and their beliefs, and they said they would henceforth treat them as "sons."

The Haudenosaunee had had some of their men up near Statacona (later, Quebec City) forcibly "adopted" eighty years earlier and taken to France on Jacques Cartier's sailing ships never to be seen again. So they covered their alarm at this proposal with diplomatic calm. "We respect you, your belief, and what you say," said the Haudenosaunee. "You pronounced yourself as our father and this we do not agree with because the father can tell his son what to do, and can punish his son. We suggest that we call each other brother."[7]

The Dutch, needing to establish friendly terms with the people who governed the region, agreed, and to indicate their understanding of the serious intent of this council of friendship, they offered to "put our friendship in writing." The Haudenosaunee replied, "This is good, but one thing we must remember, paper will not last. We must find a way to make sure that the friendship will be passed on to the next generation." The Haudenosaunee had shown the Dutch a durable, long-lasting, easy-to-read iconographic representation of their relationship in the Two Row Wampum. So the Dutch replied with a symbolic object of their own, a chain of three links, representing friendship, a good mind, and peace; this chain would represent the binding of the two peoples together. As it was made of iron, it would need to be cleaned and polished to keep off rust, just as any friendship needs review and renewal.[8]

The Dutch then affirmed, "What we do about our own ways of belief, we shall both respect having our own rights and power." To which the Haudenosaunee replied with this explanation of the *Aterihwihsón:sera Kaswentah*: "I will put in my canoe my belief and laws. In your vessel you shall put your belief and laws. All my people will be in my canoe, your people in your vessel. We shall put these boats in the water and they shall always be parallel, as long as there is Mother Earth, this will be everlasting." Then the Dutch had a question: "What will happen if your people will like to go into my vessel?" The Haudenosaunee answered: "If this happens, they will have to be guided by my canoe." But the Dutch raised another problem: "What will happen if any of our people may someday want to have one foot in each of the boats that are parallel?" The Haudenosaunee replied, "If this so happens that my people may wish to have their feet in each of the two boats, there will be a high wind and the boats will separate and the person that has his feet in each of the boats shall fall between the boats, and there is no living soul who will be able to bring them back to the right way given by the Creator but only one – the Creator himself." And thus, they concluded their pact of friendship.

The agreement recorded in the Two Row Wampum emphasizes a cultural and interrelational framework – indeed, you could see it as a model for cross-cultural reading. The threat to its values is recorded in the story itself – that one of the two parties will interpret the relationship in consumptive terms and, instead of protecting the relation of autonomous equals, will attempt to absorb the other into the same: want to own a piece of their property, grab the rudder in the other's vessel. To put it differently, the story anticipates the complications that will occur when people in later generations cross over from one boat to the other and become confused about where they belong and what kind of deal they are signing. Richard Hill notes that, like any text, the Two Row has been interpreted variously by contemporary Iroquois folks. Some, for example, have suggested that if Indigenous people want to enter the white man's vessel, then they pretty much sign over their Haudenosaunee birthright. They will lose their cultural values, suffer from a "split mind." The Thomas and Miller versions, Hill suggests, take a milder view. Because of the long history of contact and exchange between Haudenosaunee and European cultures, many Iroquois people now live, whether they want to or not, in the white man's vessel. Consider for instance the domain of language, where the majority of the Six Nations populace no longer speaks one of the original languages, with the result that concepts such as those presented in the *Aterihwihsón:sera Kaswentah* must be borne by the uncertain vessel of the English language. Thomas and Miller present the Two Row not as a document of absolute cultural separatism, but as one that suggests Native people should retain a Native value system no matter where they go (Hill, "Oral" 158).

II

The chances of Haudenosaunee people staying in their own canoe have turned out to be very few, despite their having formalized Two Row treaties at successive councils with the Dutch, French, British, and then Americans and Canadians between the seventeenth and nineteenth centuries. A history-defining catastrophe occurred when the British, with whom the Six Nations had formed a Two Row understanding, broke into two warring parties in 1776. Many Six Nations warriors felt compelled by their history of friendship with the British to side with them against the upstart rebels during the Revolutionary War. The result was that they were literally burnt out of their homes and farms by vengeful American troops during the infamous Sullivan campaign of 1779. After the Treaty of Paris (1783), which, significantly, failed to make any provisions for the First Peoples whose lands had been overtaken during the fighting, the Haudenosaunee negotiated with British Commander Sir Frederick Haldimand for a million acres of land on both banks of the Grand River in what's now Ontario. The British colonial government acceded to this arrangement not only in recognition of the Haudenosaunee contribution as military allies, but also to secure their support in case of further aggression from the Americans and their Native allies (Johnson 167–8). This land, however, was then whittled down to less than a tenth of its original size by confusing land leases and sales, and by successive reductions enforced by British and Canadian governments. Canadian observation of the Two Row agreement went from partial compliance to outright rejection. As late as 5 April 1909, Chief J.S. Johnson, deputy speaker of the Six Nations Confederacy Council, had a letter of assurance from Canada's Minister of the Interior Frank Oliver that Ottawa would respect Six Nations' right to govern themselves. "The Six Nations Indians of the Grand River came to Canada under special treaty as allies of Britain," wrote Oliver, "and the policy of the Canadian government is to deal with them having that fact always in view. [...] The system of tribal government which prevailed among the Six Nations on their coming to Canada was satisfactory to the Government at that time, and so long as it is satisfactory to the Six Nations themselves so long it will remain satisfactory to the Government of Canada" (qtd. in Woo 6). But by 1924 Canada had abandoned Two Row policy, when the Canadian government sent a detachment of armed RCMP officers to forcibly close the traditional government of the Six Nations on the Grand River and insist that the Haudenosaunee submit to the Indian Act with its Ottawa-controlled band council system (Monture 135). The chances of staying in their own canoe have been diminished not just by warfare, residential schools, and other legalized interventions; they have also been swamped by the saturating power of television and the Internet.

These circumstances have raised the Two Row for rereadings by contemporary Haudenosaunee artists and writers. Consider, for example, Mohawk artist Alan Michelson's *Two Row II* (2005), a large, thirteen-minute video installation that presents panoramic video shots of each bank of the Grand River in two parallel rows, just like the *Aterihwihsón:sera Kaswentah.* Shot separately through a purple filter from moving boats, the two banks seem to flow by in opposite directions on the huge screen. These images are accompanied by a soundtrack that superimposes a Canadian cruise boat captain's English narration about the river onto narratives in their own language by Haudenosaunee elders.

The confusion of overlaid voices and the disorientation of having the land rather than the river appear to move, and in opposite directions, highlight the complexity inhabited by the Grand River communities on both the reserve side and the "white" side of the river to this day. The racial division of the two communities by the river is not the ideal conveyed in the *Aterihwihsón:sera Kaswentah.* The two vessels were to remain independent, but they were to share the river, not divide it.

Figure 2. Alan Michelson, *Two Row II*, 2005. Four-channel video with sound, 13:05 minutes 108 × 576 inches. Courtesy of the National Gallery of Canada, Ottawa.

How long can two communities live in harmony on such a divided river, when they are administered by a government that has taken over both boats in remarkably unequal ways? How long can these communities actually maintain a respectful relationship? Do the stories of the cruise boat captain and the Haudenosaunee elders hear one another? Or are they each speaking separate stories that are obliterated by each other's noise?

Over twenty years earlier, Tuscarora visual historian, artist, and curator Jolene Rickard, a professor in the Art Department at Cornell University, produced a photo collage called "Two Canoes," which reads the *Aterihwihsón:sera Kaswentah* with similar questions in mind. In this work, Rickard presents the image of two tree trunks growing side by side in the same soil, but the feet of the two tree trunks are replaced by the feet of a moccasined groom and a European bride.

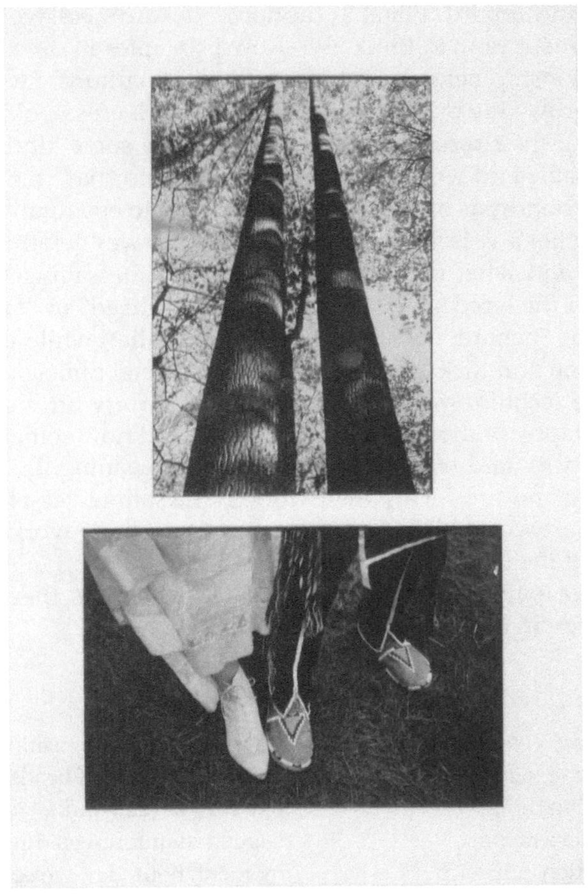

Figure 3. Jolene Rickard, *"Two Canoes,"* 1988. Chrome print, 11 × 17 inches. Courtesy of Jolene Rickard and the Burchfield Penney Art Centre.

Rickard says that the title comes from her grandfather, "who always said the Indian canoe is too swift for white culture. You had to decide which way you were going to go." The photo of the bride and groom, she says, was taken at the wedding of a white woman "who is very into her colonial background" and an Indigenous man "who is also very into his past." The bride is dressed like a nineteenth-century woman while the man is dressed for the present, and his natural, traditional, but still popular moccasins contrast with her artificial, pointed, and fashionable shoe (qtd. in Lippard, Plate 40 caption). Rickard's collage asks many questions about how to think Two Row principles in our times. What is the relationship between nature and human culture? How long can two trees grow side by side in the same ground, cross-pollinating and intertwining their roots, before they blend into some kind of hybrid? Is it reasonable and workable to expect people to share the same community for hundreds of years and for them not to eventually cross over into each other's vessels? How do we (why do we) determine what is traditional and what is modern: the canoe or the sailing vessel? The moccasin or the laced shoe? Which culture is "ahead" or "fast"? Which is "slow" or "behind"? It's significant to note that, while these works by Michelson and Rickard pose these far-reaching, philosophical questions in the techniques and media of contemporary art, they do so in the iconography of the Two Row – you have to know something of Six Nations history and tradition to plumb their meaning. If these artists are working and producing their work in the sailing vessel of the contemporary art world, they nonetheless produce these works out of the traditions of the Haudenosaunee canoe.

Onondaga painter and poet Eric Gansworth puts these considerations overtly in the following poem (2008):

Cross	**PolliNation**
And look here, you three	how you pull in opposition you
sisters growing together	jerk on the string of beads
each providing things	like seed in the wind
the others lack: support,	leaning in unforeseen directions
food, protection, and each	moment, hour, day, week, in another
time you pull away from one	place you land
another, risking everything,	and for what, to start over
you tear apart your world,	reforming yourselves as
our world. Each time you offer	us in endless variation,
the line up, we will add one	dark color, light color,
purple bead to your white strand	diluting your heritage
reminding you of the ways	we disappear for that moment
you put us all in danger	then strengthen, regenerate ourselves,
with each small tug	and embrace.

Gansworth notes that you can read the poem vertically, keeping the two rows separate, or you can read it horizontally across the two rows, your eyes following the conventions of English orthography from left to right. Whichever way you read it, the sense of the poem is made from Haudenosaunee knowledge and history, even if it circulates in the world of literary publication outside of the Iroquoian canoe: you need to know the three sisters refers to corn, beans, and squash: the three complementary food plants cultivated for millennia by Iroquoian peoples. You need to know not only the iconography of the *Aterihwihsón:sera Kaswentah* itself, but also the subsequent history of how the question of purity versus racial and cultural mixing has become increasingly loaded for Haudenosaunee communities and their neighbours.

III

The *Aterihwihsón:sera Kaswentah* is a visualization of the paradox of reading, that activity in which one can reach across the fence between oneself and the world without destroying what one finds. It is an image of simultaneous interdependency and independence, of accommodation and autonomy. The white rows do not constitute negative space, for their three rows of three beads distinctly represent the groundwork of peace, friendship, and respect that bind the two purple rows to one another. Rather than *negative space*, then, we might think of the white rows as constituting what Cree philosopher Willie Ermine calls *ethical space*. Ermine suggests that when two unequal parties enter into dialogue, the imbalance of power between them usually scuttles the possibilities of understanding. The beliefs and views of the dominant group tend to assert themselves as universal, and the beliefs and views of the subordinate group will be filtered through them. The resulting "institutionalized monoculture," Ermine explains, "creates the unfounded belief that there is a consensus about society and that the status quo of Indigenous-Western relations is the 'norm' in this country. This norm becomes so embedded that the danger exists of a society believing that the social inequities and dominant/subordinate relationships between human communities are authorized under the laws of nature or that they are the will of God" (198). This is the history of Indigenous and Euro-Canadian dialogue: Euro-Canadian languages, protocols for argumentation, ways of ordering knowledge, and legal structures have bulldozed Indigenous ones. Whether through the evacuation of Indigenous languages and beliefs through the "civilized" education delivered in residential schools, through the outlawing of ceremonies from the sundance to the potlatch, or through the removal of Indigenous people from traditional lands and therefore their capacity to protect those lands from abuse, Euro-Canadian values and systems of knowing have entertained little reciprocity with Indigenous ones. The Haudenosaunee, to return to our immediate example, were welcomed as allies of the British and given land as equals during the Loyalist migrations at the end of the Revolutionary War, but they were pretty much immediately subsumed to the dictates of the Royal Proclamation (1763) which asserted that all negotiations with Native peoples over land must be brokered by the Crown. The universalizing reach of British law commandeered their canoe even in the moment when the two parties were trying to negotiate a partnership, not between conqueror and conquered, but between allies. So the dialogue was not a dialogue. It rarely has been. Ermine argues that we need to take a step back from this assumed universalism and create ethical space by

> the unwavering construction of difference and diversity between human communities. These are the differences that highlight uniqueness because each entity is moulded from a distinct history, knowledge tradition, philosophy, and social and political reality. With the calculated disconnection through the contrasting of their identities, and the subsequent creation of two solitudes with each claiming their own distinct and autonomous view of the world, a theoretical space between them is opened. (194)

His is not an argument for permanent cultural separatism; it is an argument for clarification and respect. As signalled by Jolene Rickard's white-shoed bride and moccasined groom, by Michelson's overlaid voices of the tour boat captain and the Haudenosaunee elder, and by Gansworth's "Cross PolliNation," Ermine says that the long history of "socio-political entanglement" has created "an irritable bond" between settler-Canadian and Indigenous communities whose result is "transcultural confusion at its worst. We are now so badly entangled in our political and social lives that the principles of our existences as autonomous human communities have become blurred in that intercultural confusion. We no longer know what informs each of our identities and what should guide the association with each other" (197). Essentially, he suggests we all need room to breathe. For true dialogue to occur, all parties need to back away from coercive assertions of common ground that engulf and absorb the other, so that we can listen to what the other is actually saying. "The idea of the ethical space, produced by contrasting perspectives of the world," he explains, "entertains the notion of a meeting place" where we can "detach from the cages of our mental worlds and assume a position where human-to-human dialogue can occur" (202).

We have returned to paradox. "When you take the other's otherness away," Robert Bringhurst writes, "the other's sameness and humanity go too" (22). The paradox is that a full recognition of the autonomy and uniqueness of the other requires that we not coerce the other into the category of the same. We cannot try to incorporate the other within our own existing systems of thought, our own cultural formulations and understandings, if we are to respect the other person as a human being. The same is true if we are talking about nature. According the other respect means *valuing* the otherness of the other for itself, valuing its difference just as we value ourselves for our own uniqueness. This kind of valuing requires the paradox of similarity and difference, of finding the similarity in unassimilated difference, the universal in the divergently particular. All life deserves care and respect, but each life is distinct and unique and must not be stripped of its distinction if it is to be what it is.

For this reason, instead of common ground, we need uncommon ground. To build uncommon ground, the parties on both sides of a dialogue need to read *away from* rather than towards the self. Rather than importing the signs of the other into our existing frameworks in order to find value in them, we need to engage actively and attentively to the frameworks that are foreign to us, not neglect them as incommensurable. We need to notice and learn from them, even as we remember that they are not our own. We need to map the uncommon ground where differences meet. In the words of Sarah Ahmed, rather than fixing difference in the incomprehensible strangeness of the other, we need to attend to the mode of encounter itself, reading away from selves and instead focussing on the unequal circumstances and histories that produced the encounter as strange in the first place (145). The reason to read away from the self and our familiar frameworks is not to push the other away, not to diminish or dismiss its value nor that of the culture from which it emerged. Rather, we read away from ourselves so that we do not eat the other, do not reduce the other into serving merely as a foil for the self. We read away from ourselves to turn private consumption into work that is publicly intellectual. If we as neighbouring societies are to work towards respect, peace, and friendship with each other as well as with the natural world in which we live, we need to learn how to build nonconsumptive relationships with one another. We need to rediscover Two Row consciousness.

IV

So, what can be achieved by rereading the Two Row Wampum in the twenty-first century? And why have I taken as my example of nonconsumptive reading this text from oral culture, rather than from the long and rich tradition of written literature? Didn't I begin by asserting that there is hope to be found in the act of reading, and isn't reading tied intimately to that particular tradition?

To begin with the last two questions, it seems to me that we live in a period when the media we read are changing. Many people read and write on screens these days more than they do on books and paper. I am not interested here in the red-herring debates about whether book culture will survive and whether literacy in the twenty-first century is going to hell in a handbasket. What I am interested in is the value there is in the act of reading itself, which paradoxically emphasizes vulnerable solitude and worldly interconnection. Both ends of this paradox are about attentiveness: we go into solitude when we read, not in order to sink into our own egos, but in order to pay closer attention to the voice of the other as we trace it on the page, on the computer screen, or on a seventeenth-century ceremonial bead belt. By reading a seventeenth-century oral document such as the *Aterihwihsón:sera Kaswentah*, I want to show that far-reaching philosophical and publicly crucial reading is not restricted to books, nor to the Euro-American literary or philosophical canon. By tracing the history of interpretations of the Two Row Wampum from its formulation between the Dutch and the Iroquois in 1613 through to its recent rereadings in contemporary art and poetry (I haven't even touched on its many readings in political and legal debates),[9] I have wanted to demonstrate that a rich tradition of reading and rereading exists around documents that emerge from oral culture. That tradition is far from dead; you can easily see it circulating today, not just in museums, your local library, or even on the Internet. It is circulating in roadblocks set up to assert land claims such as the ongoing land dispute in Caledonia, Ontario, in the editorial pages of the newspaper, and in ongoing debates in the House of Commons. From its inception, the Two Row Wampum was an intercultural document. It is literally about reading others across the lines of difference, about the value to be found in difference, especially for those who live together in the same environment.

But what is the point of rereading historical texts such as the *Aterihwihsón:sera Kaswentah* today? What hope can there be in reading documents like this that have been smothered by centuries of disavowal, dismissal, and wilful ignorance? Julia Kristeva writes that, despite her early disillusionment with the idea of revolution in communist-era Bulgaria, she did not abandon hope in social change. Rather, she says, it emphasized for her the etymology of *revolt*, as revolving movement, and how it might be understood, then, as a "return to the past, and innovation, renewal of the self – in other words a process of re-evaluation of the psyche" (75). For substantial public change to take place, she suggests, we must engage in "constant symbolic re-evaluation" (77). For Kristeva, revolution can only take place when we return to the past and reinterpret, renarrate its symbols and meanings for the present. Kristeva is a psychoanalyst, so it's not hard to see that this approach to social change rises out of the mission of psychotherapy: the therapist works with the patient to renarrate the troubled past so as to liberate the present from its toxicity and to liberate new self-realization for the future.

Rereading the Two Row Wampum is not just a way to review what went wrong in the past between European newcomers and the Haudenosaunee; it is a way of rethinking the present relationship between the hungry self and the larger world – not just between Europeans and First People, but between humans and the river itself, the watershed and the life it represents. To do this kind of revolutionary resymbolization, we need to reconceive reading, the central activity of the humanities, in broader terms than we often do. We need to reinvigorate the traditional disciplines of mindful and alert interpretation that have been called close reading: the capacity to attend to the signs left by others, to consider their details and nuances, to bring our own experience of the world into dialogue with these signs and see not just how they reflect what we know, but how they differ from and challenge it. To realize the public intellectual potentials in this activity, however, we must be willing to challenge the boundaries of some of these traditional humanities disciplines. We must expand from the idea that the most relevant texts are captured solely in books and read a wider set of signs, from ink on a page or a computer screen to quahog shells in a wampum belt to the presence or absence of honeybees and songbirds in an ecosystem. We need to read these signs to reanimate their histories, so we can remember what has been suppressed or devalued, so they can be resymbolized, and we can learn from the otherness that we previously missed. We need to read for differences, not to push the world and others away from ourselves, but so that we can understand more clearly the nature of the uncommon ground which we share and on which our lives depend. In this way, we can learn to reach across the fence between ourselves and the world and not destroy what we touch.

NOTES

This is a revised and expanded version of a lecture "Beyond the Book: Reading as Public Intellectual Activity," the 2011 Augustana Distinguished Lectures, presented in January in Camrose, Alberta, and published with the same title by the Ronning Centre in their series *Reading Beyond the Book: Reading, Spirituality and Cultural Politics.*

1 See Gramsci 5–14.

2 It's a tussle because Gramsci insists that it is an error to define the intellectual on the basis of "the intrinsic nature of intellectual *activities,* rather than in an ensemble of the system of relations in which these activities [...] have their place" (8; my emphasis). Because the activities of intellectuals can support hegemonic elites, making what Gramsci calls "traditional intellectuals" the "deputies" of dominant groups for example (10, 12), Gramsci advocates instead for "organic intellectuals" (12), who arise from the nondominant classes and provide persuasive analysis and organizing models for intervening in the existing "system of relations." While we differ on whether to emphasize the person or the activity, we agree that the key criterion is an "active participation in practical life" (10) that re-calibrates the "system of relations." In seeing the public intellectual as a set of activities in which many engage, rather than being embodied in the individual of the romantic hero, this chapter also picks up on one of this volume's larger concerns: the notion of the public (or various publics) *as* intellectual.

3 See chapter 2, "Reading as Counter-Culture," esp. 26–31.

4 As postcolonial and feminist scholars from Edward Said to Gloria Anzaldúa showed in the 1970s and 1980s, the history of reading is rife with the consumption and dispossession of the knowledge and cultural systems of racialized and gendered others. My comments here must be read with alertness to the colonial history of "cognitive imperialism" (the term is that of Mi'kmaq scholar Marie Battiste, "Unfolding" xvii) which has generated multiple instances of what Boaventura de Sousa Santos has called "epistemicide" (xix). The radical potential of reading, however, consists in its *différance,* the fact that the ultimate meaning of a text can never be finally fixed or imprisoned. There is always a remainder that eludes the consuming power of even the most oppressive system. There is always the possibility

of a rereading, or to use language I will return to in this chapter, "re-symbolization," and this possibility is clearly demonstrated by the resistant and regenerative readings carried out by the writers I have mentioned in this note.

5 See Tahenetorens, Jennings, and Foster.

6 Various English spellings exist for Haudenosaunee terms in part because the English spellings attempt to emulate how these words sound in different ones among the six languages of the confederacy and in part because of the historical layering of French and English transcriptions of Haudenosaunee terms. Because much of my information on the Two Row Wampum comes from the work of Richard Hill, I am following his spelling as presented in "Linking Arms" (2009).

7 This and subsequent quotations from the exchange between the Haudenosaunee and the Dutch come from Richard Hill's "Oral Memory of the Haudenosaunee: Views of the Two Row Wampum."

8 See Hill's "Linking Arms: The Haudenosaunee Context of the Covenant Chain" for a discussion of how the iron covenant chain evolved into the Silver Covenant Chain.

9 The Two Row Wampum is referred to repeatedly in Six Nations documents tracing the history of the Confederacy's legitimacy as the government of Six Nations and of Haudenosaunee independence from Canada as allies rather than subjects of the Crown. For an example of discussion of the Two Row in legal and political contexts, see John Borrow's *Rediscovering Canada.*

WORKS CITED

Ahmed, Sara. *Strange Encounters: Embodied Others in Post-Coloniality.* London: Routledge, 2000. Print.

Anzaldúa, Gloria. *Borderlands / La Frontera: The New Mestiza.* San Francisco: Spinsters/Aunt Lute, 1987. Print.

Battiste, Marie. "Introduction: Unfolding the Lessons of Colonialization." *Reclaiming Indigenous Voice and Vision.* Ed. Marie Battiste. Vancouver: U of British Columbia P, 2000. xvi–xxx. Print.

Battiste, Marie. "Print Culture and Decolonizing the University: Indigenizing the Page: Part 1." *The Future of the Page.* Ed. Peter Stoicheff and Andrew Taylor. Toronto: U of Toronto P, 2004. 111–23. Print.

Borrows, John. *Recovering Canada: The Resurgence of Indigenous Law.* Toronto: U of Toronto P, 2002. Print.

Bringhurst, Robert. *The Tree of Meaning Thirteen Talks*. Kentville, NS: Gaspereau P, 2006. Print.

Coleman, Daniel. *In Bed With the Word: Reading, Spirituality, and Cultural Politics*. Edmonton: U of Alberta P, 2009. Print.

Ermine, Willie. "The Ethical Space of Engagement." *Indigenous Law Journal* 6.1 (2007): 193–203. Print.

Foster, Michael K. "Another Look at the Function of Wampum in Iroquois-White Councils." *The History and Culture of Iroquois Diplomacy*. Ed. Francis Jennings et al. New York: Syracuse UP/Newberry Library, 1985. 99–114. Print.

Gansworth, Eric. "Cross PolliNation." *A Half-Life of Cardio-Pulmonary Function: Poems and Paintings*. Syracuse: Syracuse UP, 2008. 9. Print.

Gramsci, Antonio. *Selections from the Prison Notebooks of Antonio Gramsci*. Ed. and Trans. Quintin Hoare and Geoffrey Nowell Smith. London: Lawrence, 1971. Print.

Hill, Richard. "Linking Arms: The Haudenosaunee Context of the Covenant Chain." *Mamow Be-Mo-Tay-Tah: Let Us Walk Together*. Ed. José Zárate and Norah McMurtry. Toronto: Canadian Ecumenical Anti-Racism Network, the Canadian Council of Churches, 2009. 17–24. Print.

Hill, Richard. "Oral Memory of the Haudenosaunee: Views of the Two Row Wampum." *Indian Roots of American Democracy*. Ed. José Barreiro. Ithaca: Akwe:kon P, Cornell UP, 1992. 149–59. Print.

Jennings, Francis. "Introduction." *The History and Culture of Iroquois Diplomacy*. Ed. Francis Jennings et al. New York: Syracuse UP/Newberry Library, 1985. xiii–xviii. Print.

Jennings, Francis, William N. Fenton, Mary A. Druke et al., eds. *The History and Culture of Iroquois Diplomacy*. New York: Syracuse UP/Newberry Library, 1985. Print.

Johnson, Charles M. "The Six Nations in the Grand River Valley, 1784-1847." *Aboriginal Ontario: Historical Perspectives on the First Nations*. Ed. Edward S. Rogers and Donald B. Smith. Toronto: Dundurn P, 1994. 167–81. Print.

Kristeva, Julia. "Joyful Revolt." *An Interview with Mary Zournazi. Hope: New Philosophies for Change*. Ed. Mary Zournazi. New York: Routledge, 2002. 64–77. Print.

Lippard, Lucy R. *Mixed Blessings: New Art in a Multicultural America*. New York: Pantheon, 1990. Print.

Monture, Rick. "'Beneath the British Flag': Iroquois and Canadian Nationalism in the Work of Pauline Johnson and Duncan Campbell Scott." *Essays on Canadian Writing* 75 (2002): 118–41. Print.

Said, Edward. *Orientalism*. London: Routledge and Kegan Paul, 1979. Print.

Santos, Boaventura de Sousa, et al. "Introduction." *Another Knowledge Is Possible: Beyond Northern Epistemologies*. London: Verso, 2007. xix–lxii. Print. Reinventing Social Emancipation Ser. 3.

Tehanetorens (Ray Fadden). *Wampum Belts of the Iroquois*. Summertown, Tenn.: Book Publishing, 1999. Print.

Woo, Grace Li Xiu. "Canada's Forgotten Founders: The Modern Significance of the Haudenosaunee (Iroquois) Application for Membership in the League of Nations." *Law, Social Justice, and Global Development* 5 (2003): n. pag. Web. 12 Dec. 2006.

10 The Political Nature of Things: David Suzuki and Narratives of Change

IMRE SZEMAN

Dr David Suzuki is one of Canada's most important – if not *the* most important – public intellectuals. Bestselling author of more than forty books, recipient of twenty-two honorary doctorates (in addition to his own PhD in Zoology from the University of Chicago), and ranked fifth in the Canadian Broadcasting Corporation's (CBC) 2004 "The Greatest Canadian" series (he was the highest-ranked living individual), he is a familiar enough figure to Canadians to require no introduction in his appearances in a series of humourous powerWise energy-conservation TV ads in 2009. For four decades, Suzuki has relentlessly forced our attention on an issue that has only recently come to be an inescapable part of social and political debate: the present state of the environment and the necessity for us to address it *now* in order to offset a whole range of collective problems in our (near) future.[1] Through his activities on numerous fronts – from his work as a media personality and popular broadcaster to the multiple activities of the David Suzuki Foundation (incorporated in 1990) – he has endeavoured to do what public intellectuals are, traditionally, meant to do: use critique, analysis, and public discourse to generate social change that they see as essential to our collective well-being.

I want to engage here with some of Suzuki's most recent activity as a public intellectual in order to consider his specific approach to and understanding of the nature of the political pedagogy and activism enacted by figures such as him. In focussing on the figure of the public intellectual, I engage the larger concerns of this volume by also raising broader and more general questions about intellectual activity in relation to the public today. I want to look in particular at Suzuki's second autobiography, *David Suzuki: An Autobiography* (2006) and what he claims will be his final book, *The Legacy: An Elder's Vision for Our Sustainable Future* (2010). These two books represent a small fraction of Suzuki's activity as an intellectual over a long career that has seen him engage the public in multiple ways: as a newspaper columnist (for the *Globe and Mail* and *Toronto Star*); the host and originator of a long-running radio program (CBC's weekly science program *Quirks and Quarks*, started in 1975); and host since 1979 of the celebrated (and globally disseminated) television program *The Nature of Things*. Nevertheless, in these two career-capping books, one can find in condensed form Suzuki's ongoing reflections on the activities of the public intellectual and the approaches, pathways, and mechanisms that one might use in order to help animate significant social and political change.

The history of Suzuki's public impact and reception has been ambivalent. On one hand, as evidenced by his own popularity and the seriousness with which his claims and criticisms continue to be treated by the public and politicians alike, Suzuki has been a stunningly successful public intellectual. He is considered to be one of the globe's most important environmental voices – a vocal presence whose own career as a research scientist lends his claims and arguments especial force and gravitas. On the other hand, Suzuki's activities as a public intellectual have to be counted as a failure. Though there is no doubt that his involvement in the environmental movement has played a significant role in shaping the way in which publics view the environment – the environmental movement in Canada in particular would not be the same without him – the extent of real action on the part of either governments or individuals in the face of an impending, unprecedented, and systemic ecological calamity has been minimal, and has proven in recent years to be *regressive* rather than forward looking. At the time of writing, the current Canadian government's stated intentions towards greenhouse gas reduction is meeker than it was under (for instance) the governments of Prime Minister Jean Chrétien or Paul Martin; the fact that it is not formalized in policy but is merely a stated intention suggests that even these relatively modest goals are unlikely to be met.[2] What is true of Canada is also true of the rest of the world in the wake of the 2008 financial crash: the outcome of the 2009 United Nations Climate Change Conference meeting in Copenhagen (COP 15) was deemed by many to be an abject failure, and in his 2011 State of the Union address, President Barack Obama – the leader of the country whose economy has the biggest impact on the planet's ecology – made little or no reference to climate change or the environment.[3]

It might seem harsh to say that Suzuki's activities have been a failure; at a minimum, the demand that his advocacy on behalf of the environment should lead to wholesale political and social change seems to posit a measure of success that might be deemed unrealistic or impossible. Yet Suzuki's own assessment of his impact is no less stark and bleak: "Quite frankly, as far as I'm concerned, I feel all the effort that I've been involved in has really failed. We're going backward" (qtd. in Dixon R2). This issue of success or failure draws attention to precisely the issues I want to consider with respect to the activities of public intellectuals such as Suzuki and what form they take (or should take). Failure should be treated here as an analytic concept rather than a normative judgment; at a minimum, it helps to outline the nature of the demands for change which Suzuki and other intellectuals make, and the ways in which they narrate the movement from today's failure to tomorrow's (potential, hopeful) success. But, before turning to a discussion of Suzuki, I want to offer a quick (and necessarily crude) taxonomy of public intellectuals that will frame my subsequent discussion.

Public Intellectuals: Politics vs. Structure

Allow me to start with an admission. I have a natural suspicion of the public intellectual and the vision of the world it presumes. I say this even of those public intellectuals that interest me most – those who are willing to take on the state and existing centres and form of power, as opposed to those (also clearly public) intellectuals who tend to speak on behalf of existing social forms and warn of the need to maintain and even expand dominant ideas and existing forms of political hegemony (e.g., everyone from Allan Bloom to Canada's Margaret Wente and Rex Murphy, from Christopher Hitchens in his latter days to many of Fox News' prominent commentators). I applaud the brave interventions by those public intellectuals who take on the powerful commonplace and quotidian beliefs, ideas, and behaviours that shape social life today; I admire, too, their addition to the possibilities of what society might yet become in the future. There's no question that those voices that challenge all manner of social and political injustice, and who draw attention to the limits of the status quo have a role to play in helping to transform the societies we have into the societies we want. But even at first blush, there are a whole range of questions and problems that arise when one begins to consider the figure of the Left, critical public intellectual (which is whom I will be focussing on below) – issues that I would feel remiss in passing over without (at least brief) comment.

First, the activity of public intellectuals and their social impact depends on a notion of expertise and of the application of Reason to problems that has been challenged by numerous critics for numerous reasons – from the Frankfurt School's powerful critique of instrumental reason (most famously in Max Horkheimer and Theodor Adorno's *Dialectic of Enlightenment*) to more recent arguments concerning the importance of affect and passion in addition to reason in the drama of the political.[4] Second, while the importance of the kind of public pedagogy enacted by public intellectuals is celebrated by many critics (from Edward Said to Henry Giroux), others, most notably Jacques Rancière, have challenged both the theoretical claims and political necessity of the model of instruction and/or emancipation that is presumed by critique that understands itself as revealing the truth that exists behind (ideological) falsehood. At a minimum, Rancière has suggested that the impact of such activity is other than what its proponents might believe: while critique might generate difference (or newness), this is within an existing schema of concepts and beliefs rather than the full-scale paradigm shift that is often hoped for.[5] Third, there is a vanguardism associated with the activities of the public intellectual that is at odds with how political change has been theorized by a number of thinkers over the past several decades, especially (though not exclusively) by the Italian autonomists and in the influential work of Michael Hardt and Antonio Negri.[6] In some respects, these theorists see the figure of the public intellectual as part of the *problem* rather than the solution – as a sign of a deferral of political activity and organization to leaders and (looping back around to the first point) experts who will guide the "masses" to enact changes that intellectuals have identified as important or necessary. I could continue in this vein at some length. I've yet to mention, for instance, that the work of the public intellectual tends to presume that *ideas* generate change as opposed to substantial, structural transformations that arrive only through shifts in material conditions of possibility – which is to say: to assert the importance of public intellectuals can be to reaffirm a faith in liberalism and its (problematic) vision of change through public debate in a living, active civil society (of the kind explored by Jürgen Habermas), as opposed to challenging and troubling the presumptions of liberalism via the kind of materialist critique associated with (for instance) forms of Marxist critique.

There is, then, a misfit between the understanding of the operations of the world that I (and many other academics) have learned from contemporary Left social and political philosophy, and the one presumed by the activities of David Suzuki and other public intellectuals who take on existing structures and strictures. One could summarize the former in two basic principles: (1) knowledge is intimately connected to power, and it is thus essential to challenge all claims to knowledge, especially those premised on expertise (i.e., the legitimation of knowledge claims through existing social systems and structures, whether that of the state, the university, or the media): and (2) structure is more significant than agency: whether one has (a sense of) agency and autonomy is itself generated by the structures or systems within which one lives, as opposed to being a condition that arises when one stands (impossibly) outside structure. The first principle fuels social and cultural criticism; the second dampens it, both for epistemological reasons and due to the social and historical weight of institutions whose influence and power cannot be gainsaid.[7] It is easy to see why some students and scholars of contemporary Left social and political philosophy are stuck with a deep pessimism when it comes to imagining the possibility of generating needed political change within such coordinates – which is not the same as saying that this model of the social world and the place of critique within it is (fundamentally) incorrect.

But lest it seem that I am questioning the significance and importance of (at least Left) public intellectuals *in toto* before I even attend to the work of Suzuki, let me introduce two challenges to Left theory's understanding of the social world. First, while I think that it is essential to challenge expertise and explore the links of knowledge to power, it is also the case that late capitalist society is one that is deeply and necessarily dependent on expertise. In a vast and complicated global society made up of an array of systems (economic, social, and/or technological), some individuals – whether through training or experience – will have a better understanding of these systems than others; having them draw on this expertise to engage in discussions and debates about the direction of social life is essential, even if it remains important to criticize the values or imperatives that might shape various forms and modes of expertise. Environmentalists such as Suzuki and those on whose work he draws open up perspectives we would not otherwise have regarding the implications and significance of our collective life activity; it is, simply put, a mistake to worry so much about the cult of expertise that one might thus fail to consider the knowledge that expertise produces.[8] Second, social life is not fate. While it seems to me to be important not to imagine that social change can occur in an instant – a sudden lurch into wakefulness out of an ideological slumber, on the other side of which everything is different – it is equally important not to imagine that we are consigned to those social systems that we have created over the course of history. Nor does a suspicion about the notion of social change as a sudden revolutionary rupture or break (a perspective argued for by Slavoj Žižek and others) leave us only with the myth of progress and gradual amelioration of existing systems. Critique should point to the limits of our epistemic and economic systems, and the foundation of these limits in systems of power and social control, but do so in a manner that leaves open criticisms of what is and the political possibility of what might yet be.

There has been an enormous amount written about public intellectuals, especially over the past several decades.[9] While I don't want to repeat or provide an overview of these accounts (as tempted as I am to spend some time – as do the introduction and certain other chapters of this volume – situating such contested terms as "public" and "intellectual"), it is important when discussing the work of a figure like David Suzuki to draw a distinction between the activities of different kinds of public intellectuals – again, focussing on those critical intellectuals who are usually left of centre in their politics. There are essentially two forms of the activity of representing technical expertise or knowledge to publics as an intellectual (as opposed to a governmental official, or an expert drawn from the business class). The first is a frankly *political* mode of activism or agency. This consists of the work of shaping political positions or public policy by speaking out directly against specific actions taken (or not taken) or positions adopted (or not) by corporations, governments, international agencies, and the agents associated with all three sites of power and control. Such intellectuals include everyone from novelist Émile Zola and mathematician and physicist Henri Poincaré, who spoke out in support of Captain Alfred Dreyfus during the Dreyfus Affair at the end of the nineteenth century, to the activities of Edward Said on behalf of Palestine; from Dr Henry Morgentaler's actions on behalf of the women's access to abortion, to the work of Canadian writers and artists in support of government agencies such as the Canada Council or the Canadian Broadcasting Corporation; and many other actions directed towards a range of actors and institutions, such as Canadian political activist Maude Barlow's championing of global water rights. Much of the work of public intellectuals fits into this category of the political, which might be characterized as a form of lobbying whose impact comes about through the intellectual's capacity to draw on their particular reservoirs of technical expertise or experience, as well as their ability to shape public and governmental perspectives on the (topical) issues in question.

A second form of intervention by public intellectuals can be termed *structural*. In this case, intellectuals are less interested in shaping policy or political decisions (though this, too, can be an outcome of their activity) than in engaging with problems that are embedded in the very structure of contemporary systems – political, social, economic, and ecological, or often all of these taken together. A political public intellectual might want to challenge (say) the decision by the Canadian government to participate in the war on Afghanistan; a public intellectual interested in structural questions will want to call attention to the very limits of what constitutes democratic decision making in Canada – limits that make certain government decisions predictable, if not inevitable.[10] By "structure" I am calling attention to both the material *and* cultural systems that constitute social life in the twentieth century – everything from our belief systems, to the concrete, everyday operations of our systems of governance and the institutions associated with them, to the shape and physical coordinates of our urban spaces. This might seem too broad and indiscriminate a category to be a meaningful one. Yet I think it usefully draws attention to the level of change demanded by some public intellectuals, and points, too, to the horizon of its possibility.

In the *political* cases mentioned above, the change demanded can be accommodated within the existing parameters of state systems and capitalist economics. For example, the accusations against Captain Alfred Dreyfus, which prompted Zola's famous letter, were shown to be driven by French anti-Semitism rather than by any real evidence against him; abortion is (at a minimum) more accessible to Canadian women than it was previously due to Morgentaler's defiance of the law and advocacy on the behalf of the right of women's choice; and petitions and media campaigns by writers and artists have meant that Canadian governments continue to be cautious when it comes to making substantial cuts to funding for the arts or for the CBC. Even in the case of the causes championed by Barlow or Said, the potential resolution lies within existing politico-juridical and economic structures, however blind (in the cause of global water rights) or intransigent (in the case of Palestine) governments and nongovernmental agencies might be.

What needs to change in the case of those public intellectuals who devote themselves to *structural* causes? In a word, *everything* – not just this or that practice or decision by actually existing governments, but (for instance) the form of government itself; the manner and degree to which citizens participate in it; the values that underlie it and society at large; and its understanding of its own aims, function and purpose. There are two dominant issues that public intellectuals engaged today with structural issues tend to focus on: the environment and capitalism. In the latter case, thinkers such as Noam Chomsky or Slavoj Žižek might decry the specific actions of specific governments, but they do so in order to draw attention to the larger systems or structures that generate such decisions and actions, especially the forms of economic (and so social and political) injustice and exploitation that are a necessary outcome of capitalism. Concerns about the environment are, of course, necessarily related to capitalism. Though some might imagine that it is possible to engage in actions that would ameliorate human impacts on the environment *within* capitalism – for instance, through mechanisms such as carbon taxes or market incentives to generate alternative sources of energy – most environmentalists see the imperatives for perpetual growth and profit that animate capitalism as working at cross purposes to their own aims. Intellectuals who attend to structure make a radical and difficult demand on the publics to which they speak – not that they vote differently, or that they drive or consume less, but that they consider moving collectively in an entirely new direction – one whose form and outcome cannot be easily mapped or imagined concretely in advance.

David Suzuki's work as a public intellectual has taken place in both the political and structural registers. He locates the beginning of his career as a public intellectual in his involvement as a speaker at a rally on 4 April 1968, at the University of British Columbia, during which students and faculty came together to express sorrow about the assassination of Dr Martin Luther King and to express solidarity with all those engaged in the work of social justice. Drawing on the energies of 1968's political upheavals, at this rally Suzuki spoke out about racism in Canada and the incarceration of Japanese Canadians during World War II (*Autobiography* 52–3). Much of Suzuki's first autobiography, *Metamorphosis: Stages in a Life* (1987) addresses the racism experienced by his parents – who were "evacuated" by the Canadian government to Slocan City, BC, in the wake of the Japanese bombing of Pearl Harbor in 1941 – and by himself as he moved through the ranks of academia. His interest in discussing publicly the social responsibilities of science can be linked to his early antiracist activism. In *Metamorphosis,* Suzuki narrates his gradual shift from lab to broadcast booth as occurring via his recognition of the role that his field of scientific study – genetics – had played in legitimating racial politics over the course of its history (234–45). Though some of the environmental themes that have dominated his work over the past twenty-five years do appear in this first autobiography, they come as asides: the Suzuki of 1987 is concerned with making science a part of public discourse and political decision making, rather than pointedly and provocatively drawing our attention to the *structural* depth of the environmental and social problems we face. While he has not moved away entirely from the political to the structural – that is, from proposing "solutions" to our environmental crises (for instance, through the Suzuki Foundation's Nature Challenge[11]) or lobbying governments about the need to amend or shape policy decisions – he has increasingly focussed his energies on making an argument for the necessity of a radical paradigm shift if contemporary society is to address the problems he and other environmentalists have identified. "Only by confronting the enormity and unsustainability of our impact on the biosphere," he claims at the outset of *Legacy*, "will we take the search for alternative ways to live as seriously as we must" (3).

The challenge confronting Suzuki and other public intellectuals who address themselves to the task of redefining the fundamental structures of society is *how* they might accomplish the outcome they seek. His recent books, articles, and 2010 CBC Radio series, *A Bottom Line*, are filled with pleas for the necessity of quick action given the degree of damage already done to the environment and the length of time required to "undo" it (should this even be possible). I want now to turn to a consideration of Suzuki's understanding of his role as a public intellectual and of the strategies he employs to try to generate an awareness of the fact that the environment represents a structural challenge on an unprecedented scale. Working through the challenges he faces and some of the solutions he has developed provides insight not only into the thoughts of Canada's most prominent public intellectual, but some of the problems and possibilities of public advocacy more generally today.

Knowledge, Belief, Action

The claim or argument that some of the fundamental ways in which a society organizes itself are problematic or mistaken is easy enough to make. However, to achieve the change required – especially when it is claimed that doing so with speed is essential – is enormously difficult.

There have been few massive, rapid social or political revolutions (e.g., the Russian Revolution, the Cultural Revolution in China) in the modern period, each with its own traumas, problems, crises, successes, and failures; even by these measures, however, the social change demanded to reduce significantly the human impact on the environment is of a depth and scale that can be difficult to comprehend. Despite increasing levels of scientific evidence to the contrary, an ever-increasing number of Westerners are expressing scepticism about the reality of climate change (as Monbiot discusses); even amongst the (still) majority who believe in the deleterious impact of human activity on climate and on the environment more generally, the ever-present gap between belief and action suggests that we enact what Žižek has termed "cynical reason" on a daily basis: there is broad understanding that how our society is structured impacts the environment, and knowledge that change – at a minimum – of individual behaviour is required, but with little effective impact on (for instance) automobile usage or flights by many in the Global North to warm weather destinations for their annual vacations.[12]

Like other public intellectuals, Suzuki understands his efforts as a form of public pedagogy that works through argument and reason. Like most other public intellectuals, his sense of how broad decisions in the development of society are constituted is through the Enlightenment drama outlined by Immanuel Kant, in which history constitutes a passage of humanity from immaturity to maturity through the application of reason to the problems it encounters. In an era in which the movements and circulation of knowledge might perhaps be seen as more complex than Kant's (due in part to the sheer scale of information, in part to the speed with which it is circulated by new communication technologies), Suzuki understands his specific role to be that of an expert who can help publics navigate issues that demand significant training and time to understand, both of which are today in short supply:

> I have read many books and articles, met many people, acquired information and knowledge, and reflected a lot about issues, all of which has shaped the way I see the problems. It has become clear to me over the years that it would be very difficult and time-consuming for people who are starting to get involved to wade through the same volume of material in a short period. And if the issues are urgent, then those of us who are

> pressing those issues have a responsibility at the very least to help people avoid unnecessary material or sources and get up to speed faster, still on their own but with some shortcuts to assist them. (*Autobiography* 350)

In both *Legacy* and *Autobiography*, Suzuki repeatedly expresses faith in the power of human reason to address and overcome problems and limits. He writes in *Legacy*: "Our great evolutionary advantage was the ability to lift our sights and look ahead, to imagine the world as it could be and then make the best choices to move toward that vision" (88). Suzuki is clearly frustrated by the gap between those actions that this evolutionary foresight should manifest and the limit on the actual changes that have taken place in human social organization and behaviour in relation to the environment. This frustration shapes the rhetorical form of *Legacy* and *The Sacred Balance* (1997), an earlier book that *Legacy*'s structure mimics. In each, Suzuki resorts frequently to a form of shaming through a critique of the very intelligence that is supposed to be guiding us from present to future. "We say we are intelligent," he writes, "but what intelligent creature, knowing the role the earth plays in constructing our very bodies, would then proceed to use the earth as a dump for our waste and toxic material? [...] We are the earth, and whatever we do to the earth, we do to ourselves" (*Sacred* 78). He suggests that there is no disagreement over what the future we might want should look like (89); human beings understand, too, that our actions are damaging the environment in ways that impede the possibility of this future coming into being. So why do they not act differently, especially given the fact that reason and human intelligence suggests that they – that we – should?

This problem is the fundamental one that Suzuki addresses – or at least, *should* address – in his advocacy as a public intellectual. However, his work continues to emphasize the importance of communicating information about the environment, especially data framed in the mode of what I have termed elsewhere "eco-apocalypse": frightening statistics that are intended, it would seem, to either kick-start the intellect or engage dormant survival instincts by communicating the scale of the human impact on the planet (e.g., humanity has coopted 40% of photosynthetic activity on the planet; some scientists estimate that by 2048 there will be no commercially viable fish species left on the planet; an estimated fifty thousand species are driven to extinction annually; and so on).[13] Suzuki's dependence on the idea of public reason prompts him to continue to engage in the task of passing along such information, a task underwritten by a faith in the idea that the gap between understanding and action is simply due to a lack of relevant data or a misunderstanding of the severity of the consequences suggested by it.

This faith in the function of information drives many public intellectuals to try to maximize the impact of their ideas through the media that they use to communicate. And certainly, Suzuki's presence across multiple media – radio, newspapers, television, (adult and children's) books, film, the Internet – might be read in this way: as a frantic demand for the attention necessitated by the cause he wishes to advocate. Yet for someone whose status as a public figure owes a great deal to his televisual presence, in both *Metamorphosis* and *Autobiography* he is acutely critical of the medium's capacity to develop the kind and degree of environmental knowledge for which he might hope. Suzuki pulls no punches: "Television is an ephemeral medium; a program we might work for months to create flashes onto the screen to an audience often distracted by other activities – feeding the kids, answering the phone, going to the toilet, walking the dog, getting a drink. Viewers aren't fully engaged through the entire program, and what is ultimately remembered may be a snippet" (*Autobiography* 64). In both autobiographies, he is intent on demystifying his own role as host: far from being the expert on any and every topic that appears on *The Nature of Things with David Suzuki,* he wants it to be known that he is little more than a talking head who does the "stand ups" that come at the beginning and end of shows, as well as during short connective visual interstices. In addition to whatever information the show might convey – ephemerally, in the midst of those demands of daily life that can write them out of the picture – the primary function of a serial genre like a weekly educational or news program is to generate trust and belief in the host. Television functions not to maximize the circulation of information on an issue – in this case, an issue legitimated by an expert – but to identify Suzuki in this manner as a public figure with the capacity to act on behalf of the public that media brings into existence:

> I wanted to empower the public, but the opposite happened because of the nature of the medium. Regular viewers of *The Nature of Things with David Suzuki* watch the program on faith that what we present is important and true, and they come to expect me to tell them what to do or to act on their behalf. If I phone a politician's office, even the prime minister's, chances are very good that my call will be returned within half an hour – not because I'm an important person, but because an informed politician knows that a million and a half people watch my shows regularly. (*Autobiography* 68)

This faith and belief in the host only has significance, however, if it affords some ability to generate those changes he desires. An informed politician or businessperson – those brave enough to take Suzuki on, such as Canada's Environment Minister, Jim Prentice, and the Executive Vice President of Shell Canada, both of whom are the focus of episodes of *The Bottom Line* – might recognize that Suzuki has a considerable public presence and could impact the bottom line or the outcome of elections. Nevertheless, the degree to which such figures are able or willing to envision or make manifest the kinds of wide-scale, structural changes needed to address the environmental crisis is doubtful. As an intellectual who has had a public profile for four decades, Suzuki understands not just the limits of contemporary media in generating a change of belief – much less a change in action – but the need to produce new narratives through which it might be possible to communicate both the urgency of his message and close the gap separating knowledge, belief, and action.

I've written above that *Legacy* and *Sacred Balance* exhibit a frustration at the limits of human reason to produce action. While not abandoning the hope that rational argumentation and the purveyance of fact might reshape the views of the public, these books take up the challenge of proposing new narratives about the environment. At the core of *Sacred Balance* are chapters organized around the Greek classical elements of air, water, earth, and fire. The arguments that Suzuki makes combine scientific knowledge with myth, poetry, and literature; there are charts, tables, and figures of scientific data included in the narrative that expand on points made, but just as frequently these asides constitute excurses in history and literature. The chapter on air, for instance, includes an excerpt from Father José de Acosta's *Natural and Moral History* (1590), which describes "the sickness of the Andes" – a "disease" that turns out to be a lack of oxygen at high altitudes (*Sacred* 31); it also includes an account of the Chernobyl disaster and the movement of radioactive materials around the planet (*Sacred* 31). Spread throughout the book are short quotations from a huge range of sources, each of which speaks to the significance of the classical elements for human life, or addresses more generally the way in which humanity is ultimately dependent on nature. These include quotes from scientists such as Albert Einstein, Paul Ehrlich, and Edward O. Wilson; poets and novelists, such as George Eliot, Samuel Taylor Coleridge, and William Butler Yeats; passages from the Bible (Genesis, Ecclesiastes, etc.); and quotes from indigenous religions and ancient narratives. On one hand, this makes for a messy book that seems intent on mixing and matching very different epistemologies and ontologies, connecting them only through their (sometimes incidental) reference to one of the elements, to nature, or to human interdependence or interconnectivity. On the other hand, this shift to a multidimensional narrative of love, the sacred, and significance and meaning in one's life offers a rich, compelling, and original account of the importance of nature and of the trauma of environmental loss and devastation, and does so in a way that rubs against the grain of Suzuki's public persona as a scientist.

The structure of *Legacy* – remember, what Suzuki has said will be his last book – mimics *Sacred Balance* in almost every respect: the breakout passages (though there are no charts or figures), which put one in mind of the Spinozian-inspired scholia of Michael Hardt and Antonio Negri's *Empire* more than they do a science text; the interstitial quotations (from an equally eclectic mix of figures, such as Marcel Proust, Anita Roddick, Johann von Goethe, Inuit elder Annette Helmer, and others); and the articulation of an argument based (in part) on scientific fact via the structure of the classical elements – a structure that one might have expected to be anathema to modern science. In *Sacred Balance*, Suzuki prepares us for the mix of narratives to come by arguing that "we have much to learn from the vast repositories of knowledge that still exist in traditional societies [...] leading members of the scientific community are starting to understand that science alone cannot fulfill humankind's needs; indeed, it has become a destructive force. We need a new kind of science that approaches the traditional knowledge of indigenous communities" (26). *Legacy* adopts a similar pose, beginning with an account of the Big Bang and evolution described as "every bit as fantastic as myths of the past" (6–7) and speaking immediately to the question of the status of scientific knowledge in relation to other forms of knowledge. In "Traditional Narratives," the title of the first aside in the book, Suzuki writes:

> For most of human existence, we were oral creatures, sharing experiences, insights, and beliefs through the stories we told. Woven into the stories were implicit lessons about how to respond to the world around us [...] Until very recently, all of humankind was local and tribal, following game and plants through the seasons in a nomadic existence of hunting and gathering. Contrary to popular belief, our ancient ancestors were not slow-witted, primitive savages. They were human beings with the same genetic heritage as twenty-first century people. (8)

Sacred Balance and *Legacy* appear to constitute examples of the "new kind of science" for which he calls. In the twenty years since his first autobiography was published, indigenous knowledges and the role and place of indigenous peoples in environmental struggles have become a primary object of Suzuki's interests and energies. *Metamorphosis* makes no mention of indigenous communities or Canadian First Nations. By contrast, the main focus of *Autobiography* is on his activities in relation to and on behalf of (as a public intellectual and through the work of the Suzuki Foundation) indigenous communities in Canada (113–33), Brazil (134–93), Australia (195–216), and Papua New Guinea (288–304). In the opening pages of the second autobiography, Suzuki names himself as "an elder"; *Legacy* features this word in its subtitle. The language of "elder" is one that Suzuki draws as much from his own Japanese heritage as from the various indigenous communities with whom he has worked and lived. It represents a very different relationship to knowledge than that of the "expert" – knowledge built up out of experience rather than the communication of technical prowess, and one whose legitimacy arises less from a relationship to accepted knowledge-producing structures within society (such as universities) than from memory. Suzuki identifies a "remarkable congruence of scientific insights and traditional knowledge, as we are beginning to recognize that what were once pristine forests and shores were in fact moulded by sophisticated human activity" (*Legacy* 84–5). Despite this congruence, there are at least two reasons why science might require the insights of traditional knowledge in order to address our environmental crisis. First, contemporary societies have an increasingly short memory, a point he makes in both *Legacy* (55, 60–1) and *Autobiography* (376). The problem here is one of norms: the pace of change and (a point that brings us back to Suzuki's warnings about media) a focus on the immediate means that it becomes nearly impossible to establish baselines that might be used in the restoration of nature. In one of *Legacy*'s excurses, Suzuki tells the story of changes to the neighbourhood in which he grew up: a grove of trees in an empty lot were chopped down to make way for an apartment building; those who came to live in the building had no sense that the trees had ever existed, and as the original inhabitants grew up or moved, memory of the trees faded away. Elders provide this form of memory-knowledge that is important to create a sense not only of what was, but of what could – or should – be.

The second element that traditional knowledge can add to science is a focus on the whole rather than on the constituent parts of nature.

Suzuki values indigenous knowledges because they emphasize the deep interrelation of human life and ecology. These knowledges are not stitched together from increasingly detailed and specific forms of technical or scientific expertise, but are the outcome of an epochal or *longue durée* experience of living in nature rather than in opposition to it.[14] The fragmentation of a single system into constituent parts is a feature not only of much scientific thought, but of politics as well: "trees fall under the 'management' of the minister of forests; the salmon under the ministers of tourism (sports fishers), Indian and northern affairs (native food fishers), and fisheries and oceans (commercial fishers); eagles, bears, and wolves under the minister of the environment; the water under the minister of agriculture (for irrigation) or energy (hydro power); the rocks and mountains under the minister of mining" (*Legacy* 64). Without narratives that enable a comprehension of the deep interconnection of all aspects of the environment, it becomes impossible to generate a response to the impact of the current technical, social, and political systems that manage knowledge and memory in its component parts.

It is this emphasis on the whole that is at the heart of Suzuki's most recent writing and reflection on the environment. The mixture of different elements in *Legacy* is not meant to sideline or displace the importance (or indeed, even the centrality) of scientific knowledge in our understanding of the ecological impact of human activities. It does suggest, however, that what is required more than information is a new narrative through which human beings might understand themselves and their relationship to nature. Employing the classical elements as a structure through which to narrate his vision for a sustainable future is a way of dragging the cosmological into the quotidian. Each element points to an interconnection of humanity with nature *and* of humanity with humanity that stretches across borders and even across time: "we are air [...]. every breath we take contains argon atoms that were once in the bodies of Joan of Arc and Jesus Christ; every breath contains argon atoms that were once in dinosaurs 65 million years ago; and every breath will suffuse all life far into the future" (75); "every drink we take has water molecules that evaporated from the canopies of every forest in the world, from all the oceans and plains" (76); and "we are the earth, and whatever we do to the earth, we do to ourselves" (78). It might seem as if speaking as an elder instead of as a scientist – and in speaking often of the sacred character of these relations with air, water, earth, and fire – means that Suzuki has abandoned the position that we have come to associate with him as a public intellectual. But I think that it is a mistake to see these recent books in this way – that is, as the reflections of an elder on the sacred and the cosmological in the shadow of his own mortality (Dr Suzuki turned seventy-five in 2011). Shifting away from a mode of address through which an expert speaks to a (presumably) unknowing audience with the aim of educating them is intended to help close the gap between belief and action, and to do so with the aim of generating the necessary degree of sociostructural change required today. This is not a mere rhetorical ploy to court public interest in the environment – a "dumbing down" of science or sacralization of it to make it palatable to publics – but a way of reinforcing the degree to which the human is a single species that shares common interests. And these interests go beyond dealing collectively with a global problem that transcends national borders, but extends a shared understanding of the kinds of factors that would – in Suzuki's view – make human life genuinely meaningful and productive.

But it is with another kind of totality with which I want to end. As I claimed earlier, it seems all but impossible to address the problems of the environment without naming what is perhaps the primary structuring element of our social and political lives: *capitalism*. Yet despite the fact that Suzuki has taken up the challenge of advocating for and somehow generating large-scale structural changes, he seems careful to avoid naming capitalism directly (the word appears only once in *Legacy*). His preferred term is "economics." In *Legacy*, he is unrelenting in his criticism of the limits of economics.[15] Suzuki is aware that current forms of economics are driven by a logic of endless growth that cannot but have a deleterious impact on the environment (47); he is similarly critical of the predominance of economic value as a near universal measure, a mode of social valuation whose outcome is that "those things that matter most to us are worthless" (91). Even within its own measure of value, mainstream economics is incapable of measuring either the "input" of nature or the impact of its "output": "the economy is built on extracting raw materials from the biosphere and pouring wastes back into it without regard to [its] services. Disregarding nature and her services is ultimately suicidal, yet it is exactly what conventional economics does" (43). If the logic of growth (which is to say, profit) and value that constitutes economics is at the heart of the impact that human beings have had on the environment, one might expect more explicit arguments from Suzuki that challenge dependence on these social narratives. As I've argued above, I think this is what Suzuki *has* been attempting in his recent work; importantly, he insists: "Capitalism, free enterprise, the economy, markets, corporations, and currency are not natural elements or forces of nature [...] We created them and if they are not working, we can change them" (39).

There is something lost, though, in not naming capitalism directly and in equating capitalism with economics as such. The attempt to bridge the gap between belief and action founders in its evocation of the cosmological without an interrogation of the material (Suzuki travels as far as Feuerbach, we might say, but not as far as Marx). This last quotation extends an invitation to produce change as a result of an insight into the mechanisms of a system that doesn't work, and for that reason alone, should be fixed: we're back to the beginning, though now armed with a more detailed and deeper normative critique of the coldness with which economics (and, insofar as it, too, tends towards instrumentality, science) surveys the world. To speak of capitalism instead of economics would mean to take seriously the mechanisms through which capitalism is naturalized *as* economics, such that it becomes extremely difficult to imagine a genuine other to it, if and when it is even possible to challenge it at all. The irrationality of economics to which Suzuki appeals actively prevents a direct confrontation with what lies at the heart of the distance separating belief and action when it comes to the environment: the mechanisms of hegemony that have been studied in depth by Left humanists over the past half century. It is perhaps Raymond Williams who offers the best description of just what constitutes hegemony and why it should generate impasses even in the midst of an understanding or knowledge of one's circumstances. For Williams, hegemony is

> a lived system of meanings and values – constitutive and constituting – which as they are experienced as practices appear as reciprocally confirming. It thus constitutes a sense of reality for most people in the society, a sense of absolute because experienced reality beyond which it is very difficult for most members of the society to move, in most areas of their lives. It is, that is to say, in the strongest sense a 'culture', but a culture which has also to be seen as the lived dominance and subordination of particular classes. (110)

In the end, the problem of the environment – which is the problem of nothing less than the ability to mobilize change in a deep, systemic way – has to be addressed through a direct interrogation of the mechanisms that constitute reality, and not only through the production of another more palatable narrative of how "we" should be. Suzuki's recent work goes a long way in this direction – farther than many might recognize – but it pulls back at the last moment.[16] His criticism of the suicidal disregard of nature by economics in *Legacy*, for instance, ends with an unexpected turn to the economic fiction of sustainability: "The tragedy – and the opportunity – is that if done properly, many renewable resources can be harvested indefinitely" (39).

Perhaps Suzuki's reluctant to speak about capitalism directly is to be expected. After all, can a *scientist* speak about capitalism as a public intellectual – that is, someone whose expertise seems to stop short of those whom have legitimacy to speak knowingly about capitalism, that is, economists? The larger question may be whether any public intellectual can today challenge capitalism directly and remain legitimately *public* while doing so. Even if capitalism is at the heart of the failure of imagination in contemporary social life, it seems to have become difficult to speak about such matters directly and unabashedly instead of appealing (for whatever purposes) only to changes *within* our contemporary social and political system.[17] Suzuki's brave work on behalf of public education about our present global circumstances is laudable. So too, is his experimentation with imagining and producing new social narratives that might allow us to unthink our servile dependence on the dream and drama of an endless economic growth that appears as natural as the seasons themselves. Whether it will produce the changes needed, within the time they are needed, may well depend on a more direct and fearless confrontation with that system of quotidian intelligibility from which we have thus far seemed unable – or unwilling – to shake ourselves loose.

NOTES

I want to thank Justin Sully, Sarah Blacker, and the editors of this volume for their comments and criticisms of an earlier draft of this chapter.

1 Along with many others, Suzuki identifies the publication of Rachel Carson's *Silent Spring* in 1962 as the founding moment of the contemporary environmental movement. As he points out, "in 1962, there wasn't a single department or ministry of the environment on the planet" (*Autobiography* 267).

2 Canada was a signatory to the Kyoto Protocol (adopted December 1997 and ratified in Canada in 2002), which mandated a reduction of total greenhouse gas emissions by 5.2% from the 1990 level. The government of Stephen Harper has largely ignored Kyoto, which is one of the reasons that Canada was singled out for criticism by protestors and participants at the 15th Conference of the Parties (COP) to the United Nations Framework on Climate Change in Copenhagen in December 2009. The Harper government has suggested that it would try to support the outcome of COP 15, which is not binding and which drops Kyoto's stated aim of reducing emissions by 80% by 2050. While this volume was in process, Canada announced its formal withdrawal from Kyoto. For the newer figures on greenhouse gas emissions, consult the most recent *How Canada Performs*, specifically the section "GHG per capita," on the Conference Board of Canada's website (See "GHG Emissions per Capita").

3 See Cazdyn and Szeman 32–3 and Hertzberger 21–2.

4 For examples of the latter, see Connolly and Panagia.

5 See Rancière, *The Ignorant Schoolmaster* and *The Emancipated Spectator* 25–49; for a different take on the relationship between Rancière's work and the public (as) intellectual, see Jason Haslam's contribution to this volume.

6 Hardt and Negri's *Empire* and Paolo Virno's *A Grammar of the Multitude* are two representative texts.

7 I follow Pierre Bourdieu's understanding of how structure and agency are framed in relation to one another: "The social world is accumulated history, and if it is not to be reduced to a discontinuous series of instantaneous mechanical equilibria between agents who are treated as interchangeable particles, one must reintroduce into it the notion of capital and with it, accumulation and all its effects. Capital is accumulated labor (in its materialized form or its 'incorporated,' embodied form) which, when appropriated on a private, i.e., exclusive, basis by agents or groups of agents, enables them to appropriate social energy in the form of reified or living labor. It is a *vis insita*, a force inscribed in objective or subjective structures, but it is also a *lex insita*, the principle underlying the immanent regularities of the social world. It is what makes the games of society – not least, the economic game – something other than simple games of chance offering at every moment the possibility of a miracle" (26).

8 This is perhaps especially the case when it comes to environmental issues and concerns. In "Two Faces of the Apocalypse: A Letter from Copenhagen," Michael Hardt points out that unlike many forms of

political and social oppression, "the basic facts of climate change – for example, the increasing proportion of CO_2 in the atmosphere and its effects – are highly scientific and abstract from our daily experiences. Projects of public pedagogy can help spread such scientific knowledge, but in contrast to the knowledge based in the experience of subordination, this is fundamentally an expert knowledge" (273).

9 For a useful overview, see McLaughlin.

10 For recent accounts of the limits of liberal democratic elections as they are presently constituted, see Rancière, *Hatred of Democracy* and Badiou and Žižek. For Badiou, there is a lack of radical possibility in existing Western political systems because in "standard parliamentarianism, in its usual functioning, the majority and the opposition are commensurable. There is obviously a common measure between the majority and the opposition, which means you do not have the paradoxical relation. You have differences, naturally, but these differences do not amount to a paradoxical relationship; on the contrary, they constitute a regular, law-governed relationship. This is easily grasped: since sooner or later (this is what is referred to as 'democratic alternation') the opposition will replace the majority, or take its place, it is indeed necessary for there to be a common measure between the two. If you don't have a common measure, you will not be able to substitute the one with the other. So the terms are commensurable, and to the extent that they are commensurable you do not have the situation of radical exception" (17–18).

11 The Nature Challenge posed ten possible ways individuals could reduce their impact on the environment, and asked them to adopt at least three of them in the year ahead. The ten "steps" are

1. Reduce home energy by 10 percent
2. Choose energy-efficient home and appliances
3. Don't use pesticides
4. Eat meat-free meals one day a week
5. Buy locally grown and produced food
6. Choose a fuel-efficient vehicle
7. Walk, bike, carpool or take public transit one day a week
8. Choose a home close to work or school
9. Support alternative transportation
10. Learn more and share information with others. (*Autobiography* 262)

12 On the role played by cynical reason in relation to environmental crisis, see Žižek 420–61. Žižek's notion of cynical reason is drawn from Peter Sloterdijk's groundbreaking *Critique of Cynical Reason*. The first part of Sloterdijk's wide-ranging book probes the constitution of what he

identifies as the "new attitude of consciousness toward 'objectivity,'" which he names "enlightened false consciousness." This "new cynicism" draws on the productive negativity of the enlightenment but also rejects any possibility of hope or new values that might result from it. The cynicism (or sarcasm) Sloterdijk detects in contemporary thought is "a matter of the social and existential limits of enlightenment. The compulsion to survive and desire to assert itself have demoralized enlightened consciousness. It is afflicted with the compulsion to put up with preestablished relations that it finds dubious, to accommodate itself to them, and finally even to carry out their business" (5–6). It is easy to see the implications of this form of enlightened false consciousness for contemporary explorations of the gap between belief and action on environmental issues.

Cynicism was not always thus. The Greek Cynics (for instance, Diogenes) might be said to have advocated a form of anarchist environmentalism: a disavowal of power and money, a rejection of property and social distinctions, and an embrace of a simple life in harmony with the natural world. Cynicism might well be what is needed to counteract (contemporary) cynical reason.

13 These examples are taken from Suzuki, *Legacy*. For a discussion of eco-apocalypse, see Szeman.

14 Suzuki makes this point in *Autobiography* as well: "One of the terrifying aspects of globalization and economics is that this kind of knowledge is not seen as having value in a modern industrialized world, and what has taken thousands of years of careful observation, experimentation, and insight is being lost all over the planet in just a few generations and will never be recovered. This information is far more profound than current science, because it has been tested over time with the survival of those who possessed the knowledge" (212).

15 In recent years, Suzuki returns again and again to a criticism of economics. See, for instance, Suzuki and Moola.

16 The long feature story on Suzuki in *Maclean's* practically gloats at the necessity of "Saint Suzuki" to have to reign in his "revolutionary" impulses in order to deal with corporations in a less critical and dismissive fashion, especially with respect to the work and funding of his Foundation (see MacQueen). Even so, it is clear that Suzuki remains generally critical of the activities of corporations (see Babiak).

17 In a slightly different context, Nancy Fraser has described such critique as "affirmative," that is, as "aimed at correcting inequitable outcomes of social arrangements without disturbing the underlying framework that generates them" (23).

WORKS CITED

Babiak, Todd. "Suzuki scoffs at Syncrude offer." *Edmonton Journal* A1 (22 September 2010): 3. Print.

Badiou, Alain, and Slavoj Žižek. *Philosophy in the Present*. Cambridge: Polity, 2009. Print.

Bourdieu, Pierre. "The Forms of Capital." *Handbook of Theory and Research for the Sociology of Education*. Ed. John G. Richardson. New York: Greenwood, 1986. 241–58. Print.

Cazdyn, Eric, and Imre Szeman. *After Globalization*. London: Wiley-Blackwell, 2011. Print. http://dx.doi.org/10.1002/9781444396478.

Connolly, William E. *Neuropolitics: Thinking, Culture, Speed*. Minneapolis: U of Minnesota P, 2002. Print.

Dixon, Guy. "The bottom line? He has some regrets." *Globe and Mail* (30 June 2010): R2. Print.

Fraser, Nancy. *Justice Interruptus: Critical Reflections on the "Postsocialist" Condition*. London: Routledge, 1997. Print.

"GHG [Greenhouse Gas Emissions] Per Capita." *How Canada Performs. conferenceboard.ca*. Conference Board of Canada. Web. 1 April 2011.

Hardt, Michael. "Two Faces of the Apocalypse: A Letter from Copenhagen." *Polygraph* 22 (2010): 265–74. Print.

Hardt, Michael, and Antonio Negri. *Empire*. Cambridge, Mass.: Harvard UP, 2000. Print.

Hertzberger, Hendrik. "Cooling on Warming." *New Yorker*. 6 February 2011: 21–2. Print.

MacQueen, Kent. "The Remarkable Transformation of Saint Suzuki." *Macleans. Macleans.ca*. 25 October 2007. Web. 1 April 2011.

McLaughlin, Neil. "Global Public Intellectuals, Autonomy, and Culture: Reflections Inspired by the Death of Edward Said." *Cultural Autonomy: Frictions and Connections*. Ed. Petra Rethmann, Imre Szeman, and William D. Coleman. Vancouver: U of British Columbia P, 2010. 111–31. Print.

Monbiot, George. "Death Denial" *Monbiot.com*. 2 November 2009. Web. 1 April 2011. Rpt. of "Clive James isn't a climate change sceptic, he's a sucker – but this may be the reason." *Guardian*. Web.

Panagia, Davide. *The Political Life of Sensation*. Durham, NC: Duke UP, 2009. Print.

Rancière, Jacques. *The Emancipated Spectator*. Trans. Gregory Elliott. New York: Verso, 2009. Print.

Rancière, Jacques. *Hatred of Democracy*. New York: Verso, 2006. Print.

Rancière, Jacques. *The Ignorant Schoolmaster: Five Lessons in Intellectual Emancipation*. Trans. Kristin Ross. Palo Alto, Calif.: Stanford UP, 1991. Print.

Sloterdijk, Peter. *Critique of Cynical Reason*. Trans. Michael Eldred. Minneapolis: U of Minnesota P, 1987. Print.

Suzuki, David. *David Suzuki: The Autobiography*. Vancouver: Greystone Books, 2007. Print.

Suzuki, David. *The Legacy: An Elder's Vision for Our Sustainable Future*. Vancouver: Greystone Books, 2010. Print.

Suzuki, David. *Metamorphosis: Stages in a Life*. Toronto: Stoddart, 1987. Print.

Suzuki, David, and Faisal Moola. "David Suzuki: The absurdity of endless growth." *The Georgia Straight. straight.com*. Vancouver Free Press. 18 Nov. 2008. Web. 1 April 2011.

Suzuki, David, with Amanda McConnell. *The Sacred Balance: Rediscovering Our Place in Nature*. Vancouver: Greystone Books, 1997. Print.

Szeman, Imre. "System Failure: Oil, Futurity, and the Anticipation of Disaster." *South Atlantic Quarterly* 106.4 (2007): 805–23. http://dx.doi.org/10.1215/00382876-2007-047.

Virno, Paolo. *A Grammar of the Multitude*. New York: Semiotext(e), 2004. Print.

Williams, Raymond. *Marxism and Literature*. Oxford: Oxford UP, 1977. Print.

Žižek, Slavoj. *In Defense of Lost Causes*. New York: Verso, 2008. Print.

11 The Immaterial Matters

R. DARREN GOBERT

In recent years, like other humanities scholars, I have worked in the face of calls to justify my work in terms of the skills and "practical outcomes" that it facilitates in its audience; these calls, I fear, herald the direction of public higher education policy more generally. In the UK, after all, the Chancellor of the Exchequer, George Osborne, has declared British universities the "jewels" in the country's "economic crown" (qtd. in Vasagar) while announcing massive funding cuts to higher education to be levied according to a crude material logic: the teaching of science, technology, engineering, and mathematics will continue to be funded by the state, while the teaching of humanities will presumably have to be borne largely, if not entirely, by tuition costs (Morgan; Richardson). It would be tempting to blame this logic entirely on Prime Minister David Cameron and his coalition government but for the awkward fact that it had shown itself well before their election. In 2009, the Labour government had changed the name of the department responsible for higher education from "Innovation, Universities, and Skills" to "Business, Innovation, and Skills" – downgrading innovation, in an apparently un-ironic gesture, as business supplanted the universities. And the new department's minister, Lord Peter Mandelson, had recommended (a) that degrees be labelled with their dropout and employment success rates as well as their earning potential, and (b) that employers fund courses in return for helping to design them (Curtis; Tickle). If the Labour argument was buttressed by an implicit claim that no kind of knowledge cannot be assigned a material value, the Conservative/Liberal Democrat exploitation of this argument explicitly claims that those who care about philosophy, or about theatre, or about history – that is to say, about culture – can pay for it themselves, because such studies do not benefit the state (or its "economic crown") materially as the study of medicine does. Needless to say, government research budgets in these areas have been gutted, too: victims of the same pragmatic logic that will soon decimate British funding for the fine arts.

It is wearying though hardly impossible to mount a counterclaim that the study of the humanities materially contributes to society in ways unaccounted for by the blunt mathematics of government budgets. I would mount a different counterclaim: that some contributions of this domain are no less essential for being quite immaterial. In what follows, I turn to a contemporary British play, Sarah Kane's *Phaedra's Love,* which might be said to represent a culture that can only understand itself in material terms. In one regard, Kane's project recalls that of Antonin Artaud, who had called for a "theatre of cruelty" that could transform the material body of society through the immaterial force of theatre[1]; like Artaud, Kane stages a certain violence as a step towards engaging the significance of the immaterial. However, she also directs us to the impossibility of such a project in contemporary Britain. That Kane's version of the famous story of Hippolytus and Phaedra condemns consumer materialism – she focuses the opening action on Hippolytus's electronic toys and fast-food snacks – is clear enough. But what interests me more is the way that she emphasizes materiality more generally, by literalizing so many of the immaterial elements in Euripides, Seneca, or Racine. For example, Phaedra's love (the subject of all versions of the story but now bluntly the title) is crudely physicalized in a degrading sex scene, and, indeed, the metaphorically fiery ardour that Racine had so famously bestowed on the queen – "et moi je brûle encore," she proclaimed (791) – is replaced by an even more distinctly material fire: the "awesome fucking thing" that "burns" in Kane's Phaedra seems to be gonorrhoea (71), an affliction made all the more unremarkable by its being shared with her daughter and even the Priest, Hippolytus's confessor, all of whom get their "burn" from the same royal source.

Kane's role as a playwright of intense formal experimentation and deep ethical commitment was established with her debut play, *Blasted,* premiered in 1995 at the Royal Court, London, in a production directed by James Macdonald. It is suggestive both of the play's difficulty and of journalist critics' kneejerk refusal to engage that *Blasted* was initially (and unanimously) dismissed in hyperbolic and condescending terms: most notoriously, Jack Tinker of the *Daily Mail* declared himself "utterly and entirely disgusted by a play which appears to know no bounds of decency," condemning its seemingly relentless onslaught of extreme stage action, including eye-gouging, cannibalism, and rape (42); Tinker suggested that the money that had gone into the play's development "might have been better spent on a course of remedial therapy" (42). But if the critics were savage, the most intellectually rigorous of Britain's playwrights, including Harold Pinter and Edward Bond, just as immediately recognized the play's thoroughgoing critique of contemporary society and its investigation of British complicity in the horrors of Bosnia. As Pinter put it, Kane was "facing something actual and true and ugly and painful" (qtd. in Sellar 33). Blasting apart the play's realistic set and its naturalistic stage idiom at the end of the second scene, Kane's *Blasted* had unmoored unities of place and situation. Moving from Ian's rape of Cate in a hotel room in Leeds – "the kind that is so expensive it could be anywhere in the world" (Kane 3) – to an unidentified war zone, the play thus explores how "the logical conclusion of the attitude that produces an isolated rape in England is the rape camps in Bosnia," as the playwright put it (qtd. in Urban, "Ethics" 45). When the play received its first major London revival in 2001, the journalistic reviews resembled public acts of contrition. For example, Michael Billington, the *Guardian*'s primary reviewer, began his 2001 review by noting, "Five years ago I was rudely dismissive of Sarah Kane's *Blasted*. Yet watching its revival last night I was overcome by its sombre power" (421). The shift was in no small part the result of thoughtful considerations of the play by scholars such as Graham Saunders and Ken Urban and such public intellectuals as Bond, who helped a snarky press corps, along with the larger public, to navigate the play's considerable difficulties. Kane was a new stripe of political playwright, weaned on eleven years of Margaret Thatcher's rule and disillusioned with the Labour party's moves towards the political centre; her apparent cruelty, Urban argued, was "a means of both reflecting and challenging the despair of contemporary urban life" ("Cruel" 39).

When Kane took on the story of Phaedra and Hippolytus in *Phaedra's Love,* she was engaging with a daunting genealogy of adaptations. The story was undoubtedly dramatized in several Greek plays, of which only one survives: Euripides's *Hippolytus* (c. 428 BCE), which focuses on the goddess Aphrodite's plan to smite the prince who hubristically disdains her. The vessel and collateral damage of Aphrodite's plan is Hippolytus's stepmother, Phaedra, who comes into sharper focus in another well-known classical representation: Seneca's *Phaedra* (?50 CE).

Inspired by the playwright's Stoicism, *Phaedra* de-emphasizes the supernatural aspects of Euripides's play, shifting focus onto the emotional actions of Phaedra (and her nurse) and heightening Phaedra's moral responsibility both for her love for her stepson and the allegation of rape she makes against him to her husband, Theseus. Seneca's Stoic preoccupation with the problem of the passions and the tension between fate and free will was sharpened still further in the play's most famous rendering, Racine's *Phèdre* (1677), which is deeply suffused with the playwright's Jansenist background.[2] For Racine, what Phaedra confronts is her own psychology and humankind's inherent sinfulness, which pull her – as inexorably as Aphrodite had in Euripides's play – towards Hippolytus. In keeping with this theme, Racine de-emphasizes Aphrodite (here Venus) and indeed writes out Artemis; rather, in a striking parallel to his stepmother, Hippolytus loves someone forbidden to him: the captive princess Aricia, the remaining daughter of a family implacably hated by Theseus.

Kane's *Phaedra's Love* premiered in 1996 at the Gate Theatre, London, in a production directed by the playwright. Like *Blasted*, it was initially greeted with an ad-hominem hostility. Charles Spencer of the *Telegraph*, for instance, wrote that "It's not a theatre critic that's required here, it's a psychiatrist" (653). And as with *Blasted*, a reassessment of the play – and an examination of its ethical interventions – began with its academic critics. Here I wish to pursue an observation made by the English philosopher Simon Critchley, who used Kane's play heuristically in his exploration of Racine's *Phèdre*. In Racine's play, Critchley writes, "the corpse onstage at the end of the play is not Phaedra's, it is that of the illusion of the *polis*, the city, the state, the political order" (36). For Critchley, Racine's play is anti-political insofar as it is thoroughly Christianized; it moves away from Euripides's focus on the political order and towards a "rejection of the temporal world" and embrace of the "tragic vision of Jansenism" (Critchley 37, 38). (Racine, after all, could never escape the Jansenism of his educators, whose worldview saturates his plays; following Lucien Goldmann's famous analysis of the playwright in *Le dieu caché*, we might say that Racine presents a world in which God is hidden and yet ever present and ever watchful.) Pursuing Critchley's analysis, I note that, for Kane, not only the political order of Euripides and his day but also the theological frame of Racine and his day are missing. Her Phaedra exists in a culturally incoherent void in which there is room for neither emotion nor ethics, both of which rely on a governing cultural context. For what grounds a well-functioning society, Kane implies, is not only its material elements. In the play, she heavily foregrounds the institutional structures – such as church and government – that might create frameworks of belief within which emotions and ethics could be generated; but she shows that, absent considerations of the immaterial, these structures will founder.

According to Clifford Geertz's well-known articulation, culture is "an historically transmitted pattern of meanings embodied in symbols, a system of inherited conceptions expressed in symbolic forms by means of which men communicate, perpetuate, and develop their knowledge about and attitudes toward life" (89). Culture thus provides factual information, normative beliefs, and perceptual frames that collectively constitute the reality of an agent situated within it. Of course, the line of cultural transmission and inheritance does not extend with unproblematic continuity. It mutates as it is relayed (and theorized), as it interacts with other cultural traditions, and as it absorbs the influential contributions of individuals embedded within it. Edward Bond eloquently expressed the importance of individual agents, noting that rare individuals can change cultural reality. This ability, he says, is the hallmark of great artists, among whose few he places Kane: "Half-way through seeing *Blasted* in a small, cramped theatre, in an adequate production, I realised that reality had changed. I do not exaggerate. This century's horrors do not change reality, they merely draw its conclusions and we could go on as if we had learnt nothing from them. *Blasted* changed reality because it changed the means we have of understanding ourselves. It showed us a new way in which to see reality, and when we do that reality is changed," he writes (190). Through these interactions, the line of cultural transmission becomes riven by contradictions and laden with interpretive baggage, as expressed in the rich and difficult texts that humanities scholars make it their business to explicate.

Kane's play theatrically embodies the ruptures and burdens of Phaedra's cultural transmission even as it dramatizes an ethical wasteland founded on an unstable cultural context. While the play seems to take place in contemporary Britain, Kane undermines this setting with a typically postmodern overlay of contradictory locators, including, for example, the play's references to funeral pyres and vultures and her characters' un-contemporary and un-British names. (Phaedra's daughter Strophe, for instance, takes her name from one part of the Greek choral ode.) The uneasy coexistence of these cultural and geographical references highlights the mutations undergone by Greek "history" as Kane has inherited it – a "history" whose earliest beginning (at least that can be seen from our perspective) is Euripides's literary representation, and a history transfigured by its many interactions, including those with Seneca, Racine, and their own respective cultural contexts.[3] Kane winks at the illusive contemporary Britishness of her setting when the disguised Theseus asks a denizen of the mob: "Come far?" (98). The man's answer – "Newcastle" – provides a specific detail whose precise significance remains elusive, since his current location remains unknown. Thus, Kane's play can be read as a palimpsest of Phaedra and Hippolytus's theatre history, with their "original" story signalling through the murk of its cultural elisions, revisions, updates, and commentaries. At the same time, the play demonstrates the savagery of a population incapable of recognizing this history. As I will explore at greater length, if the mob's desire for catharsis is frustrated, this frustration is tied to the lack of a stable cultural inheritance whose exegetical accretions they can never adequately understand and, therefore, whose emotional meanings they cannot access.

Phaedra's Love, like any cultural product, is an agent in the "creation and maintenance" of a cultural sensibility, as Geertz would have it (451), and, as a palimpsest, it also reflects assumptions about its immediate cultural context and bears traces of the complicated history of its antecedent texts. And just as there is cultural and ethical value in difficult art, like Kane's, so too is there cultural and ethical value in the sort of humanities scholarship that helps to illuminate such difficult art and such complicated histories. The mounting disregard for the immaterial considerations of humanities scholars suggests that this value is not being recognized, and that a cruder material logic, such as that pilloried in the play, may be on the ascent.[4] The consequences are rigorously explored by Kane, whose dénouement to *Phaedra's Love* occurs "[o]utside the court" (98) – a delectably indeterminate phrase, given the play's contextually indeterminate setting. The phrase recalls, for me, a clinical term of Sigmund Freud and Josef Breuer, *bewusstseinsunfähig,* a neologism they coined by analogue to *hoffähig* ("admissible to court") (Breuer and Freud 225 n.1). Freud and Breuer had argued that the *Unfähigkeit* (inadmissibility) of certain emotions to the sovereign *Bewusstsein* (consciousness) arrested the emotional development of the agent. Here, the mob's placement outside the court signals the failure of a judicious foundation from which to construct coherent emotional and ethical meaning. If, as Critchley claims, the *polis* is dead already in Racine, Kane shows us a world in which there is no compensatory framework, such as religion or even psychology – in which there is, indeed, no immaterial connection between individuals.

Alienation results. Kane links Hippolytus's declaration that he feels "[n]o remorse" about the death of Phaedra to another of his declarations: "Don't need tat" (92). And if Hippolytus has "no desires" – as Tom Stoppard's Guildenstern, similarly divorced from his original cultural context, puts it[5] – these desires are absent because the prince's once-fervent worship of Artemis (which Euripides had yoked to his single-minded hatred of Aphrodite)[6] cannot inhere in Kane's irreligious setting as it would have, though signifying differently, in Racine's Jansenism-soaked Paris. Kane's Priest struggles to provide emotional lustration to the prince in order to preserve "the stability of the nation's morals," as the mob gathered outside begins to press in (94). But having struck out in every attempt at catechistic argument ("Is there anything you need?" – "Do you feel remorse?" – "Do you know what the unforgivable sin is?" – "Do you believe in God?" – "What do you think forgiveness is?" [92, 92, 94, 96, 96]), the Priest ultimately performs sacramental absolution by undoing Hippolytus's trousers and fellating him (97). The scene's parodic coupling of ecstasy and contagion – the prince's gonorrhoea having been established – seems to mock the long-held idea that theatre-going effects a cathartic release that sweeps over the audience: "There is a kind of purity in you," the Priest proclaims before undoing the prince's trousers and getting on his knees to do what passes, in Kane's grim representation, as God's work (97).

For Breuer and Freud, the emotional arrest of an individual could only be overcome with the purgation – catharsis, again! – of the arrested emotions through his or her mimetic representation in language, a cultural product shaped and dramaturged (and its *mise en scène* facilitated) by the analyst.[7] Named the "talking cure" by their famous patient Bertha Pappenheim,[8] the process suggests the role that a play might serve not only for its playwright – Tinker's and Spencer's references to the playwright's mental health were particularly unfortunate, in light of Kane's mental illness[9] – but also for its audience. It is no accident that *Phaedra's Love* features an analyst-like figure, who tries to determine the etiology of Hippolytus's illness in Kane's second scene. Summoned by Phaedra to discuss her stepson, the Doctor has some unsurprising observations: "He should change his diet"; "He should tidy his room and get some exercise"; "He has to help himself"; "Perhaps your son is missing his father"; "Perhaps he's missing his real mother"; and "He's bound to be feeling low, it's his birthday" (65, 66, 66, 68, 68, 68). But while the Doctor's diagnosis – "He's depressed" (65) – is similarly unsurprising, his prescription for cure is not: "Get over him," he tells Phaedra (68). The Doctor's unprompted analytic slippage from the object of observation to the observer herself performs the principal move of Freudian catharsis, in which the hero's neurosis facilitates not his own emotional abreaction but rather that of the spectator who watches him. And, correspondingly, Kane ties the mob's – and the play's – inability to achieve dramatic closure to the incapacity of the literally dis-affected Hippolytus to experience emotion.

Typically, the hero's overcoming of his or her emotional difficulties serves to effect the emotional benefits of theatre-going for the play's audience, according to a well-theorized logic of dramatic theory that begins with Aristotle's *Poetics* (where the notion of dramatic catharsis is first established) and extends to Freud's "Psychopathic Characters on the Stage" and beyond.[10] But holding no beliefs, having no needs, Hippolytus is emotionless. The play begins with his "impassive" viewing of a "particularly violent" film and his masturbation into a dirty sock "without a flicker of pleasure" (Kane 65). Like Euripides, Kane positions the prince as an object of spectatorship – she focuses the action on him and his electronic toys, fast-food snacks, and filthy socks – but Kane's onstage spectators, like their spectacle, seem emotionally compromised. For example, Theseus "does not cry" at his wife's suicide (97), and this suicide has been spurred by her failure to enjoy herself when her stepson finally consents to be fellated: "*Hippolytus*: You enjoyed that? [...] *Phaedra*: (*Doesn't respond*)" (82). Kane herself had extended her critique of the onstage spectators to include the members of her 1996 audience. In the premiere production that she directed, the entire space was ontologically continuous, with the audience seating incorporated into the set. Thus, when the mob descended to participate in Hippolytus's murder, its members rose up from among the paying spectators, where they had been preset.[11] One might have felt complicit – there might have been a union of character and audience citizenry such as that imagined by Aristotle, or even by Artaud, who borrowed from Augustine his central metaphor of theatre as a plague that overcomes its audience[12] – except that Kane's black humour, and the near-farcical extremity of the scene, prevented it. Aleks Sierz reported nervous laughter at the premiere (108): a reaction that he presumes was unintended but one that, in fact, well reflects the queasy implications of Kane's critique.

In the failed union of the citizenry, Kane stages the impossibility in contemporary Britain of the sort of theatre advocated by Artaud (who, it may be relevant to consider, had attempted to reassert immaterial prerogatives in the face of involuntary medical treatments[13]). Artaud's theatre, he wrote in a 1932 essay, would be like the mystery cults of ancient Greece; like alchemy, it would transfuse matter and find its "*fin*" and its "*réalité*" in its impact on the spectator (*Oeuvres* 4:46).[14] In the mystery rites to which Artaud alludes in this article, the initiate undergoes an irreversible transformation, a purification that experientially enacts the infant Demophoön's terrifying brush with the goddess Demeter, who had put him in the fire in order to confer immortality.[15] This initiation destroys and remakes its subject just as the theatre of cruelty, "sans tuer, provoque dans l'esprit non seulement d'un individu, mais d'un peuple, les plus mystérieuses altérations" (Artaud, *Oeuvres* 4:25).[16] However, by grounding his theory in the image of religious mystery cults, Artaud also reveals why his project would be doomed to fail in an entirely material culture such as that represented by Kane. As he explained in a letter to Jean Paulhan, the theatre of cruelty should confront the principle of theatre itself, which is metaphysical[17] – Artaud's version of the truism that (in Karl Jaspers's formulation) "there is no tragedy without transcendence" (41). Similarly, there can be no catharsis – neither ethics nor emotions – without the immaterial.

To say that ethics and emotion are grounded in a stable cultural framework is not to advocate for a return to Euripides's or Seneca's or Racine's worldview, to this or that religious hegemony, and of course many of the practises of those cultures are ethically repugnant to us. Rather, I am arguing that a society's self-questioning and self-knowledge is essential to its emotional and ethical development, and that the intellectual, like the artist, has a pivotal role to play in leading this self-questioning and disseminating this self-knowledge. In one of her boldest provocations, Kane claimed to be uninterested – even unaware – of the play's earlier incarnations, thus positioning herself as the product of a culture whose ignorance she pilloried.[18] To understand Racine's context, or Seneca's or Euripides's or even Artaud's, means to submit the cultural documents of their times – the symbolic forms by which ethical and emotional knowledge and attitudes were developed, to paraphrase Geertz – to scrutiny; it is the work of scholars. And doing so also proves pivotal in understanding our own culture. The critical machinery that scholars bring to their analyses of other cultures is, at its best, self-reflexive: it acknowledges the limitations of its own cultural location and thus encourages self-examination, even if, as Stanley

Fish has articulated, critical analysis requires not only the demotion of the cultural norms under scrutiny but also an unexamined allegiance to new norms that will enable such analytic scrutiny (53). It is a hoary humanistic cliché, perhaps, but I believe it to be true: by learning about the there and then, we better understand the here and now.

That there are culturally specific ethical standards may seem self-evident, but increasingly evident too is the fact that there are culturally specific emotions that are constituted within and by particular cultures. Such a view has become common in both psychology and the philosophy of mind,[19] and the claims and observations in these fields run parallel to – and, indeed, are persuasively substantiated by – those of such cultural anthropologists as Catherine Lutz, who have significantly influenced contemporary understandings of and beliefs about emotion.[20] First, thick descriptions of emotions from other cultural contexts (emotions understood as "natural" from within but recognizably foreign from an outside perspective) have helped to undermine the universalist and essentialist views that have dominated so much of the concept's history, steering attention to the more profitable notion that emotions are, in the words of anthropologist Michelle Rosaldo, "*embodied* thoughts" expressed in the behaviour of individual agents: "thoughts seeped with the apprehension that 'I am involved'" ("Toward" 143; her emphasis). Second, anthropological analyses have demonstrated that the content of these thoughts is largely determined by the agent's cultural context – learnt by the agent as part of an acculturation into a set of social values and expectations that require negotiation. Thus, the failure of emotional coherence in Kane's play is explained.

My argument here has been that scholars do important work in helping us to understand our own cultural context, because, in doing so, we make possible the ethical and emotional adjustments essential to a society's development. And just as this work sometimes seems immaterial, so too do its benefits. Reading Kane's play as an allegory, I have suggested that the absence of catharsis stands in for the absence of such ineffable benefits, and that the play's comment on the culture of its day is that the immaterial matters. In this way, Kane's play demonstrates by omission what earlier versions of the play had sought to put on stage and, indeed, to effect offstage. At the end of Euripides's *Hippolytus*, for example, the titular prince is trampled by horses after his father's rash curse, and the populace is called upon by the Chorus to lament his death: "This is a common grief for all the city; / it came unlooked for. There shall be / a storm of multitudinous tears for this" (221). This public lamentation effects a catharsis of the play's once-hidden, private grief – the impious love that had tormented Phaedra at the play's beginning and instigated the play's conflict (149–50) – and thus facilitates "an emotional participation that binds 'all' the members of the theatre together in the collective experience of the tragic suffering," in Charles Segal's assessment (157). Declaring to Theseus that "I free you from all guilt in this" (220), Euripides's Hippolytus accepts a sacrificial role, absorbing Theseus's guilt (an emotion that threatens social harmony) and positioning himself as the object of collective grief (an emotion that facilitates social harmony). But in *Phaedra's Love*, Hippolytus will have none of it. Despite an excess of possibilities – in addition to Phaedra's suicide, Strophe is raped and murdered, and Theseus slashes his own throat – the mob's need for cathartic relief remains frustrated, even as they hold their grisly barbecue in a perverse parody of public ritual that outdoes anything in Seneca's *Phaedra*. As the vultures descend on him, Hippolytus can only "manag[e] a smile" (102). Keen for anything resembling emotional connection, the alienated prince speaks his last words: "If there could have been more moments like this" (103).

If Kane's Hippolytus "apparently get[s] pleasure from neither" his electric car nor his television (74), this incapacity reflects more than his heartlessness (Strophe's estimation [89]), his adolescent disenchantment, or the playwright's premillennial malaise. If Phaedra's love cannot find expression, this incapacity reflects the absence of a stable cultural context within which her emotions can be generated. For Kane's most flagrant challenge to Aristotelian tragedy is her disavowal of the universal truth that the *Poetics* emphasizes in Book 9 (Aristotle 18), a challenge she expresses in the play's unstable unity of place. On one level, this unstable unity of place embodies Phaedra's cultural history, acknowledging that the play has been brought to vivid life in various ways in the various contexts that have anchored it. But on another level Kane's unstable unity of place serves to allegorize a brutal citizenry whose ignorance of their cultural history leaves them with no stable foundation for emotional or ethical expression.

Emphasizing the material – exercising a logic analogous to that of much current public higher education policy – Kane shows us what is missing from its picture. Most tellingly, the eviscerating charge of great tragedy is rendered physical in the macabre picnic scene, where the rabble eats Hippolytus's barbequed genitals and bowels. In the midst of all of the play's literalizations, the quintessential immaterial – even ineffable – aspect of tragic spectatorship goes missing: catharsis, the goal of all of Kane's dramatic forebears since Euripides. And with it goes missing the possibility of social cohesion that the theatre has been believed, since at least Aristotle, to engender. (Kane emphasized her choice of genre repeatedly, once stating of her play *Cleansed*, for example, that "I decided I wanted to write a play that could never be turned into a film; it could never ever be shot for television; could never be turned into a novel; the only thing that could ever be done with it was that it could be staged" [qtd. in Saunders, "Apocalyptic" 127].) Kane's play, in other words, might be said to allegorize our fixation on the quantifiable, the tangible, the material, even as it reveals that something essential is lost when we pay insufficient heed to the immaterial. Catharsis, after all, requires a shared experience of emotion, but neither emotions nor ethics are possible without an intelligible cultural framework to anchor them. I have suggested some ways that Kane, in her characteristically inscrutable way, reveals the seemingly intangible roots through which culture might anchor our emotional and ethical lives; these roots can be more clearly traced by resituating *Phaedra's Love* within the history that it reflects. In its allegory, then, the play makes a case for both the theatre artist and the arts scholar in civic life, and, indeed, departing from a popular view that both ought dispassionately to study culture instead of passionately seeking to lead it, Kane suggests that their work – whether plays or academic writing – can serve as positive agents in cultural stability and a society's emotional and ethical development. Professor Natalie Fenton, the deputy head of media and communications at Goldsmiths, University of London, criticized the UK government's funding cuts to humanities departments by saying that "By only protecting science, they're signalling that arts, humanities and social sciences are worthless. But these are the disciplines that engender civility" (Williams). Such a claim may seem at first blush to be hyperbolic. But by illuminating both Kane's play and the cultural accretions it carries, I hope to have limned the importance to society of intellectual life – and articulated why we must attend carefully to matters that have been deemed immaterial.

NOTES

1 For example, Artaud writes: "Mais qu'on n'oublie pas qu'un geste de théâtre est violent, mais qu'il est désintéressé; et que le théâtre enseigne justement l'inutilité de l'action qui une fois faite n'est plus à faire, et l'utilité supérieure de l'état inutilisé par l'action mais qui, *retourné*, produit la sublimation" (Artaud, *Oeuvres* 4:99) ["But let it not be forgotten that though a theatrical gesture is violent, it is disinterested; and that the theatre

correctly teaches the uselessness of the action which, once done, is not to be done again, and the superior usefulness of the state unused by the action but which, *transformed,* produces sublimation" (translation mine)]. The other meanings of the word *sublimation* – in aesthetics, religion, or psychoanalysis, for example – enrich its meaning as Artaud uses it here. He distinguishes between a chemical action (useless in the sense that it can only happen once and is immediately finished – a lesson, he says repeatedly, that theatre teaches us) and the state of matter upon which it acts. This state undergoes sublimation, the process of changing from solid to gas without becoming liquid.

Therefore, the standard English edition of this passage misses Artaud's central metaphor – rendering *retourné* as "restored," *mais* as "and," and *utilité* as "use" – and thus obfuscates entirely Artaud's already somewhat obscure meaning (*Theater* 82).

2 Racine had been educated by Port-Royal's Jansenist theologians, at the time the theatre's most implacable enemies. Eventually, his adult rapprochement with them would lead him to abandon secular theatre. An account of Racine's retirement as a playwright and his reconciliation with his Port-Royal teachers is provided by Geoffrey Brereton's *Jean Racine* (234–7, 253–4, 305–11).

3 Kane's use of the funeral pyre derives from Seneca, whose Theseus commands one not for his "ungodly" wife, as in *Phaedra's Love,* but for Hippolytus: "Let fire cremate, […] what we have here […] / Kindle the flames, men, for a royal pyre" (Seneca 242, 241–2). The vultures migrate into Kane's play from a more unexpected source: Bertolt Brecht's *Baal,* which she had been adapting at the time (Saunders, *Love Me* 81).

4 For another discussion of the relation between material criticism and the immaterial images of culture, see Jason Haslam's contribution to this volume.

5 See *Rosencrantz and Guildenstern Are Dead*:

GUILDENSTERN: Are you happy?
ROSENCRANTZ: What?
GUILDENSTERN: Content? At ease?
ROSENCRANTZ: I suppose so.
GUILDENSTERN: What are you going to do now?
ROSENCRANTZ: I don't know. What do you want to do?
GUILDENSTERN: I have no desires. None. (Stoppard 17)

6 Hippolytus's intransigence – "Men make their choice: one man honours one God, / and one another," he says (Euripides 167) – would have been

viewed as "ostentatious" and a "perversity" even by his original audience, according to classicist Richard Lattimore (qtd. in Euripides 159).

7 On the connection between Aristotelian dramatic catharsis and Freudian psychoanalytic catharsis, see my "Dramatic Catharsis, Freudian Hysteria and the 'Private Theatre' of Anna O." I address the explicit aestheticization of the psychoanalytic patient's narratives under the dramaturgical assistance of the analyst (327–9).

8 Pappenheim – better known as Anna O., the name used in the *Studies on Hysteria* – coined the phrase, which Breuer and Freud retained (Breuer and Freud 30).

9 The connection between Kane and Hippolytus is by now a mainstay of Kane criticism; see, for example, Saunders, *Love Me* (79–80). Kane herself said: "I suppose I set out to write a play about depression because of my state of being at that time. And so inevitably it did become more about Hippolytus" (qtd. in Saunders, *Love Me* 73).

10 Freud argues that the efficacy of tragic heroes is determined by the particular emotional blocks of the audience who are to witness and identify. In this way, the audience member engages in a vicarious experience in *Schauspiel* just as children do at *Spiel*, which Freud underscores by spelling the former word as a hyphenated compound: "*Being present* as an interested spectator at a spectacle or play [*Schau-Spiel*] does for adults what play does for children, whose hesitant hopes of being able to do what grown-up people do are in that way gratified" ("Psychopathic Characters" 305; my emphasis) ["Das teilnehmende Zuschauen beim Schau-Spiel leistet dem Erwachsenen dasselbe wie das Spiel dem Kinde, dessen tastende Erwartung, es dem Erwachsenen gleichtun zu können, so befriedigt wird" ("Psychopathische Personen" 163).]

11 For details of the staging of this production, see Campbell 175.

12 See Artaud, *Oeuvres* 4:25. Augustine, of course, was condemning the theatre, while Artaud celebrates it.

13 During his nine years of confinement in asylums (1937–1946), Artaud reconverted to (1937) and rerenounced (1945) Christianity, and dabbled in Hinduism and various occult practices (Hayman 116–30). Artaud's attitude towards both mysticism and rational psychology is captured well in the following passage from his reading notes:

> Plus l'homme se préoccupe de lui, plus ses préoccupations échappent en réalité à l'homme,
> égocentrisme individualiste et psychologique
> opposé à l'humanisme,

l'homme quand on le serre de près, cela aboutit toujours à trouver ce qui
n'est pas l'homme. …
La psychologie n'est pas la science de l'homme, au contraire.

[The more preoccupied man is with himself, the more irrelevant his preoccupations are to human reality,
individualistic and psychological egocentrism
opposed to humanism,
squeeze a man and you will always find something not human. …
Psychology is not the science of man, on the contrary.] (*Oeuvres* 8:144; translation mine)

14 Artaud, *Oeuvres* 4:50.

15 While the exact content of the mysteries remains unknown, their origin myth is recorded in the Homeric *Hymn to Demeter*: declaring that she will "lay down the rites so that hereafter / performing due rites you may propitiate my spirit," Demeter "revealed / the conduct of her rites and taught her Mysteries to all of them, / holy rites that are not to be transgressed, nor pried into, / nor divulged" (Foley ll. 273–4, 475–8). On the mysteries, see Helene Foley's commentary (esp. 30, 69–70, and 86).

16 "[W]ithout killing, [theatre] provokes the most mysterious alterations in the mind [i.e., spirit] of not only an individual but an entire populace" (Artaud, *Theater* 26). Mary Caroline Richards's translation of "esprit" as "mind" here is unsatisfactory, for "mind" fits ill with "un peuple" and bears inappropriate connotations of cognition. "Spirit" is truer to Artaud's sense in this passage.

17 "[Le] principe même du théâtre, qui est métaphysique" (Artaud, *Oeuvres* 4:111).

18 In light of the play's sophisticated borrowings from its predecessors, it is likely that Kane was being disingenuous when – living up to her bad-girl reputation – she winked at her postmodern disinterest in origins and claimed to rely, scantily, on Seneca alone:

in the end it was the Gate [Theatre] which suggested something Greek or Roman, and I thought, "Oh, I've always hated those plays. Everything happens off-stage, and what's the point?" But I decided to read one of them and see what I'd get. I chose Seneca […] I read Euripides only after I'd written *Phaedra's Love*. And I've never read Racine so far. Also, I only read Seneca once. I didn't want to get too much into it. (qtd. in Saunders, *Love Me* 72)

19 In her overview "The Thesis of Constructionism," Claire Armon-Jones identifies pioneers of this view: Jeff Coulter's *The Social Construction of Mind* (1979) in philosophy and James Averill's "A Constructivist View of Emotion" (1980) in psychology.

20 This work is indebted to Geertz's methodology: for example, work on Utku Eskimos (Jean L. Briggs's *Never in Anger*) or among the Ilongot of the Philippines (Michelle Z. Rosaldo's *Knowledge and Passion*). More recent studies, more narrowly focused on culturally specific emotions, include that of Lutz, whose work on the emotional life of the Ifaluk is seminal. See, for example, her *Unnatural Emotions: Everyday Sentiments on a Micronesian Atoll and their Challenge to Western Theory* (1988) and "Need, Nurturance, and the Emotions on a Pacific Atoll" (1995).

WORKS CITED

Aristotle. *On Poetry and Style*. Trans. G.M.A. Grube. Indianapolis: Hackett, 1989. Print.

Armon-Jones, Claire. "The Thesis of Constructionism." *The Social Construction of Emotions*. Ed. Rom Harré. Oxford: Blackwell, 1986. 32–56. Print.

Artaud, Antonin. *Oeuvres complètes*. 16 vols. Paris: Gallimard, 1970–1984. Print.

Artaud, Antonin. *The Theater and its Double*. Trans. Mary Caroline Richards. New York: Grove, 1958. Print.

Averill, James R. "A Constructivist View of Emotion." *Emotion: Theory, Research, and Experience*. Ed. Robert Plutchik and Henry Kellerman. New York: Academic, 1980. 305–39. Print.

Billington, Michael. Rev. of *Blasted*. *Guardian* 4 Apr. 2001. Rpt. in *Theatre Record* 21 (2001): 421. Print.

Bond, Edward. "Afterword: Sarah Kane and Theatre." *"Love Me or Kill Me": Sarah Kane and the Theatre of Extremes*. By Graham Saunders. Manchester: Manchester UP, 2002. 189–91. Print.

Brereton, Geoffrey. *Jean Racine: A Critical Biography*. London: Methuen, 1973. Print.

Breuer, Josef, and Sigmund Freud. *Studies on Hysteria*. Trans. and ed. James Strachey. New York: Basic, 1957. Print.

Briggs, Jean L. *Never in Anger: Portrait of an Eskimo Family*. Cambridge, MA: Harvard UP, 1970. Print.

Campbell, Peter A. "Sarah Kane's *Phaedra's Love*: Staging the Implacable." *Sarah Kane in Context*. Ed. Laurens de Vos and Graham Saunders. Manchester: Manchester UP, 2010. 173–83. Print.

Coulter, Jeff. *The Social Construction of Mind: Studies in Ethnomethodology and Linguistic Philosophy*. London: MacMillan, 1979. Print.

Critchley, Simon. "I Want to Die, I Hate My Life—Phaedra's Malaise." *New Literary History* 34 (2003): 17–40. Print.

Curtis, Polly. "University drop-out rates and graduate earnings to be tagged." *Observer* 1 Nov. 2009. Web. 3 Nov. 2010.

Euripides. *Hippolytus. Euripides I.* Trans. David Grene. Ed. David Grene and Richard Lattimore. Chicago: U of Chicago P, 1955. 157–221. Print.

Fish, Stanley. "Is There a Text in this Class?" *The Stanley Fish Reader*. Ed. H. Aram Vesser. Oxford: Blackwell, 1999. 38–54. Print. http://dx.doi.org/10.2307/1772220.

Foley, Helene P., trans, ed., and commentary. *The Homeric* Hymn to Demeter. Princeton: Princeton UP, 1994. Print

Freud, Sigmund. "Psychopathic Characters on the Stage." *The Standard Edition of the Complete Psychological Works*. Vol. 7. Trans. James Strachey. Ed. James Strachey et al. London: Hogarth, 1953–1974. 305–10. Print.

Freud, Sigmund. "Psychopathische Personen auf der Bühne." *Studienausgabe*. Vol. 10. Ed. Thure von Uexküll et al. Frankfurt: Fischer Taschenbuch, 1982. 161–8. Print.

Geertz, Clifford. *The Interpretation of Cultures*. New York: Basic, 1973. Print.

Gobert, R. Darren. "Dramatic Catharsis, Freudian Hysteria and the 'Private Theater' of Anna O." *Emotions: A Cultural Studies Reader*. Ed. Jennifer Harding and E. Deidre Pribram. New York: Routledge, 2009. 321–35. Print.

Goldmann, Lucien. *Le dieu caché: Étude sur la vision tragique dans les* Pensées *de Pascal et dans le théâtre de Racine*. Paris: Gallimard, 1969. Print.

Hayman, Ronald. *Artaud and After*. Oxford: Oxford UP, 1977. Print.

Jaspers, Karl. *Tragedy is Not Enough*. Trans. Harald A.T. Reiche et al. Boston: Beacon, 1952. Print.

Kane, Sarah. *Blasted. Complete Plays*. London: Methuen, 2001. 1–62. Print.

Kane, Sarah. *Phaedra's Love. Complete Plays*. London: Methuen, 2001. 63–104. Print.

Lutz, Catherine. "Need, Nurturance, and the Emotions on a Pacific Atoll." *Emotions in Asian Thought: A Dialogue in Comparative Philosophy*. Ed. Joel Marks and Roger T. Ames. Albany: SUNY P, 1995. 235–52. Print.

Lutz, Catherine. *Unnatural Emotions: Everyday Sentiments on a Micronesian Atoll and Their Challenge to Western Theory*. Chicago: U of Chicago P, 1988. Print.

Morgan, John. "Fears made flesh: only STEM teaching grants spared CSR scythe." *Times Higher Education* 20 Oct. 2010. Web. 21 Nov. 2010.

Racine, Jean. *Phèdre. Oeuvres complètes*. Vol. 1. Ed. Raymond Picard. Paris: Gallimard, 1950. 745–803. Print.

Richardson, Hannah. "Humanities to lose English universities teaching grant." Bbc.co.uk 26 Oct. 2010. Web. 21 Nov. 2010.

Rosaldo, Michelle Z. *Knowledge and Passion: Ilongot Notions of Self and Social Life*. New York: Cambridge UP, 1980. Print. http://dx.doi.org/10.1017/CBO9780511621833.

Rosaldo, Michelle Z. "Toward an Anthropology of Self and Feeling." *Culture Theory: Essays on Mind, Self, and Emotion*. Ed. Richard A. Shweder and Robert A. LeVine. New York: Cambridge UP, 1984. 137–57. Print.

Saunders, Graham. "The Apocalyptic Theatre of Sarah Kane." *British Drama of the 1990s*. Heidelberg: *Universitätsverlag Winter*. 2002. 123–35. Print.

Saunders, Graham. *"Love Me or Kill Me": Sarah Kane and the Theatre of Extremes*. Manchester: Manchester UP, 2002. Print.

Segal, Charles. "Catharsis, Audience, and Closure in Greek Tragedy." *Tragedy and the Tragic: Greek Theatre and Beyond*. Ed. M.S. Silk. Oxford: Oxford UP, 1996. 149–72. Print.

Sellar, Tom. "Truth and Dare: Sarah Kane's *Blasted*." *Theater* 27.1 (1996): 29–34 Print. http://dx.doi.org/10.1215/01610775-27-1-29.

Seneca. *Phaedra. Seneca: Three Tragedies*. Trans. Frederick Ahl. Ithaca: Cornell UP, 1986. 171–242. Print.

Sierz, Aleks. *In-Yer-Face Theatre: British Drama Today*. London: Faber and Faber, 2001. Print.

Spencer, Charles. Rev. of *Phaedra's Love. Daily Telegraph* 21 May 1996. Rpt. in *Theatre Record* 16 (1996): 652–3. Print.

Stoppard, Tom. *Rosencrantz and Guildenstern Are Dad*. New York: Grove, 1967. Print.

Tickle, Lois. "What did the Romans ever teach us?" *Guardian* 10 Nov. 2009. Web. 3 Nov. 2010.

Tinker, Jack. Rev. of *Blasted. Daily Mail* 19 Jan. 1995. Rpt. in *Theatre Record* 15 (1995): 42–3. Print.

Urban, Ken. "Cruel Britannia." *Cool Britannia: British Political Drama in the 1990s*. Ed. Graham Saunders and Rebecca D'Monté. London: Palgrave, 2007. 38–55. Print.

Urban, Ken. "An Ethics of Catastrophe: The Theatre of Sarah Kane." *PAJ a Journal of Performance and Art* 23.3 (Sept. 2001): 36–46 Print. http://dx.doi.org/10.2307/3246332.

Vasagar, Jeevan. "Universities alarmed by 40% cut to teaching budgets." *Guardian* 20 Oct. 2010. Web. 21 Nov. 2010.

Williams, Rachel, and Gozde Zorlu. "Spending review: how the cuts affect me." *Guardian* 21 Oct. 2010. Web. 30 Nov. 2010.

12 Higher Education and the End(s) of Time

PATRICK DEANE

In October 1929, W.H. Auden articulated the aspirations of his age in a poem of petition. "Look shining," it concluded in a peculiarly undirected imprecation, "at / New styles of architecture, a change of heart" ("XXIII," *English Auden* 36). A parody of prayer, although not quite parodic enough to justify the description, the poem's hunger for social and cultural transformation is passionate but hedged, forward looking but also sentimentally, treacherously, attached to the imperfections of the here and now.

In that ambivalence the poem effectively captures its historic moment. In the same month, the Judicial Committee of the Privy Council announced that women were persons, and in Canada enlightenment of a similar sort dawned when it was decided women could be appointed to the Senate. On 24 October, however, the Wall Street Crash began, and even if the socialist Auden might on occasions have seen the Crash in positive terms – it was construed by many, after all, as a sign of the imminent collapse of capitalism and the end of economic injustice – the human suffering it implied could never allow him to imagine with much conviction the new world waiting. Intimations of plenitude in Auden's poetry are invariably social, more likely to be linked to a fulfilled humanity and empathy than to asceticism, suffering, or self-denial. He was famously sustained, for example, by a "Vision of Agape" he experienced while teaching at the Downs School near Malvern in the thirties,[1] and poignant humanity typically coexists in his work with a sense of all that threatens it.

Notwithstanding "the crumpling flood" that looms ("A Summer Night," *Collected Poems* 118), to imagine "new styles of architecture" was, however, one of the defining activities of 1929, a year which saw come into effect the Kellogg-Briand Pact renouncing war as an instrument of foreign policy, the signing of the Geneva Convention on the treatment of prisoners, and the beginning of Gandhi's resolute campaign against British rule in India. It was characteristic of Auden to understand world events in personal terms; thus these phenomena could be taken as evidence of an impending "change of heart."

John Charles Polanyi, winner of the 1986 Nobel Prize for Chemistry, is a child of this same moment – he was born earlier in 1929, on 23 January – and he represents a link between the interwar years in Britain and our own time in Canada. "Pugwashite" and for decades an articulate spokesman for disarmament, in the nuclear age he has argued urgently for a new ideological architecture, one appropriately responsive to the lessons of Hiroshima and Nagasaki. Thus we find him a signatory to the statement made by Laureates on the occasion of the 100th anniversary of the Nobel Prize, 11 December 2001. As it looks forward to the next 100 years, the statement ends in a manner reminiscent of Auden: "To survive in the world we have transformed we must learn to think in a new way. As never before, the future of each depends on the good of all" (Polanyi et al., "Nobel Statement").

More than seventy years have intervened between Auden's plea for a new mental architecture and this more recent insistence that we need to think in a new way. The echo is obvious, but it is important to note a subtle difference in the more recent formulation: we must now learn to think in a new way precisely because of the effect our past thinking has had on the world we inhabit. If science has brought us to the brink of self-annihilation either by nuclear weapons, nuclear accidents, or potentially irreversible environmental degradation, it is obvious we have no choice but to count on a combination of even better science and enhanced wisdom ("a change of heart") to deliver us.

Learning to think in new ways, and teaching others to do so as well, has acquired an urgency of magnitude and type unknown in the pre-nuclear age. Education and research – which during certain periods of history have themselves been saved from complete obliteration by the spirit of benign amateurism – now have a saviour's role to play, and their propagation and advancement are so important to our species that they cannot be left to village explainers and the merely curious. When Auden wrote in 1939 that "We must love one another or die," he certainly indicated that humanity's progress – indeed, its survival – will depend upon the "affirming flame" of the heart as conventionally understood ("September 1, 1939," *English Auden* 246), as the root of civil society and the basis of his "vision of agape." But this poet, in whose works it is not unusual to find human existential challenges explored in the language of post-Einstein physics, sees advances in science and progress in human values as consubstantial: "So, hidden in his hocus pocus, / There lies the gift of double focus" ("New Year Letter," *Collected Poems* 220). "The future of each depends on the good of all," the "good" in that context being both well-being and moral or ethical soundness.

Such a focus is apparent in the Nobel Laureates' statement. What is wanted is a scientific mode inextricably interwoven with a complementary (because compensatory) mode of living, being and feeling. Nothing less than the survival of humanity depends upon our achieving this synthesis, so it follows that nothing less should be the goal at all levels of education, informal to formal, amateur to institutional. And if there is agreement on the goal, we must next ask whether we are achieving it, or are at least on course towards doing so. And in this Great Age of Indicators, do we have a means of measuring effectively the outcomes of this process? That we are apparently surviving as a species may be a promising indicator, but one is haunted by the possibility that we are still moving towards our deserved end, and our survival is merely temporary.

To assess our chances of survival, we might consider almost any of our society's mechanisms of intellectual and personal formation. Perhaps most telling of these are the universities, those human institutions at the formalized and advanced extreme of the spectrum, which have been founded and funded specifically to promote critical, creative, integrated, and innovative thinking. How good a job are we doing? The world is profoundly invested in the answer. If to find new ways of thinking is not possible in the hothouses that are our campuses, watered by public monies and fertilized by guaranteed freedoms of every sort, its future may be grim.

Problems attach to the definition of "new," of course, and Thomas Kuhn (whom I frequently quote in this connection) and the author of Ecclesiastes (whom I do not), both warn that absolute novelty is a chimera. To avoid becoming caught in an infinite regress of definition and counter-definition, I would propose to alter the question to read not, "how good a job are we doing at fostering new ways of thinking?" but rather, "are we satisfied that our institutions of academic inquiry are set up so as to encourage and support 'new styles of architecture,' to be properly responsive to changes in the human heart?"

Students are probably better able to answer this question than are university presidents such as myself, for if there is any part of our institutions in which it can be said that a hankering for a new global architecture has taken root in recent years, it is the student body. On every campus, and between campuses, the last decade has seen an apparently unprecedented surge in student volunteerism, and in particular a proliferation of "without borders" student organizations. Members of faculty who have welcomed the return of student activism have possibly found its contemporary form disconcerting: passionate, insistent, and determined as in previous decades, but also practical, constructive, and often informed by a mature business sense. Is it even appropriate to identify this as student activism? Is it not perhaps something entirely and wonderfully new? The infinite regress of definition and counter-definition threatens.

In *Save the World on Your Own Time,* Stanley Fish has recently underlined a discrepancy between, on the one hand, institutions and programs of higher education and, on the other, the ethical and social claims that are frequently made for them, within and without the academy. For example, between the questionable university rhetoric of "global citizenship" – ubiquitous nationally and internationally at present – and the real, admirable activities and attitudes of many students falls a shadow, cast partly by a failure of imagination and curiosity on the part of institutional leaders and perhaps also by the presence of a comparatively less respectable financial motive in those leaders' embrace of internationalism.

Until very recently, in fact, "global citizenship" has been something students have been required to cultivate almost entirely through extra-curricular activities, which naturally raises questions about the curriculum and its shortcomings. What should a globally informed curriculum look like? And how should it be taught? It is regrettable enough that the hopeful and constructive mood of our students and the young faculty with whom they identify is sometimes co-opted into a bloodless institutional discourse driven by dubious motives; even more alarming is the role of administrators, faculty members, and university senates in perpetuating atrophied pedagogies and an approach to curriculum that together prevent engagement with "the world" from becoming central to the educational experience and a matter for formal credit.

If it is not proper to want to save the world on university time, I do not know why else our institutions should continue to exist – or at least why they should continue to benefit from public support. Fish prejudices the discussion by formulating the terms in an exceedingly reductive fashion, but notwithstanding the point just made about internationalization, the ways in which the academy can and does intervene to the benefit of people and planet are many, various, sophisticated, and often indirect. Even the "pure" spirit of enquiry – and the education of students in that spirit – redounds in some way to the benefit of the world. The asking of questions, the framing and testing of hypotheses, the interrogation of received wisdom and government proclamation: the process is itself a good, and no less valuable for being ultimately impure, for having consequences in the world.

That last assertion has been disputed in a different context by Fish, who argues somewhat oddly that curiosity is neither an inalienable right nor an absolute good.[2] To be sure, curiosity in one form can be a type of narcissism, with the questioner caught up in a tautology cycling between his overpowering desire to know and his vain delight in knowing. Open-ended questioning, however – the kind which we pursue out of interest in the second, third, and fourth questions to which a first will lead – is the means by which we are drawn out of ourselves and into dialogue with the world around us. At the very least it is the only known antidote to intellectual atrophy. There can be no new architecture, no change of heart, without it, and from our universities every day come astonishing accounts of the fruits of "pure" inquiry in research, of curiosity-driven approaches to learning at all levels, and of new programs integrating the insights and methods of science with those of the humanities and social sciences. Even in professional schools it has become widespread practice to require students to consider the relationship between the fulfilment of their personal skills and the achievement of a greater human good. Such is the consequence of approaching life in all its aspects in the interrogative mood.

This is all very hopeful and positive. Even if Fish is correct, and our institutions of higher learning are for the most part not set up as they might be had "saving the world" been their explicit and historical aim, it remains true that they do contribute incalculably to the progress of our species. While in recent years that progress has certainly come to be understood as inseparable from the fortunes of our planet, such was not always the case, however. There is a need to balance optimism with caution. As the statement by the Nobel Laureates makes clear, human progress in one area of enquiry can have potentially cataclysmic ramifications in another, so in assessing the role of universities in our future, nothing – particularly not the compatibility of all our activities and ambitions – should be taken for granted. Perhaps the greatest danger to be addressed in universities is therefore the presumption of our own alliance with the global good, a presumption reinforced daily by breakthroughs of one kind or another and underwritten in recent years by identification of the "knowledge economy" as a kind of operating system for the world at large.

The effect of such presumption, however defensible on the evidence it might seem to be, is in subtle but very real ways to close down avenues of enquiry, and in that respect to limit the potential for further advance. Regardless of our triumphs, to keep those avenues open we obviously have to subvert or at least to question whatever the academy seeks to present as self-evident truth, including especially its own claim to authority. The universities' presumed alliance with good – defined differently over the centuries, of course – lies at the base of that claim, and it also does service to justify the fundamental paradox of the academy, which is that we exist to institutionalize the fluid, unstable, and corrosive pursuit of knowledge and new perspectives.

Such a conclusion does not vitiate the dream of a new human "architecture," of new ways of thinking that will be adequate to the challenges of our future. Still less does it preclude the universities from continuing in their historical role as both mother and midwife to transformative thinking. It does, however, stand as a reminder to educators that the institutionalization of knowledge and enquiry – which can so easily be, and is so often mistaken for, their true mission – is always potentially an obstacle to success in the greater and more critical enterprise of humanity.

The dark side of the institutionalization of knowledge need not be elaborated here. Anyone who has worked in a university knows about the bizarre conflagrations that arise over changes to the curriculum, to modes of delivery, to what represents a proper contribution to research, to the way in which a course of study might be designed. Amongst jaded administrators there is a joke too often made that the stakes in any academic debate appear inversely proportional to the magnitude of the subject. There is truth to that assertion, and it is certainly dispiriting to reflect that closed mindedness is certainly no less common – and may even be worse – in the academy than in the world at large. But the fierceness of academic debate, no matter how large or small the issue, is also a consolation in that it confirms the continuing vitality of universities as places of debate and exploration through dialogue. The institution-as-monolith-and-monument is countered by the institution-as-polyform-and-process.

If we are careful to contrive it that the second of these always outweighs the first, there is the possibility that our survival will be a continuing rather than a temporary – even if not absolute – phenomenon. Auden, for one, would have appreciated this distinction and derived consolation from it. A lover of limestone landscapes, he came to find contentment in perpetual transformation rather than timeless order. A somewhat idiosyncratic Freudian, he understood why "we'd rather / Be perfect copies of our father, / Prefer our *idées fixes* to be / True of a fixed Reality." Thus, "How hard to stretch imagination / To live according to our station," he wrote in *New Year Letter* in 1940, "For we are all insulted by / The mere suggestion that we die / Each moment and that each great I / Is but a process in a process / Within a field that never closes [...]" (*Collected Poems* 208). Our "station" is paradoxically not stationary, and anyone who aspires to discover a new human architecture must take this into account. In the universities in particular, the institutionalization of learning and thinking may be both positive and negative in its effects – its expression may be a "paralysing smile," to borrow yet again from Auden's *New Year Letter* – and against that threat "Our best protection is that we / In fact live in eternity" (210). To the refractory desire to replicate our intellectual fathers we must be sure to add the full Oedipal correction.

NOTES

1 See Auden, Forewords and Afterwords.
2 See Fish, "Does Curiosity Kill."

WORKS CITED

Auden, W.H. *Forewords and Afterwords*. London: Faber and Faber, 1973.
Auden, W.H. *Collected Poems*. New York: Vintage, 1991. Print.
Auden, W.H. *The English Auden: Poems, Essays and Dramatic Writings 1927–1939*. Ed. Edward Mendelson. London: Faber and Faber, 1977. Print.
Fish, Stanley. "Does Curiosity Kill More Than the Cat." *New York Times.* 14 September 2009. *NYTimes.com*. Web. 9 July 2011.
Fish, Stanley. *Save the World on Your Own Time*. New York: Oxford UP, 2008.
Polanyi, John Charles et al. "Nobel Statement." 11 December 2001. *John Polanyi*. Web. 9 July 2011.

List of Contributors

James Robert Allard is Associate Professor in the Department of English Language and Literature and Participating Faculty in the interdisciplinary MA in Popular Culture programme at Brock University. He is coeditor of the collection *Staging Pain, 1580–1800: Violence and Trauma in British Theater* (2009) and the author of *Romanticism, Medicine, and the Poet's Body* (2007), as well as essays on such topics as Joanna Baillie, William Wordsworth, Frances Burney, John Thelwall, Matthew Lewis, and Rhetoric of Science. His current project examines the emergence of the concept of the "patient" in the Romantic Century. He is recipient of the 2006 Polanyi Prize for Literature.

Nandi Bhatia is Professor of English and Associate Dean (Research) in the Faculty of Arts and Humanities at Western University. She is the author of *Acts of Authority/ Acts of Resistance: Theater and Politics in Colonial and Postcolonial India* (2004) and *Performing Women/Performing Womanhood* (2010). She is coeditor of *Partitioned Lives: Narratives of Home, Displacement, and Resettlement* (2008) and editor of *Modern Indian Theatre: A Reader* (2009). She has also guest edited special issues of *Feminist Review* on "Postcolonial Theatres" and *TOPIA: Canadian Journal of Cultural Studies* on "Bollywood and the South Asian Diaspora" (2011), and coedited a special issue of *Fashion Theory* on "Fashion and Orientalism." Her work on colonial and postcolonial theatre, film, and literature has appeared in *Theatre Journal, Modern Drama, Centennial Review, Feminist Review, South Asia Graduate Research Journal, Alif: Journal of Comparative Poetics, Gramma,* and various book collections. Currently she is working on a SSHRC funded project, "Colonial Censorship and

Literary Movements in India: 1858–1947." Bhatia won the 1999 Polanyi Prize for Literature.

Daniel Coleman is Professor at McMaster University. He teaches and researches in Canadian Literature; the literary and cultural production of categories of privilege such as whiteness, masculinity, and Britishness; and the spiritual and cultural politics of reading. He has published *Masculine Migrations: Reading the Postcolonial Male in "New Canadian" Narratives* (1998), *The Scent of Eucalyptus: A Missionary Childhood in Ethiopia* (2003), and *In Bed With the Word: Reading, Spirituality, and Cultural Politics* (2009), and has coedited nine scholarly volumes. His book, *White Civility: The Literary Project of English Canada* (2006), won the Raymond Klibansky prize for the best English-language book in the Humanities in Canada for 2006–2007. With Smaro Kamboureli, he has recently coedited a volume entitled *Retooling the Humanities: The Culture of Research in the Canadian University* (2011). He received the Polanyi Prize for Literature in 1998.

Patrick Deane is President and Vice Chancellor of McMaster University, where he is also Professor of English and Cultural Studies. Among other administrative positions, he has served as Vice President (Academic), Acting President, and Provost at the University of Winnipeg, and Vice Principal (Academic) at Queen's University. Previously he has taught at the University of Toronto and Western University, where he also served as Chair of the Department of English. His areas of teaching and research expertise are Twentieth-Century British Literature and Culture; South African Literature and Culture Literature and Society/Politics; Criticism and Theory; and Postcolonial Literature. Among his numerous publications, he is author of *At Home in Time: Forms of Neo-Augustanism in Modern English Poetry* (1994) and editor of *History in Our Hands: A Critical Anthology of Writings on Literature, Culture, and Politics from the 1930s* (1998). He won the Polanyi Prize for Literature in 1988.

Angela Esterhammer is Principal of Victoria College and Professor of English at the University of Toronto. Her publications include *Creating States: Studies in the Performative Language of John Milton and William Blake* (1994), *The Romantic Performative: Language and Action in British and German Romanticism* (2000), *Romanticism and Improvisation, 1750–1850* (2008), and the edited volumes *Romantic Poetry* (2002) and *Spheres of Action: Speech and Performance in Romantic Culture* (2009). Her current research concerns experimental uses of textual, visual, and performative media during the 1820s. She is a founding member of the North American Society of the Study of Romanticism (NASSR) and sits on the Executive Boards of NASSR, the International Comparative Literature Association, and the Wordsworth Summer Conference Foundation. She won the Polanyi Prize for Literature in 1990.

Joel Faflak is Professor of English and Theory in the Department of English at Western University, where he is also Director of the School for Advanced Studies in the Arts and the Humanities He is author of *Romantic Psychoanalysis: The Burden of the Mystery* (2008), coauthor of *Revelation and Knowledge* (2011), editor of Thomas De Quincey's *Confessions of an English Opium-Eater* (2009), and editor or coeditor of seven volumes, including *The Romanticism Handbook* (2011) and *The Handbook to Romanticism Studies* (2012). He won the 2002 Polanyi Prize for Literature.

R. Darren Gobert is Associate Professor of English and Theatre Studies at York University, Canada, where he specializes in dramatic theory and the philosophy of theatre. He is on the editorial board of *Modern Drama*, for which he edited a special issue on contemporary playwriting from the United Kingdom, and he is the author of *The Mind-Body Stage: Passion and Interaction in the Cartesian Theater* (2013) and the forthcoming *Theatre of Caryl Churchill*. His published work has considered English, French, and German drama ranging from the seventeenth through the twenty-first centuries. What unites these threads is a belief that the history of theatre and performance can illuminate the history of emotion. He won the 2007 Polanyi Prize for Literature.

Jason Haslam is Associate Professor in the Department of English at Dalhousie University. He is the author of *Fitting Sentences: Identity in Nineteenth- and Twentieth-Century Prison Narratives*, and the coeditor of *Captivating Subjects: Writing Confinement, Citizenship, and Nationhood in the Nineteenth Century* (both 2005). His publications also include scholarly editions of Constance Lytton's suffragette autobiography, *Prisons and Prisoners: Some Personal Experiences* (2008) and Edgar Rice Burroughs's *Tarzan of the Apes* (2010), as well as essays on topics ranging from the history of the prison and its representation in literature, to science fiction's engagement with race and gender, to gothic film and sexuality. He has recently served as the President of the Canadian

Association for American Studies. He won the Polanyi Prize for Literature in 2005.

Katherine R. Larson is Assistant Professor of English at the University of Toronto. Her research and teaching centre on early modern literature and culture, women's writing, language and gender, and the function of music in literature. She is the author of *Early Modern Women in Conversation* (2011), and coeditor of three special issues: "The Song Is You: Opera, Lyrics, and Literary Studies" and "Operatics: The Interdisciplinary Workings of Opera," both for *The University of Toronto Quarterly*, and "Gendering Time and Space in Early Modern England" for *Renaissance and Reformation*. Her work has also appeared in *English Literary Renaissance, Milton Studies, Early Modern Women: An Interdisciplinary Journal*, the *Sidney Journal, Life Writing, The Journal of Popular Culture*, and *Canadian Literature*. Her current book project integrates her training as a singer in its exploration of the relationship between rhetoric, gender, and song performance in early modern English literature. She received the 2008 Polanyi Prize for Literature.

Andrea Most is Associate Professor of American Literature and Jewish Studies in the Department of English at the University of Toronto. She teaches and conducts research in the areas of modern American literature and culture, Jewish cultural studies, theatre, performance, and food studies. Her book *Making Americans: Jews and the Broadway Musical* (2004) won the 2005 Kurt Weill Prize for distinguished scholarship on music theatre. Her second book, *Theatrical Liberalism: Jews and Popular Entertainment in America*, is forthcoming from NYU Press in 2013. Prof. Most's new project, *Holy Lands*, focuses on food, agriculture, and religion in Canada and the United States. She received the Polanyi Prize for Literature in 2004.

John Charles Polanyi is faculty member in the Department of Chemistry at the University of Toronto. His awards include the 1986 Nobel Prize in Chemistry, the Royal Medal of the Royal Society of London, and over thirty honorary degrees from six countries. He is a Fellow of the Royal Societies of Canada, London, and Edinburgh, as well as the American Academy of Arts and Sciences, the U.S. National Academy of Sciences, the Pontifical Academy of Rome, and the Russian Academy of Sciences. He is a member of the Queen's Privy Council for

Canada and Companion of the Order of Canada. He has served on the Prime Minister of Canada's Advisory Board on Science and Technology, the Premier's Council of Ontario, as Foreign Honorary Advisor to the Institute for Molecular Sciences (Japan), and as Honorary Advisor to the Max Planck Institute for Quantum Optics (Germany). He was a founding member of both the Committee on Scholarly Freedom of the Royal Society, and a further international human rights organization, the Canadian Committee for Scientists and Scholars, of which he is the current President. He was the founding Chairman of the Canadian Pugwash Group in 1960, and has been active for forty years in International Pugwash. He has written extensively on science policy, the control of armaments, and peacekeeping. He is coeditor of *The Dangers of Nuclear War,* and was a participant in the recent "Canada 21" study of a 21st-century defence posture for Canada. He was co-chair (with Sir Brian Urquhart) of the Department of Foreign Affairs International Consultative Committee on a Rapid Response Capability for the United Nations. In honour of Polanyi's achievement, in 1987 the Government of the Province of Ontario instituted the Polanyi Prizes.

Imre Szeman is Canada Research Chair in Cultural Studies and Professor of English and Film Studies at the University of Alberta, Canada. He is author of *Zones of Instability: Literature, Postcolonialism and the Nation* (2003) and coauthor of *Popular Culture: A User's Guide* (2004, 2nd. ed. 2009). He is also coeditor of *Pierre Bourdieu: Fieldwork in Culture* (2000), *The Johns Hopkins Guide to Literary Theory and Criticism* (2005), *Global-Local Consumption* (2009), *Canadian Cultural Studies: A Reader* (2009), and *Cultural Theory: An Anthology* (2010). He received the John Polanyi Prize in Literature in 2000.

Julia M. Wright is Professor of English at Dalhousie University, and has recently held a Canada Research Chair (2002–12). She is the author of *Blake, Nationalism, and the Politics of Alienation* (2004); *Ireland, India, and Nationalism in Nineteenth-Century Literature* (2007); and numerous articles, as well as the editor or coeditor of a number of volumes, most recently a two-volume *Companion to Irish Literature* (2010) and *Reading the Nation in English Literature* (2009). She was awarded the Polanyi Prize for Literature in 1999.

Index

www.ingramcontent.com/pod-product-compliance
Lightning Source LLC
Chambersburg PA
CBHW030423310726
48979CB00009B/1594/J